SYMBOLIC COMPUTATION

Artificial Intelligence

Managing Editor: D. W. Loveland

Editors: S. Amarel   A. Biermann   L. Bolc
          A. Bundy   H. Gallaire   P. Hayes
          A. Joshi   D. Lenat   A. Mackworth
          E. Sandewall   J. Siekmann   W. Wahlster

Springer Series
SYMBOLIC COMPUTATION - *Artificial Intelligence*

N. J. Nilsson: Principles of Artificial Intelligence. XV, 476 pages, 139 figs., 1982

J. H. Siekmann, G. Wrightson (Eds.): Automation of Reasoning 1. Classical Papers on Computational Logic 1957-1966. XXII, 525 pages, 1983

J. H. Siekmann, G. Wrightson (Eds.): Automation of Reasoning 2. Classical Papers on Computational Logic 1967-1970. XXII, 638 pages, 1983

L. Bolc (Ed.): The Design of Interpreters, Compilers, and Editors for Augmented Transition Networks. XI, 214 pages, 72 figs., 1983

R. S. Michalski, J. G. Carbonell, T. M. Mitchell (Eds.): Machine Learning. An Artificial Intelligence Approach. XI, 572 pages, 1984

L. Bolc (Ed.): Natural Language Communication with Pictorial Information Systems. VII, 327 pages, 67 figs., 1984

J. W. Lloyd: Foundations of Logic Programming. Second, extended edition, XII, 212 pages, 1987

A. Bundy (Ed.): Catalogue of Artificial Intelligence Tools. Second revised edition, IV, 168 pages, 1986

M. M. Botvinnik: Computers in Chess. Solving Inexact Search Problems. With contributions by A. I. Reznitsky, B. M. Stilman, M. A. Tsfasman, A. D. Yudin. Translated from the Russian by A. A. Brown. XIV, 158 pages, 48 figs., 1984

C. Blume, W. Jakob: Programming Languages for Industrial Robots. XIII, 376, 145 figs., 1986

L. Bolc (Ed.): Natural Language Parsing Systems. XVIII, 367 pages, 155 figs., 1987

L. Bolc (Ed.): Computational Models of Learning. IX, 208 pages, 34 figs., 1987

Computational Models of Learning

Edited by Leonard Bolc

With Contributions by
G. L. Bradshaw   P. Langley   R. S. Michalski
S. Ohlsson   L. A. Rendell   H. A. Simon
J. G. Wolff

With 34 Figures

Springer-Verlag
Berlin Heidelberg New York
London Paris Tokyo

Leonard Bolc
Institute of Informatics, Warsaw University
PKiN, pok. 850, PL-00-901 Warszawa, Poland

ISBN-13:978-3-642-82744-0   e-ISBN-13:978-3-642-82742-6
DOI: 10.1007/978-3-642-82742-6

Library of Congress Cataloging in Publication Data.
Computational models of learning.
(Symbolic computation. Artificial intelligence) Includes index.
Contents: Learning strategies and automated knowledge acquisition / R.S. Michalski -
Heuristics for empirical discovery / P. Langley, H.A. Simon, and G.L. Bradshaw - Transfer
of training in procedural learning / S. Ohlsson - [etc.]
1. Machine learning. 2. Artificial intelligence.
I. Bolc, Leonard, 1934- . II. Bradshaw, G.L. III. Series.
Q325.C626 1987 006.3'1 87-16527
ISBN-13:978-3-642-82744-0 (U.S.)

This work is subject to copyright. All rights are reserved, whether the whole or part of the material is concerned, specifically the rights of translation, reprinting, reuse of illustrations, recitation, broadcasting, reproduction on microfilms or in other ways, and storage in data banks. Duplication of this publication or parts thereof is only permitted under the provisions of the German Copyright Law of September 9, 1965, in its version of June 24, 1985, and a copyright fee must always be paid. Violations fall under the prosecution act of the German Copyright Law.

© Springer-Verlag Berlin Heidelberg 1987
Softcover reprint of the hardcover 1st edition 1987

The use of registered names, trademarks, etc. in this publication does not imply, even in the absence of a specific statement, that such names are exempt from the relevant protective laws and regulations and therefore free for general use.

2145/3140-543210

Preface

In recent years, machine learning has emerged as a significant area of research in artificial intelligence and cognitive science. At present, research in this field is being intensified from both the point of view of theory and of implementation, and the results are being introduced in practice.

Machine learning has recently become the subject of interest of many young and talented scientists, whose bold ideas have greatly contributed to the broadening of our knowledge in this rapidly developing field of science. This situation has manifested itself in an increasing number of valuable contributions to scientific journals. However, such papers are necessarily compact descriptions of research problems.

"Computational Models of Learning" supplements these contributions and is a collection of more extensive essays, which provide the reader with an increased knowledge of carefully selected problems of machine learning.

Ryszard S. Michalski (Massachusetts Institute of Technology, USA) describes in his contribution "Learning Strategies and Automated Knowledge Acquisition: An Overview" basic learning strategies in the context of knowledge acquisition for expert systems. He gives special attention to inductive learning strategies, that is, strategies that involve performing inductive inference on the information given to the learner. These strategies include learning from examples and learning from observation and discovery. A form of learning from observation, called conceptual clustering, is described in detail and illustrated with an example.

Pat Langley, Herbert A. Simon, and Gary L. Bradshaw (Carnegie-Mellon University, USA) present in their work "Heuristics for Empirical Discovery" a review of their experiences with the BACON project. The six versions of BACON focused on the empirical discovery of numeric laws. The authors examine methods for finding a functional relation between two numeric terms and methods for discovering complex laws including many terms. The notions of intrinsic properties and common divisors are introduced and methods for inferring intrinsic values from symbolic data are examined.

Stellan Ohlsson (University of Pittsburgh, USA) presents in his work "Transfer of Training in Procedural Learning: A Matter of Conjectures and Refutations?" an analysis of heuristic learning, in which he identifies five global characteristics of human learning, and proposes a theory to explain them. The five characteristics are: (a) improvement is gradual and continues after a correct solution has been found, (b) practice effects transfer from one problem to another, (c) errors are frequent during practice, (d) multiple trials are needed before a problem is mastered, and (e) the effects of practice depend upon the order of the practice problems.

The problem solving system postulated in Ohlsson's theory represents a heuristic as two sets of rules. The rules in the first set propose problem solving steps, while the rules in the second set censor (some of) those proposals. According to Ohlsson's theory, learning proceeds by using positive experiences to extend the set of proposers, and negative experiences to extend the set of censors. Ohlsson develops a detailed argument to show that this theory predicts the five global characteristics outlined above.

The second component of Ohlsson's theory is a component which discovers the appropriate breakdown of a top-goal into subgoals. A general rule is given for how to identify a subgoal during problem solving. The system built on the basis of this theory is one of the few learning systems which can discover novel subgoals.

Computer implementation proves that the proposer-censor mechanism and the subgoaling mechanism work well together. The most interesting computational result in Ohlsson's contribution is that his system adapts its learning style to the structure of the task it is working on. In simple and regular problem spaces, it learns by acquiring proposer rules. In the complex but regular problem spaces, it learns mainly by discovering the right goal-hierarchy. Finally, in irregular problem spaces, it learns mainly from its mistakes, i.e., by acquiring censor rules.

Larry A. Rendell (University of Illinois at Urbana-Champaign, USA) examines in his work "Conceptual Knowledge Acquisition in Search" several issues of induction and concept formation, to illustrate some emerging principles of incremental learning. While the ideas and methods described are domain independent, the particular domain of state-space search was selected for illustration and experimentation. This domain is difficult enough to tax any learning system, since the search spaces may be large and possibly irregular, and the learning must often be incremental and uncertain.

Rendell is concerned with general, effective, and efficient learning. Unlike most machine learning work, Rendell's research has addressed uncertain environments, particularly when learning is incremental (and intermediate results of learning are used in task performance).

In this paper, Rendell first describes his early probabilistic learning system PLS1, and its layered successor PLS2. Experimental results include the efficient discovery of locally optimal evaluation functions. Probabilistic "conceptual clustering" introduced in PLS1 may be extended to "second order" clustering. Second order clustering categorizes not the original object, but rather "utility" functions over the objects. This (efficiently) creates a structure of relations.

Rendell also begins to examine the question of how much learning a system is doing, versus the amount of resources required. One conclusion is that efficient learning demands both data-driven statistical methods (for speed and noise immunity), and also model-driven biasing constraints (for effective results and reduced complexity). Learning should be both data- and model-driven.

Gerry Wolff (Dundee University, Scotland) describes in the work "Cognitive Development as Optimisation" the latest phase of a research programme to create a comprehensive theory of linguistic and cognitive development. The foundation of the theory is the idea that learning is a process in which knowledge structures are built and refined towards a form which is optimally efficient for the several functions they must serve. Optimisation depends on the proper application of a small range of data compression principles. This paper examines the application of six such principles which are apparently sufficient for the efficient representation of a wide variety of cognitive structures.

The contributions presented in this book provide the readers with quite detailed descriptions and results for selected systems and problems. They complement the selection of articles presented in the two volumes "Machine Learning", edited by Michalski, Carbonell, and Mitchell[1].

We hope that the publication of our volume, "Computational Models of Learning", with contributions from different countries, will further our understanding of the current problems of machine learning, create greater interest in this field of science, and be an inspiration for further research.

Warsaw, September 1987   Leonard Bolc

---

[1] R. S. Michalski, J. G. Carbonell, T. M. Mitchell (eds): *Machine Learning. An Artificial Intelligence Approach*. Morgan Kaufmann, Los Altos 1983 and Springer-Verlag, Berlin Heidelberg New York 1984; *Machine Learning. An Artificial Intelligence Approach*. Vol. II. Morgan Kaufmann, Los Altos 1986

Table of Contents

Learning Strategies and Automated Knowledge Acquisition:
An Overview
   R. S. Michalski 1

Heuristics for Empirical Discovery
   P. Langley, H. A. Simon and G. L. Bradshaw 21

Transfer of Training in Procedural Learning: A Matter of Conjectures
and Refutations?
   S. Ohlsson 55

Conceptual Knowledge Acquisition in Search
   L. A. Rendell 89

Cognitive Development as Optimisation
   J. G. Wolff 161

Subject Index 207

Learning Strategies and Automated Knowledge Acquisition

An Overview

Ryszard S. Michalski[1]

Abstract

Fundamental learning strategies are discussed in the context of knowledge acquisition for expert systems. These strategies reflect the type of inference performed by the learner on the input information in order to derive the desired knowledge. They include learning from instruction, learning by deduction, learning by analogy and learning by induction. Special attention is given to two basic types of learning by induction: learning from examples (concept acquisition) and learning from observation (concept formation without teacher). A specific form of learning from observation, namely, *conceptual clustering,* is discussed in detail, and illustrated by an example. Conceptual clustering is a process of structuring given observations into a hierarchy of conceptual categories.

An inductive learning system generates knowledge by drawing inductive inferences from the given facts under the guidance of *background knowledge*. The background knowledge contains previously learned concepts, goals of learning, the criteria for evaluating hypotheses from the viewpoint of these goals, the properties of attributes and relations used to chracterize observed events, and various inference rules for transforming concepts or expressing them at different levels of abstraction.

1. Introduction

Learning ability is no doubt central to human intelligence. This ability permits us to adapt to the changing environment, to develop a great variety of skills, and to acquire expertise in an almost unlimited number of specific domains. The human ability to learn is truly remarkable: people are capable of learning from information carried by multiple physical media and expressed in an unbounded variety of forms. This information can be stated at different levels of abstraction, with different degrees of precision, with or without errors, and with different degrees of relevancy to the knowledge ultimately acquired.

Implanting learning capabilities in machines is one of the central goals of Artificial Intelligence. It is the subject of a new field of Machine Learning. Due to the enormous complexity of learning processes, development of general-purpose, versatile learning systems is a long-term goal. With the development of expert systems, however, implementing some forms of machine learning has become an urgent task, even if the forms of such implementation are very limited.

The urgency of this task stems from an explosive growth of interest and social need to develop expert systems for many different applications, from medicine and agriculture to law, education and computer design. Expert systems are com-

---

[1] Department of Computer Science, University of Illinois, Urbana, Illinois 61801

puter programs (or devices) that simulate the expertise of a human expert in solving problems in some specific domain. They are capable of conducting formal inference on their knowledge base in the interaction with the external information provided by a user, in order to provide a solution to a problem or an advice in decision making. Examples of some early expert systems include:
- DENDRAL (developed at Stanford University) for determining the molecular structure of organic compounds from mass spectrograms.
- MACSYMA (developed at MIT) which serves as a general mathematical aids system (e.g., for symbolic integration, simplification of mathematical expressions, etc.).
- R1 (developed at Carnegie-Mellon University) for determining configurations of VAX computer systems.
- INTERNIST (developed at the University of Pittsburgh) for diagnosing diseases of interest in internal medicine.
- PLANT/ds and PLANT/cd (developed at the University of Illinois) - two related agricultural expert systems, the first for diagnosing soybean diseases, and the second for predicting black cutworm damage to corn.

The major component of an expert system is its knowledge base, i.e., formally represented knowledge in the given domain of application. Building such a knowledge base is typically done as a cooperative effort between a "knowledge engineer" and a domain expert. The knowledge engineer conducts interviews with an expert and codifies the expert's knowledge in some knowledge representation system.

Such a system often consists of production rules (condition-action rules) or a semantic network. A semantic network is a graph whose nodes represent concepts and whose links represent relations between the concepts. These two forms of knowledge representation have special appeal, because of their comprehensibility and relative ease of use for implementing inference processes. For some applications, however, these forms may not be sufficient. For example, in system PLANT/cd, a large part of the domain knowledge is encoded as a set of procedures that form a simulation model of the growth of corn and the growth of black cutworms (Boulanger, 1983).

Encoding expert knowledge into a system is a time-consuming, difficult process that is prone to error. For this reason, knowledge acquisition is a "bottleneck" in the development of expert systems. The process of knowledge acquisition can be simplified by applying interactive programming aids for developing and debugging rule bases. Such an aid is provided, for example, by the system TEIRESIAS, developed by Davis (1978). A long term solution, however, is seen in the development of machine learning. The importance of the field of machine learning to further progress in the development of expert systems has been indicated by many authors (e.g., Waltz et al., 1983).

In this paper we review basic strategies of learning and discuss them in the context of automated knowledge acquisition. We specifically concentrate on knowledge acquisition through inductive learning. The latter encompasses two strategies: learning from examples, and learning by observation and discovery.

2. Fundamental Learning Strategies

The knowledge acquisition process can be greatly simplified if an expert system can learn decision rules from examples of decisions made by human experts, or from its own errors. This type of learning strategy is called *learning from examples* (or *concept acquisition*). It has been studied widely in the last ten years or so, and many important results have been obtained (e.g., Winston, 1970; Michalski, 1972; Lenat, 1976; Mitchell, 1978; Buchanan et al. 1979; Pao and Hu, 1982, Hu and Pao, 1982; Dietterich and Michalski, 1983; Langley, Bradshaw and Simon, 1983; Michalski, 1983; Reinke, 1984; Quinlan, 1986; Winston, 1986).

Learning from examples is one of several fundamental learning strategies. These strategies are identified by viewing a learning system as an inference system. Namely, they are distinguished by the major type of inference the learning system (human or machine) performs on the information provided, in order to derive the desired kowledge. At one extreme, the system performs no inference, but directly accepts and uses the information given to it (or built into it). At the other extreme, the system performs a complex, search-based inductive inference that on occasion leads to discovery of new knowledge. The following learning strategies are important points along the above spectrum:

A. Direct Implanting of Knowledge

This strategy requires little or no inference on the part of the learner. It includes rote learning, learning by imitation, learning by being constructed or by being programmed. This strategy is a widely used method for providing knowledge to a computer system: we incorporate knowledge into its hardware, we program it, and we build databases for all kinds of applications. Although building databases is not typically considered as machine learning, it can be considered as a special case of such a process. Some databases go beyond this learning strategy, if they can perform some amount of inference, usually mathematical or statistical.

B. Learning from Instruction

In this form of learning, also called *learning by being told,* a learner selects and transforms the knowledge from the input language to an internally-usable representation and integrates it with prior knowledge for effective retrieval and use. This is the most widely used strategy of human learning: it includes learning from teachers, books, publications, exhibits, displays, and similar sources. A machine version of this strategy is a system capable of accepting instruction or advice and applying the learned knowledge effectively to different tasks. Simple versions of this strategy constitute the basic method for providing knowledge to expert systems today (e.g., Davis, 1978, Hass and Hendrix, 1983).

C. Learning by Deduction

A learning system that uses this strategy conducts deductive (truth-preserving) inference on the knowledge it possesses and knowledge supplied to it. This is done in order to restructure given knowledge into more useful or more effective forms, or to determine important consequences of the knowledge. For example, given a set of numbers: 1, 2, 6, 24, 120, 720, a learning system might represent them in an equivalent, but shorter form as n!, n = 1 ... 6. To do so, the system must, of course, know the concept of a factorial.

A form of deductive learning, called *analytical* or *explanation-based learning*, has recently become an active research area. In analytical learning, the system is already equipped with a description of the target concept, but the description is expressed at the level of abstraction too high to be directly usable (operational). The system uses the domain knowledge to determine or explain why a given fact is an example of the concept. This process takes a form of formal proof, and produces a new concept description that is operational. This typically means that the concept is reexpressed in terms of properties used in the concept example.

As an illustration, consider a system that already knows that a cup is a stable, open, liftable vessel. Suppose that it is now presented a specific instance of a cup, described in terms such as an upward concavity, flat bottom, the presence of a handle, color, size, and other features. By using the domain knowledge that links the known high level concept description of the cup with the features used in the instance, the system constructs an operational description stating that a cup is an upward concave object with a flat bottom and a handle (Mitchell, Keller and Kedar-Cabelli, 1986; DeJong and Mooney, 1986).

The explanation-based learning is a useful technique, applicable to many problems. In order to be used, however, the system has to be equipped with a sufficient amount of relevant domain knowledge. This domain knowledge has to be inputed to the system somehow – either by handcrafting it to the system, or by analogical or inductive learning.

D. Learning by Analogy

This strategy involves transforming or extending existing knowledge (or skill) applicable in one domain to perform a similar task in another domain. For example, the learning-by-analogy strategy might be applied to learn water skiing when a person already knows snow skiing. Learning by analogy requires a greater amount of inference on the part of the learner than does learning from instruction. Relevant knowledge or skill must be retrieved from the memory and appropriately transformed to be applicable in a new situation or to a new problem. Examples of systems capable of learning by analogy are described by Carbonell (1983), Winston (1984) and Burstein (1984).

E. Learning from Examples

Given a set of examples and (optionally) counter-examples of a concept, the learner induces a general concept description. The amount of inference performed by the learner is greater than in learning by deduction or analogy, because the learner does not have prior knowledge of the concept to be learned, or knowledge of a similar concept. Thus, it cannot create the desired knowledge by deduction, or by analogy to what it already knows. The desired knowledge must be created anew by drawing inductive inference from available examples or facts, i.e., by inductive learning. Learning from examples, also called *concept acquisition,* can be a one-step (batch) process or a multi-step (incremental) process. In the batch case, all examples are presented at once. In incremental learning, examples (positive or negative) are introduced one-by-one or in small groups; the learner forms one or more tentative hypotheses consistent with the data at a given step, and subsequently refines the hypotheses after considering new examples. The latter strategy is commonly used in human learning.

Adaptive control systems can be viewed as a special case of systems learning from examples. A distincitve feature of them is that they improve their performance by adjusting internal parameters rather then by structural changes.

Examples of a concept may be provided by a human teacher, by the environment in which the system operates. They can be generated by a deliberate effort of a teacher, or by a random, heuristic or exhaustive search through a space of operators acting upon given situations. If an operator produces a desired result, then we have an positive example, otherwise a negative example. The inductive learning system then generalizes these examples to form general decision rules or control heuristics.

When a system determines examples by a search or other active effort, we have a form of learning called *learning by experimentation.* Such a method was used, for example, in the LEX symbolic intergration learning system (Mitchell, Utgoff and and Banerji, 1983).

Learning from examples is one form of inductive learning. Another form is learning by observation and discovery.

F. Learning by Observation and Discovery

This "learning without teacher" strategy includes a variety of processes, such as creating classifications of given observations, discovering relationships and laws governing a given system, or forming a theory to explain a given phenomenon, or The learner is not provided with a set of instances exemplifying a concept, nor is given access to an oracle (or teacher) who can classify internally-generated instances as positive or negative. Also, rather than concentrating attention on a single concept at a time, the learner may have to deal with observations that represent several concepts. This adds a new difficulty, namely solving the focus-of-attention problem, which involved deciding how to manage the available time and resources in acquiring several concepts at once.

Learning from observation can be subclassified according to the *degree of*

interaction between the learner and the external environment. Two basic cases can be distinguished:
(a) *passive observation*, where the learner builds a description of a given set of observations. For example, such a description may be a taxonomy of the observations (e.g., Michalski and Stepp, 1983), or an empirical law characterizing the observations, as in the BACON system (Langley, Simon & Bradshaw, 1983).
(b) *active experimentation*, where the learner makes changes in the given environment and observes the results of those changes. The changes may be random or dynamically controlled by some heuristic criteria. The choice of tasks and directions in the experimentation can be controlled by criteria such as *interestingness* (e.g., Lenat, 1976) or utility (e.g., Rendell, 1983a).

The learning strategies, (a) to (f), were presented above in order of increasing amounts of effort required from the learner and decreasing amounts effort required from the teacher. This order thus reflects the increasing difficulty of constructing a learning system capable of given learning strategy.

In human learning, the above order of strategies often reflects also an increasing confidence in the acquired knowledge. We all know that when we are given a general rule (a directive, a theory) without any explanation and examples supporting it, our confidence in it will not be very high; it will directly depend on the trust we have in the giver. Our confidence in a rule will be greater if we can try the rule on examples, and still greater, if we develop the rule through our own experience.

On the other hand, it is much more difficult to determine correct or highly useful knowledge by induction than to acquire it by instruction. This holds, of course, only if the teacher's knowledge is correct and/or highly useful, i.e., if we have a "perfect" teacher. Because this assumption may not hold in reality, the learning by instruction strategy is also associated with a risk of acquiring incorrect or low-grade kowledge. This explains the emphasis educators place on providing students with best teachers.

The higher the learning strategy, the more complex inference has to be performed by the learner, and thus the more cost and effort is involved in deriving the desired knowledge. It is much easier for the student to learn how to solve a problem by just being told the solution than by having to discover it on his/her own. Learning by instruction requires, however, a teacher who knows the algorithm or the concepts to be learned, and is capable of articulating them in the language of the learner. But when such a teacher is not available, another strategy must be used. For example, it is difficult to define the concept of a chair, or the shape of the characters of the alphabet. Therefore, such concepts are taught by showing examples rather than by instruction.

In many situations, the best way to explain a concept is to relate it to a similar concept and describe the differences. This is learning by analogy. In order to learn this way, however, the learner must know the referenced concepts. The more knowledgeable a learner is, the more potentially effective learning by analogy is. One can expect therefore that learning by analogy should tend to be in general more effective with adults than with children.

There are lessons for machine knowledge acquisition to be drawn from the above considerations. One is that if we know precisely how to solve a problem, we should tell the computer the solution directly (i.e., program it). Teaching by instruction will be simpler and more productive than using a deductive or inductive learning strategy. Such teaching will be facilitated by having an appropriate knowledge representation language and debugging tools. As there are many areas in which precise solutions are known and relevant concepts can be defined, this strategy has wide applications. Therefore, the development of appropriate knowledge representation languages and support tools (both general and specific to a given domain) constitutes a major research area.

When a learner already possesses a relevant knowledge, but the knowledge is not directly applicable to the given task, a deductive learning strategy may be applied, e.g., explanation-based learning. This strategy will produce operational, useful knowledge from an abstract, unusable knowledge. Equipping expert systems with such deductive inference capabilities, that is, with mechanisms for deductively transforming knowledge bases from one form to another, logically equivalent or more specific, is thus an important direction of research.

There are many application areas where precise concept definitions or algorithms are unknown or difficult to construct even in an abstract, non-operational form. Examples of such areas are technical, medical or agricultural diagnosis, visual pattern recognition, speech recognition, machine design, robot assembly, and many others. Also, people often have difficulties in articulating their expertise, even when they know well how to perform a given task or are able to recognize a given concept without any difficulty. In such cases, applying an analogical or inductive machine learning strategy seems quite desirable.

As mentioned earlier, a prerequisite for analogical learning in that the system possesses a knowledge base of concepts and solutions to problems that are similar to the ones the system will be solving. Moreover, the system must be able to recognize the similarity between any new problem and a problem for which it already knows a solution, and must be able to modify the known solution appropriately. These are difficult and complex operations. For that reason it is often easier for the system to start from scratch than to modify a known solution. This phenomenon is well known to programmers, who sometimes prefer to write a program anew rather than to modify an existing program that performs a task similar to the desired one. An interesting problem arising here is how to decide which way is better in any given situation. The decision requires estimates of costs involved in applying both methods in a particular situation.

Analogical inference can be viewed as a combination of inductive and deductive learning. The inductive part determines the existence of analogy between problems (or concepts) and formulates appropriate knowledge transformations that unify the base and the target problems or concepts. The deductive part performs these transformations on the known solution or concepts to derive the desired solution. An interesting variant of learning by analogy is *derivational analogy* (Carbonell, 1986) in which the experience transfer involves recreating lines of reasoning and their justifications in solving problems similar to the one encountered.

The remainder of the paper will discuss in greater detail the inductive learning strategy. Through this strategy a fundamentally new knowledge can be created, and thus this strategy is of special importance to machine learning. We will start by giving a more precise meaning to this type of learning.

3. Inductive Learning: General Description

Inductive learning is a process of acquiring knowledge by drawing inductive inferences from teacher- or environment-provided facts. This process involves operations of generalizing, transforming, correcting and refining knowledge representations in order to accomodate given facts and satisfy various additional criteria. An important property of inductive learning is that knowledge acquired through it cannot, in principle, except for special cases, be completely validated. This is so because inductive inference produces hypotheses with a potentially infinite number of consequences, while only a finite number of confirming tests can be performed. This is a well-known predicament of induction, already observed by Hume in the 18th century.

Inductive inference is an underconstrained problem. Given any set of facts or input premises, one can potentially generate an infinite number of hypotheses explaining these facts. In order to perform inductive inference one thus needs some additional knowledge *(background knowledge)* to constrain the possibilities and guide the inference process toward one or a few most *plausible* hypotheses. In general, this background knowledge includes the goals of learning, previously learned concepts, criteria for deciding the preference among candidate hypotheses, the methods for interpreting the observations, and the knowledge representation language with corresponding inference rules for manipulating representations in this language, as well as the knowledge of the domain of inquiry.

There are two aspects of inductive inference: the generation of plausible hypotheses, and their confirmation. Only the first is of significance to machine inductive learning. The second one (impossible in principle except for special cases) is considered of lesser importance, because it is assumed that the generated hypotheses will be judged by human experts and tested by known methods of deductive inference and statistical confirmation.

Bearing in mind these considerations, let us formulate a general paradigm of inductive inference:

Given:
(a) *premise statements (facts),* F, that represent initial knowledge about some objects, situations or processes,
(b) *a tentative inductive asertion* (which may be null),
(c) *background knowledge* (BK) that defines the goal of inference, the preference criterion for ranking plausible hypotheses, assumptions and constraints imposed on the premise statements and the candidate inductive assertions, and any other relevant general or domain specific knowledge.

Find:
an inductive assertion (hypothesis), H, that, together with background knowledge BK, tautologically implies the premise statements.

An hypothesis together with background knowledge tautologically implies a set of facts, if the facts are a logical consequence of the hypothesis and background knowledge, that is the implication H & BK $\Rightarrow$ F holds under all interpretations.

Since for a given BK an infinite number of assertions H can satisfy such an implication, a *preference criterion* (also called *bias*) is used to reduce the choice to one hypothesis or a few most preferable ones. Such a criterion may require, for instance, that the hypothesis be the shortest or the most economical description of all given facts, among all candidate descriptions.

Inductive learning programs already play an important role in the acquisition of knowledge for some expert systems. In some relatively simple domains they can determine decision rules by induction from examples of decisions made by experts. This form of knowledge acquisition relieves the expert from the tedious task of defining rules himself. Moreover, it requires the expert to do only what he can do best: make decisions. Experts are typically not trained to analyze and explain to others their decision making processes, expecially if they must express them in a formal way; therefore, such tasks are usually difficult for them to perform. Once rules are acquired from examples, expert can usually do a good job in evaluating them.

A less direct yet important application of inductive learning is to the refinement of knowledge bases initially developed by human experts. Here, inductive learning programs together with other supporting software can be used to detect and rectify inconsistencies, to remove undesirable redundancies, to cover gaps or to re-express the given rules in a simpler way (e.g., Reinke, 1984). Also, starting with initial human expert-based rules, an inductive learning program can improve these rules through feedback representing an evaluation of expert system's decisions.

Another use for inductive learning is to generate meaningful classifications of given sets of data, or to organize the sets of data (e.g., collections of rules) into a structure of conceptually simple components (Michalski and Stepp, 1983). We will illustrate this application by an example in section 5.

Most of the above applications have already been tried successfully on some relatively simple problems (e.g., Michalski, 1980; Quinlan, 1983). Current research tries to extend current machine learning techniques in a number of directions, such as: employing richer knowledge representation languages (e.g., Michalski, 1983), exploring constraints of a domain to control generalization (e.g., Mitchell 1986, Mooney and Bennett, 1986), constructing causal explanations and models (e.g., Doyle, 1986), automating the process of generating new attributes and operators by utilizing the domain knowledge (i.e., the *constructive induction,* or the *new term* problem; e.g., Michalski, 1983), coping with the uncertainty and noise in the data (e.g., Quinlan, 1986; Michalski et al, 1986), integrating different learning strategies (e.g., Lebowitz, 1986), constructing conceptual classifications of structured objects (e.g., Stepp and Michalski, 1986; Norhausen, 1986), infering components of structures (e.g., Rose and Langley, 1986).

As mentioned above, we can distinguish between two types of inductive learning: learning from examples and learning by observation and discovery. Let us discuss these two strategies of learning in greater detail.

4. Learning from Examples

Within the category of learning from examples we can distinguish two major types: *instance-to-class* generalization and *part-to-whole* generalization. In the instance-to-class generalization, given are independent instances (examples) of some class of objects, and the task is to induce a general description of the class. The instances can be representations of physical objects, sounds, images, actions, processes, abstract concepts, etc. Most research on learning from examples is concerned with this type of problem. For example, such research includes learning descriptions of block structures (e.g., Winston, 1977) or automatically inducing diagnostic rules for soybean diseases (Michalski and Chilausky, 1980). For a review of methods of such generalization see (Dietterich and Michalski, 1983).

In part-to-whole generalization, given are only selected parts of an object (a scene, a situation, a procress) and the task is to hypothesize a description of the whole object. A simple example of this type of problem is to determine a rule characterizing a sequence of objects (or a process) from seeing only a part of the sequence (or process). A specific case of such a problem occurs in the card game Eleusis, where players are supposed to discover a "secret" rule governing a sequence of cards. A computer program capable of discovering such rules has been described by Dietterich and Michalski (1983). A more advanced version of the program has been described by Michalski, Ko and Chen (1985).

The problem of discovering Eleusis rules is an instance of a more general problem of *qualitative prediction,* that is concerned with predicting behavior of any discrete processes in a qualitative way (Michalski, Ko and Chen, 1987).

In instance-do-class generalization, facts can be viewed as implications of the form

$$Event ::> Class$$

where *event,* is a description of some object or situation, and *class* represents a decision class or concept to be assigned to this object or situation. (We denote the implication between a fact or pattern, and the class associated with it by the symbol "::>", in order to distinguish it from the general implication symbol "⇒".) The result of learning is a rule:

$$Pattern ::> Class$$

where *Pattern* is an expression in some formal language describing events that belong to the given *Class,* and no events that do not belong to this class. When an unknown event satisfies the *Pattern* then it is assigned to *Class*.

The pattern description can be expressed in a many forms, e.g., a propositional or predicate logic expression, a decision tree, a formal grammar, a sematic network, a frame, a script, a computer program. The complexity of the process of inducing a pattern description from examples depends on two factors: 1) the complexity of the description language used (e.g., the number and the type of operators the system understands), and 2) the intricacy of the pattern description itself. If the pattern description involves no intermediate concepts then the above rule describes one-level class descriptions. In multi-level class descriptions there are intermediate rules between the lowest level concepts involving only measurable properties of objects, and a top level description involving higher level concepts directly related to the given class or concept.

Another important classification of learning techniques is based on the degree to which *descriptors* (attributes, relations, predicates, operators) used in the observational statements are relevant to the decision classes. The degree measures the relationship between initially given descriptors and the descriptors used in the final class description. At the lowest level, the descriptors used in the observational statements are the same as the ones used in the class descriptions. That means that the given descriptors are directly relevant to class descriptions. Such a case is assumed in many methods. At the next level, the initial descriptors contain the relevant ones, but not all of them are relevant. In this case, the system must have the ability to determine the relevant descriptors among many given descriptors. At the highest level, initial descriptors may be completely different from the ones used in the final concept description. We illustrate this case in Sect. 5, where given descriptors are simple physical properties of some objects (in this case trains), and the final descriptors are not directly observable, abstract concepts (such as "trains with toxic or non-toxic loads").

Let us illustrate *learning from examples (concept acquisition)*, and differentiate it from *learning from observation,* by an example problem known as "East-bound and West-bound trains" [Michalski & Larson, 1977] shown in Fig. 1. In the original

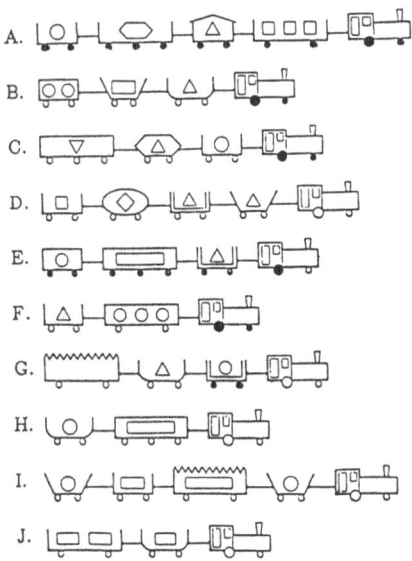

Fig. 1. The Unclassified TRAINS Problem

problem, given are two collections of trains, those that are "East-bound" (A to E) and those that are "West-bound" (F to J). The task is to determine a simple descriptive rule distinguishing between the East-bound and West-bound trains using examples of the trains.

These trains are highly structured objects. Each train consists of a sequence of cars of different shapes and sizes. The trains have different number of cars, and cars have different lengths. Thus, an adequate description of trains involves both qualitative and quantitative descriptors, e.g., numerical attributes such as *number of trains*, the *length of a car*, or the *number of loads in a car*, categorical attributes such as *shape of a car*, and relations such as *contains, in-front-of*. To illustrate one possible solution, let us present the discriminant descriptions of East-bound and West-bound trains found by the program INDUCE/2 [Hoff, Michalski, Stepp, 1983]. These discriminant descriptions, i.e., rules for distinguishing between the two classes of trains are expressed in the Annotated Predicate Calculus (APC). APC is a typed predicate calculus with additional operators (Michalski, 1983). The descriptions are:

East-bound (train) < :: ∃ (car) [contains(train, car)] & [length(car)=short] [shape(car)=closed]
("A train is East-bound if it contains a short, closed car.")
West-bound (train) < :: [num-cars(train)=2] ∨
 ∃ (car) [contains(train, car)] [shape(car)=jagged top]
("A train is West-bound if there are two cars in the train or if there is a car with a jagged top.")

These solutions are not easy to find without an aid of a computer program, but once found, they seem to be obvious.

An early practical application of the learning from examples strategy to building the knowledge base of an expert system is described in the paper by Michalski and Chilausky (1976). In the follow-up paper (Michalski and Chilausky, 1980), the learning from examples strategy was compared with the strategy of learning by being told in the context of building the afore-mentioned expert system PLANT/ds. This experiment resulted in inductively derived diagnostic rules (i.e., those obtained by machine learning from examples) that outperformed the rules determined by interviewing an expert (i.e., those acquired by the learning from instruction strategy). Reinke (1984) described a system for testing the consistency and completeness of a rule base using techniques of inductive inference. A recent example of an application of learning from examples to diagnostic problems in medicine is described in [Michalski et al, 1986].

5. Learning from Observation

The learning form observation strategy is applied when a collection of facts (observations) is given and one wants to develop a general description (a theory) explaining the facts. It is assumed that there is no teacher who can explain the facts or identify important or relevant concepts applicable to them.

The first step in developing a theory about a collection of facts is usually the creation of a classification (taxonomy). Such a classification can be considered a general description of these facts. Creating simple yet useful classifications is a challenging intellectual process of great importance.

So far, the problem of automatically creating classifications has been studied mainly in the areas of numerical taxonomy and cluster analysis. In these areas, the basic principle for creating a classification is to form classes of objects using some mathematical measure of similarity between the objects. This measure is defined over a finite, an a priori defined set of attributes characterizing the objects. Objects are put to the same class if they have a high degree of similarity, and to different classes if they have a low degree of similarity.

One difficulty with this approach is that classes (concepts) formed solely on the basis of a predefined measure of similarity can be difficult to interpret conceptually. In fact, the interpretation of obtained classifications is assumed in this approach to be the task of a data analyst. This approach does not take into consideration possible varying goals for classification, nor does it use general concepts or linguistic constructs that characterize a collection of observations as a whole (i.e., concepts that capture Gestalt properties). For example, if a collection of points forms a "T-joint", then in order to describe it this way, the system must contain in its background knowledge a method for recognizing such a concept. Without it, even if the computation of similarities (here, reciprocal of distances) puts all the points forming a "T-joint" into the same class, the system still would not "know" that the collection can be described this way.

An alternative approach to creating classifications is based on *conceptual clustering* (Michalski, 1980; Michalski and Stepp, 1983). In this approach, observations are partitioned into classes that represent some conceptual entities. Instead of *similarity,* the approach uses the measure of *conceptual cohesiveness* between objects. While the similarity of objects A and B is a function only of properties of these objects, i.e., is a two-argument function f(A, B), the conceptual cohesiveness is a function of the properties of objects A and B, of the surrounding objects, E (the environment), and of a set of concepts, C, available in the given description language for describing these two objects together. Thus, the conceptual cohesiveness is a four-argument function f(A, B, E, C).

In *conjunctive conceptual clustering* objects are assembled into classes that represent conjunctive concepts closely circumscribing or "fitting" the objects in the class, and satisfying some additional criteria measuring *clustering quality* (Michalski and Stepp, 1983). These criteria take into consideration the relation of the classes to a set of possible goals of classification, the complexity of generated class descriptions, their "disjointness", and other factors (Michalski and Stepp, 1983). The conjunctive concepts are descriptions in the form of conjunctions of statements specifying properties (attribute values) of objects representing the given concept, the relations among the object parts and the properties of the parts.

For illustration, let us consider an example (borrowed from Stepp and Michalski, 1986). Suppose that trains in Fig. 1 are not assigned to any classes, and the task is to create a meaningful classification(s) of these trains. What criteria would people use to create such a classification?

To answer this question, experiments were performed with 31 subjects, who where asked to solve this problem (Medin, Wattenmaker and Michalski, 1986). The subjects devised a total of 93 classifications of the trains. The most popular criterion for classification (used in 17 classifications) was simply the number of cars in the train. Thus, trains were classified into 3 groups: 2-car, 3-car and 4-car trains respectively. The second most popular classification (7 cases) was based on the color of engine wheels. Trains were classified to two groups: a group in which all engine wheels are white, and the group in which engine wheels have varied colors.

These results suggest that even in the absence of clear goals for a classification, people have tendency to use similar criteria for creating a classification. This similarity pattern was not very strong in the experiment, however, as indicated by a large number (40 out of 93) different classifications proposed. The same "Unclassified Trains" problem was given to the recently developed program CLUSTER/S (Stepp, 1984). The program generated several classifications. Two of them are shown in Fig. 2. The first classification A, uses as classification criterion the *num-*

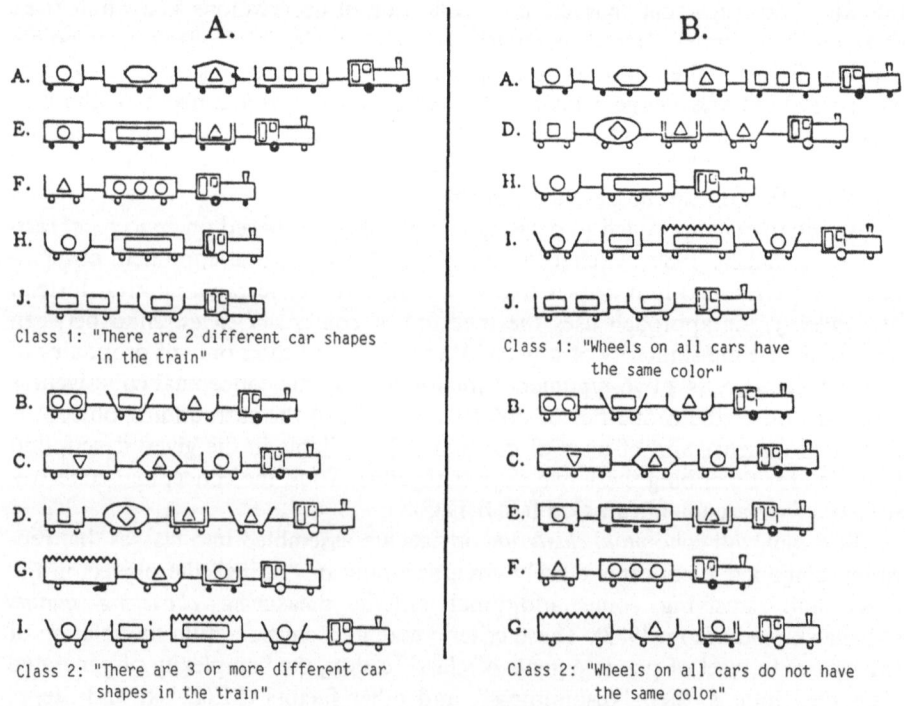

Fig. 2. Two classifications of TRAINS created by program CLUSTER/S

ber of different car shapes in the train. In the second classification B, the criterion used is whether the wheels on all cars in a train are the same or not. Although these classifications are different from the most frequent classifications made by people, they seem to be reasonable, and even appealing.

It should be mentioned that the initial descriptions of the trains (the observational statements) did not include statements about the number of different car shapes or whether the car wheels have the same color. How did the program generate such statements and use them in creating classifications?

The background knowledge of the program contained inference rules that, when applied to the original descriptions of the trains, can generate new possibly relevant descriptions (attributes and relations) characterizing given objects (here, trains) or their parts. Using various heuristics, the program selectively generates new descriptors and attempts to apply them in the process of determining candidate classifications. The program evaluates these classification according to the *classification quality* criterion LEF (lexicographic evaluation functional). The LEF criterion takes into consideration various properties of a classification, such as the degree to which it satisfies a set of goals (defined in the program's background knowledge), the degree of *fit* between a classification and the observed events (objects), and the importance of descriptors occurring in the class descriptions (see, Michalski, 1980; Medin, 1982; Michalski and Stepp, 1983 a,b; Stepp and Michalski, 1986).

To illustrate the concept of *importance* of a descriptor, let us assume that background knowledge of the system includes a rule which defines cars in the train that carry toxic chemicals. Suppose that such a rule is:

[contains(train, car)] & [car-shape(car) = opentop] & [cargo-shape(car) = circle]
[items-carried(car) = 1] ⇔ [toxic-chemicals(train)]

In this rule, the equivalence operator is used to state that the negation of the condition part is sufficient to assert the negative of the consequence. After applying this rule to each train description, the right-hand side of the rule will be appended to the description (as an additional predicate) to indicate the presence or absence of toxic-chemicals on the given train. This predicate will in turn trigger other inference rules that are part of the program's background knowledge:
- toxic chemicals are dangerous,
- dangerous things are important,
- important things should have high selection value (high preference score).

As a result of this inference the program will propose a candidate classification of trains into those containing toxic chemicals and those not containing such chemicals.

The descriptor generation process outlined above constructs new attributes from combinations of existing attributes. This process is guided by various heuristics. For example, two or more numerical attributes can be combined into a single attribute using arithmetic operators. To suggest appropriate arithmetic operators, a trend analysis can be used, as in BACON 4 (Langley, Bradshaw, Simon, 1983).

Predicates or whole rules can be combined by logical operators to form new attributes. For example, the rule

$$[\text{cold-blooded}(a1)] \ \& \ [\text{offspring birth}(a1) = \text{egg}] \Rightarrow [\text{animal-type}(a1) = \text{reptile}]$$

yields a new attribute "animal-type" with a specified value "reptile". Using this rule and similar ones, one might classify some animals into groups of reptiles, mammals, and birds (even though the type of each animal is not stated in the original data about animals).

Such classification construction problems occur when one wants to organize and classify observations that require structural descriptions. Problems of this type include classifying physical or chemical structures, analyzing genetic sequences, building taxonomies of plants or animals, structuring visual scenes, and splitting a sequence of temporal events into episodes with simple meanings. In an expert system, a classification construction program could be used, for example, to structure a large knowledge base of decision rules, or to structure the database of facts about a given problem.

6. Summary

Fundamental learning strategies have been discussed including *direct implantation of knowledge, learning by instruction, learning by deductive inference, learning by analogy, learning from examples* and, finally, *learning by observation and discovery*. The order of these strategies reflects the increasing complexity of the inference performed on the information given to a learning system in order to derive the desired knowledge.

Learning from examples and learning from observation are two basic forms of inductive learning. The paper discussed and illustrated the importance of using background knowledge in applying these learning strategies. The capability to incorporate background knowledge in inductive learning is an important prerequisite for the successful application of this form of learning.

Acknowledgement

It is this author's pleasant duty to thank Gail Thornburg and Robert Stepp for comments on the earlier version the paper. He also gratefully acknowledges the partial support of the research presented here by the National Science Foundation under grant DCR 84-06801, by the Office of Naval Research under grant N00014-82-0186, and by the Defense Advanced Research Projects Agency under the Office of Naval Research contract No. N00014-K-85-0878. A part of this paper was written while the author was with the MIT Artificial Intelligence Laboratory. The support for the Laboratory's research is provided in part by the Defence Adavnced Research Projects Agency under the Office of Naval Research contract N00014-80-C-0505.

References

Boulanger, A: The Expert System PLANT/cd: A Case Study in Applying the General Purpose Inference System ADVISE to Predicting Black Cutworm Damage in Corn, M.S. Thesis, UIUCDS-R-83-1134, Department of Computer Science, University of Illinois, Urbana, IL, July 1983.

Buchanan BG, Mitchell TM, Smith RG, Johnson CR Jr, Models of Learning Systems, Tech Rept STAN-CS-79-692, Computer Science Department, Stanford University, 1979.

Burstein MH: Concept Formation by Incremental Analogical Reasoning and Debugging, Proceedings of the 2nd International Machine Learning Workshop, Allerton House, University of Illinois at Urbana-Champaign, June 22-24, 1983.

Carbonell JG, Learning by Analogy: Formulating and Generalizing Plans From Past Experience, chapter in Machine Learning: An Artificial Intelligence Approach, Michalski RS, Carbonell J, Mitchell T (eds.), Tioga Publishing Company, 1983.

Carbonell JG, Derivational Analogy: A Theory of Reconstructive Problem Solving and Expertise Acquisition, chapter in Machine Learning, Volume II, Morgan Kaufman Publishers, Inc., 1986.

Chilausky R, Jacobsen B, Michalski RS: An Application of Variable-Valued Logic to Inductive Learning of Plant Disease Diagnostic Rules, Proceedings of the 1976 International Symposium on Multiple-Valued Logic, Utah State University, Logan, Utah, May 25-28, 1976.

Davis R, Knowledge Acquisition in Rule Based Systems: Knowledge About Representation as a Basis For System Construction and Maintenance. Chapter in Pattern-Directed Inference Systems, Waterman DA, Hayes-Roth F (eds.), Academic Press, 1978.

DeJong G, Mooney R, Explanation-Based Learning: An Alternative Review, Machine Learning Journal, Vol I, No 2, pp 145-176, Kluwer Academic Publishers, 1986.

Dietterich TG, Michalski RS, A Comparative Review of Selected Methods for Learning From Examples, chapter in Machine Learning: An Artificial Intelligence Approach, Michalski RS, Carbonell J, Mitchell T, (eds.), Tioga Publishing Company, 1983.

Doyle RJ, Constructing and Refining Causal Explanations from an Inconsistent Domain Theory, Proceedings of AAAI-86, Fifth National Conference on Artificial Intelligence, Vol I, pp 538-544, Philadelphia, PA, August 1986.

Hass N, Hendrix GG, Learning by Being Told: Acquiring Knowledge for Information Management, chapter in Machine Learning: An Artificial Intelligence Approach, Michalski RS, Carbonell J, Mitchell T, (eds.), Tioga Publishing Company, 1983.

Hoff WA, Michalski RS, Stepp RE, INDUCE 2: A Program For Learning Structural Descriptions From Examples, Technical Report, Department of Computer Science, University of Illinois, Urbana, Illinois, September, 1983.

Hu Chi-Heng, Pao Yoh-Han, Processing of Pattern Based Information, Part II: Description of Inductive Inference in Terms of Transition Networks, Technical Report 102-82 Part II, Case Institute of Technology, Case Western Reserve University, Cleveland, Ohio 44106, 1982.

Langley P, Bradshaw GL, Simon HA, Rediscovering Chemistry With the BACON System, chapter in Machine Learning: An Artificial Intelligence Approach, Michalski RS, Carbonell J, Mitchell T, (eds.), Tioga Publishing Company, 1983.

Lebowitz M, Not the Path to Perdition: The Utility of Similarity-Based Learning, Proceedings of AAAI-86, Fifth National Conference on Artificial Intelligence, Vol I, pp 533-537, Philadelphia, PA, August, 1986.

Lenat D, AM An Artificial Intelligence Approach to Discovery in Mathematics as Heuristic Search, Computer Science Department, Rept STAN-CS-76-750, Stanford University, Stanford, CA, 1976.

Lenat D, Hayes-Roth F, Klahr PH, Cognitive Economy in a Fluid Task Environment, Proceedings of the International Machine Learning Workshop, Michalski RS (ed.), Allerton House, June 22-24, 1983.

Medin DL, Structural Principles in Categorization, Developments of Perception and Cognition, Shepp B, Tighe T (eds.), Erlbaum, Hillsdale, NJ, pp 203-230, 1983.

Medin DL, Wattenmaker WS, Michalski RS, Constraints and Preferences in Inductive Learning: An Experimental Study Comparing Human and Machine Performance, ISG Report 86-1, Computer Science Department, University of Illinois, Urbana, January, 1986.

Michalski RS, A Variable-Valued Logic System as Applied to Picture Description and Recognition, Chapter in the book Graphic Languages, Nake F, Rosenfeld A (eds.), North-Holland Publishing Co., 1972.

Michalski RS, Knowledge Aquisition Through Conceptual Clustering: A Theoretical Framework and an Algorithm for Partitioning Data Into Conjunctive Concepts, Policy Analysis and Information Systems, Vol 4, No 3, pp 219-244, 1980b.

Michalski RS, Chilausky RL, Knowledge Acquisition by Encoding Expert Rules Versus Computer Induction From Examples: A Case Study Involving Soybean Pathology, International Journal for Man-Machine Studies, No 12, pp 63-87, 1980.

Michalski RS, A Theory and Methodology of Inductive Learning, chapter in Machine Learning: An Artificial Intelligence Approach, Michalski RS, Carbonell JG, Mitchell TM (eds.), Tioga Publishing Company, 1983.

Michalski RS, Ko H, Chen K, SPARC/E - An Eleusis Rule Generator and Game Player, UIUCDCS-F-85-941, ISG Report 85-11, Department of Computer Science, University of Illinois, Urbana, February 1985.

Michalski RS, Stepp RE, Automated Construction of Classifications: Conceptual Clustering Versus Numerical Taxonomy, IEEE Trans. on Pattern Analysis and Machine Intelligence, Vol PAMI-5, No 4, pp 396-410, July, 1983a.

Michalski RS, Stepp RE, Learning From Observation: Conceptual Clustering, chapter in Machine Learning, Michalski RS, Carbonell J, Mitchell T (eds.), Tioga Publishing Company, 1983b.

Michalski RS, Mozetic I, Hong J, Lavrac N, The Multi-Purpose Incremental Learning System AQ15 and Its Testing Application to Three Medical Domains, Proceedings of AAAI-86, Fifth National Conference on Artificial Intellingence, Vol 2, pp 1041-1045, Philadelphia, PA, August 1986.

Michalski RS, Ko H, Chen K, Qualitative Prediction: A Method and Program SPARC/G, Chapter in Expert Systems, Guetler C (ed.), Academic Press, 1987.

Mitchell TM, Version Spaces: An Approach to Concept Learning, Thesis PhD, Stanford University, Stanford, CA 1978.

Mitchell TM, Utgoff PE, Banerji R, Learning by Experimentation: Acquiring and Refining Problem-Solving Heuristics, chapter in Machine Learning: An Artificial Intelligence Approach, Michalski RS, Carbonell JG, Mitchell TM (eds.), Tioga Publishing Company, 1983.

Mitchell TM, Keller RM, Kedar-Cabelli ST, Explanation-based Generalization: A Unifying View, Machine Learning, pp 47-80, Vol 1, No 1, 1986.

Mooney RJ, Bennett SW, A Domain Independent Explanation-Based Generalizer, Proceedings of AAAI-86, Fifth National Conference on Artificial Intelligence, Vol I, pp 551-555, Philadelphia, PA, August 1986.

Nordhausen B, Conceptual Clustering Using Relational Information, Proceedings of AAAI-86, Fifth National Conference on Artificial Intelligence, Vol I, pp 508-512, Philadelphia, PA, August 1986.

Pao Yoh-Han, Hu Chi-Heng, Processing of Pattern Based Information, Part I: Inductive Inference Methods Suitable For Use in Pattern Recognition and Artificial Intelligence, Technical Report 101-82, Case Institute of Technology, Case Western Reserve University, Cleveland, Ohio 44106, 1982.

Quinlan JR, Learning Efficient Classification Procedures and Their Application to Chess End Games, Chapter in Machine Learning: An Artificial Intelligence Approach, Michalski RS, Carbonell JG, Mitchel TM (eds.), Tioga Publishing Co., pp 463-482, 1983.

Quinlan JR, The Effect of Noise on Concept Learning, Chapter in Machine Learning: An Artificial Intelligence Approach, Vol II, Michalski RS, Carbonell JG, Mitchell TM (eds.), Morgan Kaufmann Publishers, pp 149-166, 1986.

Reinke R, Knowledge Acquisition and Refinement Tools for the ADVISE Meta-Expert System, Thesis MS, Department of Computer Science, University of Illinois, Urbana, Illinois 1984.

Rendell LA, A New Basis For State-Space Learning Systems and a Successful Implementation, Artificial Intelligence, Vol 20, No 4, pp 369-392, 1983

Rose D, Langley P, STAHLp: Belief Revision in Scietific Discovery, AAAI-86, Fifth National Conference on Artificial Intelligence, Vol I, pp 528-532, Philadelphia, PA, August 1986.

Stepp RE, Conjunctive Conceptual Clustering: A Methodology and Experimentation, PhD Thesis, Department of Computer Science, University of Illinois, Urbana, 1984.

Stepp RE, Michalski RS, Conceptual Clustering: Inventing Goal-Oriented Classification of Structured Objects, Machine Learning: An Artificial Intelligence Approach Vol II, Michalski RS, Mitchell TM, Carbonell JG (eds.), Morgan Kaufmann, 1986.

Waltz D, Genesereth M, Hart P, Hendrix G, Joshi A, McDermott J, Mitchel T, Nilsson N, Wilensky R, Artificial Intelligence: An Assessment of the State-of-the-Art and Recommendation for the Future Directions, AI Magazine, Vol 4, No 3, Fall 1983.

Winston PH, Learning Structural Descriptions From Examples, Tech. Report AI TR-213, MIT, AI Lab, Cambridge, MA, 1977.

Winston PH, Learning by Augmenting Rules and Accumulating Sensors, Chapter in Machine Learning: An Artificial Intelligence Approach Vol II, Michalski RS, Mitchell TM, Carbonell JG (eds.), Morgan Kaufmann Publishers, Inc. 1986.

Heuristics for Empirical Discovery[1]

Pat Langley, Herbert A. Simon and Gary L. Bradshaw[2]

Abstract

In this paper, we review our experiences with the BACON project, which has focused on empirical methods for discovering numeric laws. The six successive versions of BACON have employed a variety of discovery methods, some very simple and others quite sophisticated. We examine methods for discovering a functional relation between two numeric terms, including techniques for detecting monotonic trends, finding constant differences, and hill-climbing through a space of parameter values. We also consider methods for discovering complex laws involving many terms, some of which build on techniques for finding two-variable relations. Finally, we introduce the notions of intrinsic properties and common divisors, and examine methods for inferring intrinsic values from symbolic data. In each case, we describe the various techniques in terms of the search required to discover useful laws.

1. Introduction: An Overview of BACON

Science is a multi-faceted endeavor, encompassing such diverse activities as designing experiments, discovering empirical laws, constructing new measuring devices, formulating theories, and testing hypotheses. Yet despite its complexity, the scientific process appears amenable to analysis in terms of the same concepts that have been successfully applied to other aspects of intelligence – the notion of *search* through a problem space, and the notion of *heuristics* for directing that search. In this paper we examine one facet of science – the empirical discovery of numeric laws – and describe a set of AI systems that are capable of such discovery. The programs are successive versions of the BACON system, named after Sir Francis Bacon, since their data-driven heuristics are similar in spirit to those proposed by the early philosopher of science in the Sixteenth Century.

Before examining the BACON heuristics in detail, let us briefly review the concerns and capabilities of different incarnations of the system. BACON.1 [1] was concerned mainly with the discovery of simple numeric laws relating two variables, and employed heuristics for noting trends and constants to his end.[3] BACON.2 [2] was concerned with the same task, but employed a simple differencing technique for finding such relations. We examine methods for discovering

---

[1] This research was supported by Contract N00014-82-K-0168, NR 049-514, from the Information Sciences Division, Office of Naval Research.
[2] Carnegie-Mellon University, Pittsburgh, Pennsylvania 15213 USA.
[3] BACON.1 also included heuristics for finding conditions on laws and for noting periodicity, but since these were not concerned with numeric law discovery, we will not focus on them here. BACON.2 and BACON.3 also included additional methods that we will ignore in the present paper.

two-term laws in the first section below. BACON.3 [3] returned to the trend and constant detectors used in the first version, but combined these with a method for recursing to higher levels of description. This allowed the system to discover complex laws involving multiple variables, and this is the focus of Sect. 3 below.

The BACON.4 system [4, 5] employed all of the heuristics used in BACON.3, but also included methods for postulating intrinsic properties and noting common divisors in cases where symbolic terms were involved. We discuss these methods in some detail in Sects. 4 and 5, using examples from the history of physics and chemistry. The fifth version of the system, BACON.5 [6, 7], was identical to BACON.4, except that it incorporated a differencing technique for finding simple numeric relations (this was more general than the one used in BACON.2), as well as expectation-based methods for reducing search through the space of laws. Finally, BACON.6 [8, 9] differed from its predecessor in that it replaced the differencing method with a hill-climbing technique that was more capable of handling noisy data. Table 1 summarizes the methods used in successive versions of BACON. In this paper, we examine the various heuristics for empirical discovery, focusing on their capabilities and their requirements. We will not spend much space on the individual BACON systems, since the interested reader may find descriptions in earlier papers.

Table 1. Components of successive BACON systems

BACON.1	Trend and constancy detectors
BACON.2	Specialized method for finding constant differences
BACON.3	Trend and constancy detectors Recursing to higher levels of description
BACON.4	Trend and constancy detectors Recursing to higher levels of description Intrinsic property method Common divisor method
BACON.5	General method for finding constant differences Recursing to higher levels of description Intrinsic property method Common divisor method Expectation-based methods
BACON.6	Hill-climbing method for dealing with noise Recursing to higher levels of description Intrinsic property method Common divisor method Expectation-based methods

2. Discovering Simple Numerical Laws

Let us begin with an apparently simple problem – determining the functional relation between two numeric terms. To be more specific, given two terms X and Y, along with a set of paired observations (x1, y1), (x2, y2), and so forth, we would like to find some function F such that $Y = F(X)$ predicts the observed data as closely as possible. Analytic solutions to this problem, such as the methods of regression and correlation, have been developed in the field of statistics. Although quite robust, these methods require one to assume a linear function (or some other simple form), thus ruling out many plausible relations. A few Artificial Intelligence researchs [10, 11] have tentatively explored search-based approaches to this problem, but no systematic treatment has been carried out. Below we examine four different heuristic curve-fitting methods that vary in terms of the size of the space they search, and in their ability to deal with noisy data.

2.1 Detecting Trends and Constants

Some early versions of BACON (1, 3, and 4) included four simple heuristics for finding two-term numeric laws. The first two of the rules are responsible for noting constant values and linear relations, both of which lead directly to the formulation of a law. The second two rules come into play when neither of the first pair can be used; these define some *theoretical term* as the product or ratio of existing terms. Once defined, BACON recursively applies its rules to these theoretical terms, looking for constant values, linear relations, or other trends, continuing until some law is discovered. These heuristics can be summarized as follows:

1. If Y has the value V in a number of cases, then hypothesize that Y always has that value.
2. If X and Y are linearly related with slope S and intercept I in a number of cases, then hypothesize that this relation always holds.
3. If X increases as Y decreases, and X and Y are not linearly related, then define a new term T as the *product* of X and Y.[4]
4. If X increases as Y increases, and X and Y are not linearly related, then define a new term T as the *ratio* of X and Y.

The last two rules can be viewed as directing BACON's search through the space of theoretical terms, where each new term is defined as an arithmetic combination of directly observable variables. They focus attention on terms that show potential for leading to constant values or linear relations, while the first two rules are responsible for detecting such laws once the appropriate terms have been defined.
 The operation of these heuristics is best understood through an example. Con-

---

[4] Actually, the third and fourth rules apply only when the values of X and Y have the same sign. In cases where X and Y have opposite signs, two analogous rules propose the opposite actions; for example, when the values of X and Y increase together, and X and Y have different signs, the product XY is defined.

Table 2. Data obeying Kepler's third law

PLANET	D	P	D/P	D^2/P	D^3/P^2
MERCURY	0.382	0.241	1.607	0.622	1.0
VENUS	0.724	0.616	1.175	0.851	1.0
EARTH	1.0	1.0	1.0	1.0	1.0
MARS	1.524	1.881	0.810	1.234	1.0
JUPITER	5.199	11.855	0.439	2.280	1.0
SATURN	9.539	29.459	0.324	3.088	1.0

sider the distance D of the planets from the sun (measured in astronomical units) along with the period of those same planets (measured in years). As one can see in Table 2, neither the values of D or P are constant, nor are they linearly related. However, the values of D increase along with those of P, so our fourth heuristic tells us to define the new term D/P as the ratio of these variables. Upon computing the values of this term, we find that they are neither constant nor linearly related to any other term, but that they to increase as those of both D and P increase. At this point we might define either the product D^2/P or the product PD/P. However, the latter of these is equivalent to the distance, and so should be abandoned. When the values of D^2/P are calculated, we find that they increase as those of D/P decrease. As a result, we would define the product D^3/P^2 and compute its values. Since these have the constant value 1.0, the first heuristic would apply, hypothesizing that this holds for all planets. Acting together, our heuristics have directed us through the space of theoretical terms, arriving at the functional equivalent of Kepler's third law of planetary motion.

Although the linear relation detector was not used in the above example, it is useful in other cases, such as the discovery of Ohm's law for electric circuits. In this situation, one varies the length L of a wire and observes the resulting current I. The values of I increase as those of L decrease, but since they are not linearly related, the product IL would be defined. Upon calculating the values of this term, one finds that IL and I are linearly related by the equation $IL = bI + v$ (where the particular values of b and v depend on the battery used). This equation is equivalent to Ohm's law, with the slope b respresenting the internal resistance of the battery and the intercept v its voltage.

The above heuristics do have limitations. For example, they cannot discover polynomial functions of degree two or higher, including such simple laws as $Y = aX^2 + b$. In such cases, the heuristics actually lead the system to ignore theoretical terms that are required to state the laws. However, they have been able to discover a number of nontrivial laws from the history of physics, including Galileo's laws for the pendulum and constant acceleration, as well as Ohm's law and Kepler's law. In addition, when combined with a heuristic for recursing to higher levels of description (discussed in the Sect. 3), these methods can induce much more complex relations, such as Coulomb's law of electrical attraction. What is amazing, then, is not the absolute power of these heuristics, but the fact that such *simple* rules are so useful in directing search through the space of possible laws. For instance, in finding Kepler's law, BACON.1 examined only 4 theoretical terms, compared to some 16 terms (a conservative estimate) that would be examined by a straightforward generate-and-test approach that considers simpler terms before more complex ones. One is tempted to infer that the early scientists also employed such simple heuristics to search for regularities, but that would lead us into historical discussions for which we do not have space.

As implemented in the early versions of BACON, this method had only modest capabilities for dealing with noisy data. The system required some ability on this dimension simply to deal with round-off errors in computing the constant values of higher level terms such as D^3/P^2. However, we did not explore the effects of significant noise in our experiments with BACON.1 through BACON.4. In Sect. 3, we discuss an extension of this basic approach that has excellent noise-handling capabilities, as well as being able to discover laws relating multiple terms. First, though, let us examine some other approaches to finding simple numeric laws.

2.2 Finding Constant Differences

Despite the attraction of the trend and constancy detectors, their limitations led us to explore more robust function-finding methods. As a result, BACON.2 incorporated a heuristic that searched for constant differences, and BACON.5 included a more general version of this same method; in this paper we will describe only the more general scheme. This technique searches for polynomial relations between two variables, and with a simple extension, can discover all of the laws attainable by the earlier method (though in a different form), along with many others as well.

Again, the method is best explained with an example. Consider the law $Y=3X^2+2X+1$, where X is the independent term and Y is the dependent variable. Table 3 presents some values obeying this law, along with some differences computed by the method. The first step involves examining the fist differentials of Y with respect to X for successive values. This term is computed just as one would compute the slope of a line. For instance, the first value would be $(34-6)/(3-1)=14$, the second would be $(121-34)/(6-3)=29$, and so on, until all successive values of X and Y have been combined in this manner. Since the resulting differentials are not constant, the process is repeated. The second differentials are computed using the first differentials in the numerator and the X values in the denominator; however, differences are taken between every other X value instead of directly adjacent ones. Thus, the first of the second differentials would be $(29-14)/(6-1)=3$, the second would be $(50-29)/(10-3)=3$, and so on. These val-

Table 3. Determinig the coefficient of a quadratic term

X	Y	Y'	Y''
1	6		
3	34	14	3
6	121	29	3
10	321	50	3
15	706	77	

Table 4. Determining the coefficient of a linear term

X	Y−3X²	(Y−3X²)'
1	3	
3	7	2
6	13	2
10	21	2
15	31	2

Table 5. Determining the constant term in an equation

X	Y−3X²−2X
1	1
3	1
6	1
10	1
15	1

ues *are* constant, so the system infers that the function relating the two terms includes an X^2 terms with a coefficient of 3. (This method works equally well for real-valued coefficients.)

Given this knowledge, BACON substracts out the variance accounted for by the X^2 term, and repeats the process on the values of $Y-3X^2$. Table 4 presents the resulting values, along with the first differentials of this term. Since the values of this differential have the constant value 2, the program infers that an X term with coefficient 2 is present in the final equation. Again, this component is subtracted and the resulting values of $Y-3X^2-2X$ are examined, as shown in Table 5. The values of this term are the constant 1, so BACON infers that the final form of the equation is $Y=3X^2+2X+1$. This differencing technique lets the system discover any polynomial relation, provided enough data have been observed to compute the necessary differentials. Thus, four observations would be required if the equation is of the third degree, three would be necessary if an X^2 term is involved, and so on. However, to ensure that spurious relations are not found in this manner, BACON insists that the functions it discovers be overidentified by the data, though the exact number of additional observations is controlled by the user.

The differencing method can be viewed as carrying out a heuristic search through the space of polynomial functions. This search begins by considering candidates for the largest terms in the relationship, examining constant, linear, and quadratic terms in turn. Terms that fail the test for constant differentials are rejected, along with all branches occurring below them in the search tree. Terms that pass the constant difference test are retained, and the more fully specified functions occurring below them in the tree are considered by entertaining various possibilities for the next highest term in the function. Some of these are also rejected, but some are retained, and the process continues until one or more functions with zero residuals have been generated. By applying the test for constant differentials at each level of the search tree, this technique examines only a few of the many functional relations that it would otherwise have to consider.

A simple extension of this method lets BACON deal with more complex laws as well. In addition to considering polynomial relations between X and Y (or between any two terms), the system also considers relations between X and Y^2, X and Y^3, and so forth. This enables the discovery of Kepler's third law (in the form $P^2 = aD^3$), as well as many other numeric relations. Finally, the system can also consider transformations of both the independent the dependent terms, such as inverse(Y), sine(Y), log(Y), and so on. The first of these lets the system discover Ohm's law using the differencing method; in this case, the law is stated as $I^{-1} = aL + b$, where $a = \text{voltage}^{-1}$ and $b = \text{resistance/voltage}$. We have not yet uncovered any heuristics to direct search through the space of possible transformations, so BACON.5 considers each transformation in turn, using a simple-minded generate and test strategy. However, the user can direct the system's attention by including some transformations and excluding others.

The differencing heuristic as implemented in BACON.5 can also deal with some degree of noise, though the method has certain limitations. Rather than requiring a constant differential to be found, the system is satisfied with *near* constant values. The meaning of *near* is determined by two parameters – the *relative* error R associated with a dependent term, and the *absolute* error A associated with that term. These parameters are used to construct an interval around the observed mean of a given differential. If all values fall within that interval, BACON infers that any divergence from the mean is due to noise of one form or another.

For instance, consider the values of X and Y in Table 6. The values of Y are identical to those in Table 2, except that some variation from the law $Y = 3X^2 + 2X + 1$ has been included. Suppose that BACON is given a relative error of 0.07 for Y, along with an absolute error of 0.001. Upon examining the values of Y, the system finds a mean of 240. Multiplying this mean by the relative error gives the product 16.8, from which BACON creates the interval (223.2, 256.8) by adding and subtracting this amount from the mean. (In this case, the absolute error has negligible influence, although it becomes important when values approach zero.) Since all of the Y values fall outside this interval, the program infers that Y is not constant. When the values of the first differential are computed, the mean 43.29 results. Since these values are based on pairs of the original data points, noise can be confounded, so both the relative and absolute error terms are doubled,[5] giving the interval (37.23, 49.35). Again, most results lie outside this interval, so the process is repeated. When the second differentials are calculated, the mean 3.22 is obtained. The error terms are again doubled, since the second differentials further compound the potential noise, leading to the interval (2.31, 4.13). All of the values fall within this interval, so BACON concludes that the second differential has the near-constant value 3.22. This process is repeated after the X^2 term has been subtracted, to estimate the other coefficients of the equation.

---

[5] This is a conservative estimate. Since each value of Y may be either $RY + A$ too high or too low, it is possible that the difference of two Y values will be 2 $(RY + A)$ too high or two low.

Table 6. Noisy data obeying the law $Y = 3X^2 + 2X + 1$

X	Y	Y'	Y'
1	6.15		
3	33.15	13.50	3.36
6	124.03	30.29	2.42
10	312.98	47.24	3.88
15	723.65	82.14	

When BACON transforms the dependent values to consider more complex relations such as $\log(Y) = f(X)$ and $Y^{-2} = g(X)$, the absolute error term A must be transformed as well. If we let M represent the mean of the observed dependent values and M_t stand for the mean of the transformed dependent values, then the transformed absolute error term $A_t = AM_t/M$. This formula guarantees that the ratio A/M will remain constant across transformations. To see why this is necessary, consider the dependent term Y with mean 100, and the transformed variable Y^{-1} with mean 0.01. If the absolute error for Y is 0.1, we certainly do not want to use the same error term for the much smaller values of Y^{-1}. In this case, the transformed error term would be $(0.1)(0.01)/100 = 0.0001$, which seems much more reasonable. Fortunately, there is no need to alter the relative error term R when transformations are employed.

How robust is the differencing method with respect to noise? As long as polynomials with only a single term are involved, such as $Y = aX^3$ or $Y = bX$, it performs quite well. However, recall that in order to estimate the parameters for more complex laws, BACON must first estimate one parameter, substract out some of the variance, then estimate the second parameter, and so forth. Thus, in estimating the parameters for the law $Y = aX^2 + bX + c$, the system would first determine a, then use this estimate in determining b, and employ both estimates in finding the value of c. Unfortunately, small errors in the estimation of the quadratic term *a* can seriously affect the estimate of the linear term *b*, leading to even greater effects for the estimate of the constant term *c*. Thus, while the differencing technique has some abilities for handling noise, a better method would be desirable, and we examine such an approach below.

2.3 Hill-Climbing through the Space of Parameters

Both of the above methods carry out search through a space of functional relations, though they explore somewhat different spaces and certainly employ different operators for generating new problem states. However, in both cases, these operators actually use the data in generating the new state. Thus, the two methods may be characterized as *data-driven*. Unfortunately, this reliance on the data leads to difficulties when significant noise is present, and to deal with such situations, we have explored (in the BACON.6 program) a more enumerative approach to finding numeric laws.

In this method, the user provides BACON with one or more *forms* of law that it should consider in attempting to summarize the data. For instance, the system might be told to examine laws of the form $Y = aX^2 + bX + c$, as well as those having the form $\sin(Y) = aX + b$ (where X is independent and Y is dependent). These forms define the space of laws that BACON should consider in its search for numeric relations. Based on each of the forms, the system generates a set of initial states from which to begin the search. These states are simply instantiated versions of the abstract forms with 1, 0, or -1 inserted for the parameters. For instance, given the form $Y = aX^2 + bX + c$, BACON generates nine initial states: [a=1, b=1], [a=1, b=0], [a=1, b=-1], [a=0, b=1], [a=0, b=0], [a=0, b=-1], [a=-1, b=1], [a=-1, b=0], and [a=-1, b=-1]. These values are chosen because they are well-distributed throughout the space of parameters, so that the optimum point should lie near one of them. The constant term c is not included, since its value can be computed once the quadratic and linear terms have been estimated.

Starting from these points, BACON carries out a form of hill-climbing through a k-dimensional space (in this case k=2). At the outset, the system evaluates each of the initial points in terms of its ability to summarize the observed data. This is accomplished by substituting each combination of parameter values into the form, and predicting the value of the dependent term Y for each value of the independent term X. The system then computes the *correlation* of the redicted and observed Y values; this is required since we are concerned with relative parameter values rather than absolute ones. This process is repeated for each of the initial points in the space, and the N highest scoring parameter sets are selected for further exploration.

For each of the N points that are retained, BACON generates a new set of points by adding 0.5 to each of the parameter values. In addition, a second set of points is generated by subtracting 0.5 from the same points. For example, if the initial points [a=1, b=1] and [a=0, b=-1] had been retained (with N=2), then twelve additional points would be produced: [a=1.5, b=1], [a=1, b=1.5], [a=1.5, b=1.5], [a=0.5, b=-1], [a=0, b=-0.5], and [a=0.5, b=-0.5] by adding 0.5; as well as [a=0.5, b=1], [a=1, b=0.5], [a=0.5, b=0.5], [a=-0.5, b=-1], [a=0, b=-1.5], and [a=-0.5, b=-1.5] by substracting 0.5. Each of these points is evaluated in turn, and compared to the points from which they were generated. As before, the N best parameter combinations are selected, based on their ability to predict the observed Y values in terms of the X values.

Using the N new points, the process is repeated, this time adding and subtracting the value 0.25 from each of the parameter values. Again each of the resulting points is evaluated, with the N best combinations being retained for use on the next cycle. In this way, BACON continues to improve its ability to predict the observed data, using a method of successive approximation. This beam-search version of hill-climbing proceeds, with the size of the step being halved on each cycle, until the step size falls below a user-specified level. At this point, the system stops its search, and for each of the N best parameter sets, the program generates a specific equation that can be used to predict Y in terms of the X values.

Table 7 summarizes the path taken in summarizing noise-free data obeying the polynomial $Y = 3.1X^2 + 2.35X + 1.0$, using a beam size of one. At the outset, the

Table 7. Beam search discovery of the law Y=3.1001 X²+2.3485 X+1.0031

Step size	Quadratic term a	Linear term b	Correlation
1.00000	1.0000	1.00000	0.9999827810
0.50000	1.5000	1.00000	0.9999974065
0.25000	1.2500	1.00000	0.9999994657
0.12500	1.1250	0.87500	0.9999998815
0.06250	1.06250	0.81250	0.9999999865
0.03125	1.03125	0.78125	0.9999999999

system generated the nine initial states given above, finding that the pair [a=1, b=1] best predicted the observed data. On the next cycle, BACON used a step size of 0.5 to produce six new states, this time finding the pair [a=1.5, a=1.0] to have the highest score. This process continued until the system reached a step size of 0.03125, the user-specified condition for halting. At this point, the best set of parameters was [a=1.03125, b=0.78125], which accounted for 0.9999999999 of the variance. In other words, the Y values predicted by these parameters were highly correlated with the observed Y values. However, BACON still had to compute the actual values for these parameters, along with the value for the constant term in the equation. This was easily done using the coefficients in the regression equation relating the observed and predicted values of Y, and BACON generated the final law Y=3.1001 X²+2.3485 X+1.0031. Although the estimated coefficients are not identical to those from which the data were generated, they are remarkably close.

This method is quite robust with respect to noise, since it uses the data only to test hypotheses rather than to generate them. When noisy data are involved, the path taken is very similar to the noise-free case we have just examined. The main difference is that the correlations used in evaluating parameter combinations never reach the same heights, since the observed Y values can never the completely predicted by the X values. The greater the noise in the data, the lower the final score that BACON must accept. Still, the evaluation function generally leads the system to parameter estimates that closely approximate the correct values. Unlike the differencing technique, this method does not require the user to provide an estimate of the amount of noise in the data; it arrives at the best parameters for summarizing the data, whether these are very good or very poor predictors.

However, note that if the user has provided a number of possible forms, the system must still select between these competitors. To this end, BACON employs a second evaluation function. First, the system computes the complexity C of each hypothesis (measured by the number of non-zero terms in the expression) and the variance V explained by the rule. It then combines these values into the ratio V/C, a function that improves with better fits to the data, and decreases as hypotheses become more complex. Once the scores have been computed, BACON finds the best score and multiplies it by a user-specified system parameter; the values of this parameter must fall between zero and one (we have used 0.8 in our runs). The resulting score is treated as a threshold; all hypotheses having scores below this limit are rejected, while those with scores exceeding it are retained. This strategy has a useful property. If one or a few hypotheses are clearly superior to the others, only these are retained; however, if many of the hypotheses are basically equivalent, then all of these are kept. In our experiments with noisy data, this approach has proven much more robust than the earlier data-driven methods.

2.4 Expecting Similar Relations

The heuristics we have examined so far all rely heavily on the observed data to direct their search through the space of functional relations. However, once the system has discovered a law in one context, it makes sense to use that information to direct the search process in related contexts. To this end, we have introduced certain *expectation-driven* heuristics (in BACON.5 and BACON.6) that take advantage of early findings to aid the discovery process at later points. In this way, BACON can reduce its search without any loss in generality, since the particular class of hypotheses that the system considers depends on those found earlier by the data-dependent methods. This contrasts with the type of domain-specific expectations found in most experts systems, which greatly constrain these systems' range of application.

The simplest of BACON's expectation-driven heuristics proposes that if the system has found a law in one context (i.e., when the independent terms not included in the law are held constant), it should expect a similar *form* of law to hold in a new context (i.e., when those terms take on different values). For example, once the system has discovered that Kepler's third law holds for the planets orbiting the sun, it could employ this *similar relations* heuristic to predict an analogous law for the moons of Jupiter. Specifically, if the law $D^3 = 1.0P^2$ were found in the first situation (when the sun was held constant), BACON would expect that a law of the form $D^3 = kP^2$ would hold in the new case (when the sun was replaced by Jupiter), though it would not yet know the value of the parameter k. In the case of BACON.5's differencing method, such a prediction lets the system immediately consider polynomial functions of D^3, rather than considering functions of D, D^{-1}, D^2, and D^{-2}, which would normally be tried first. In the case of BACON.6's hill-climbing method, an additional savings occurs. Rather than searching the three-dimensional parameter space associated with the form $D^3 = aP^2 + bP + c$, the system can search the much simpler one-dimensional space to estimate the quadratic coefficient *a*, since it expects both the linear and constant terms to be zero.

The reader will recall that BACON.5's differencing method requires different numbers of observations to estimate the parameters for polynomials of different complexity. This leads to a second expectation-driven method that we will call the *data-reduction* heuristic. Initially, BACON.5 gathers more than the necessary number of observations to ensure that a law is correct. However, once the system expects a particular form of a law to hold, it can determine the number of observations necessary to estimate the desired parameters, and collects only the minimum number of observations necessary to complete its description of the current law. Thus, in the above example, BACON would need only three data points to determine the value of *k* for the Jovian moons. Of course, additional observations would be required if significant noise were present, but the principle of reduced data would remain.

This method leads to only minor computational savings for two-term laws, but for more complex multi-term relations (discussed in the following section), the savings can be quite significant. Thus, in discovering the ideal gas law, the standard version of BACON.5 (without the data-reduction heuristic) ran for some 35 CPU seconds. Using the data-reduction method, the program arrived at the same law in only 21 CPU seconds. Very similar results emerged with runs on Coulomb's law, another four-term relation with a somewhat different form.

3. Discovering Complex Numeric Laws

The methods described in the previous section can discover numeric relations between *two* variables, but more complex relations lie beyond their scope. For instance, one would like methods for discovering functions involving many variables, such as the ideal gas law and Coulomb's law of electric attraction. Upon closer examination, one finds that there exist two quite different situations in which one can attempt to discover complex laws. In the first case, one has experimental control over all but one of the terms, so that the traditional method of "varying one term at a time" can be used to separate the effects of each independent term on the dependent variable. This is the approach we explored in BACON.3 and succesive versions of the system, and we discuss the basic method below. After this, we examine an extension of the method that employs knowledge of symmetry to reduce search through the space of laws. In the second situation, there is no experimental control over any of the observable terms, and one can only observe co-occurring values. Later in the section, we examine a method for dealing with such cases, based on a generalization of the heuristics used in BACON.1. The distinction between experimental science and observational science seems a major one, and there is no a priori reason to expect that identical methods will prove useful in both contexts.

3.1 Recursing to Higher Levels of Description

In order to let BACON discover laws relating many numeric terms, we introduced another heuristic that let it summarize regularities at different *levels of description*. This method operates when the system is given a number of terms over which it has experimental control. BACON begins by holding all but one of the terms constant, and discovering a specific law in that context. The constant values found in this situation are stored along with the independent values for which they occurred. Different constants are found for different contexts, and when enough values have been found, the system treats them as dependent values at a higher level of description, and attempts to find a higher level relation. The system employs the same method to find the second level law as it did at the lower level.

Heuristics for Empirical Discovery

After a law at the second level has been found, the program recurses to still higher levels, until all of the independent terms have been incorporated into a unified law, and all of the data have been summarized.

BACON's discovery of the ideal gas law provides a useful example of this strategy. This law may be stated as $PV = 8.32N(T-273)$, where P is the pressure on a quantity of gas, the dependent term V is the volume of the gas, T is the temperature of the gas in degrees Celsius, and N is the quantity of gas in moles. In order to run an experiment, BACON must be provided with values for each independent term; let us suppose the system is told to examine $N = 1, 2$, and 3, $T = 10, 20$, and 30 (Celsius), and $P = 1000, 2000$, and 3000. In discovering this law, BACON begins by holding N at 1 and T at 10, and varying the values of the pressure P, examining the resulting values of V in each case. Suppose that for $P = 1000, 2000$, and 3000, the program observes $V = 2.36, 1.18$, and 0.78. Using one of the methods for finding simple laws we described in the last section, BACON arrives at the relation $V^{-1} = 0.000425\ P$. In addition, it introduces the theoretical term a as the coefficient of P in this equation. The constant value $a = 0.000425$ is stored with the values $N = 1$ at $T = 10$ for later use, and system moves on to a new experimental combination.

BACON's next step is to continue holding N at 1, but to examine a different value of T, say 20, and to find a new relation between P and V in this new context. Suppose in this situation, for $P = 1000, 2000$, and 3000, the system finds that $V = 2.44, 1.22$, and 0.81. Although the same form $V^{-1} = aP$ continues to hold, in this case it estimates that the parameter $a = 0.000410$, instead of the earlier value. This new value is stored with $N = 1$ at $T = 20$ for future use. Analogous events occur when BACON considers $T = 30$, with the system finding that $a = 0.000396$. At this point, the program has three values for the term a, each associated with $N = 1$ and with a different value for T. Accordingly, it attempts to find a relation between the parameter a and the temperature T. Using the same method it used at the lower level, BACON finds the linear relation $a^{-1} = 8.32\ T + 2271.4$. It also defines b and c, two theoretical terms that correspond to the two parameters in this equation. The values $b = 8.32$ and $c = 2271.4$ are stored with $N = 1$ for later use, and the system continues.

This process is repeated for $N = 2$, with BACON finding different estimates of the parameter a, and relating them to the values of T. In this case, it finds the relation $a^{-1} = 16.64\ T + 4542.7$, and stores the values $c = 16.64$ and 4542.7 with $N = 2$. Analogous events occur for $N = 3$, giving the value 24.96 for b and 6814.1 for c. At this stage, BACON has enough values of N and b to search for a relation between the two terms, and it arrives at the law $b = 8.32\ N$. Similarly, it looks for a law relating N and the parameter c, this time finding $c = 2271.4\ N$. In addition, it defines two terms d and e, having the values 8.32 and 2271.4, respectively. These two values are not conditional upon the values of any other term (at least as far as BACON knows), and so the system halts, having summarized all of its data, and relating the terms V, P, T, and N to one another.

Let us examine the mapping between BACON's laws and the ideal gas law. The first level law has the form $V^{-1} = aP$, while the second level law has the form $a^{-1} = bT + c$. Substituting $(bT + c)^{-1}$ for a in the first law, we get $V^{-1} = (bT + c)^{-1} P$. From the two third level laws, we know that $b = 8.32\ N$ and $c = 2271.4\ N$, and sub-

Table 8. Summary of ideal gas law discovery

BACON's version	Standard version	Constant terms
$V^{-1} = aP$	$PV = k$	T, N
$V^{-1} = P/(bT+c)$	$PV = k(T-273)$	N
$V^{-1} = P/(dNT+eN)$	$PV = 8.32N(T-273)$	

stituting for b and c, we obtain $V^{-1} = (8.32 \, NT + 2271.4 \, N)^{-1} P$. Dividing through by P, inverting both sides of the equation, and factoring out 8.32 N, we get $PV = 8.32 \, N \, (T+273)$. The standard version of the law is $PV = 8.32 \, NT$, where T is measured in degrees Kelvin. Since adding 273 degrees Celsius converts the Celsius scale into the Kelvin scale, the above equation is equivalent to the standard form of the ideal gas law. In a sense, BACON has generated its own measurement scale for the temperature, in order to state the relation succinctly. Table 8 summarizes the steps taken in this discovery, comparing BACON's version of the law with the standard version, and showing the independent terms held constant at each level of description.

Taken together, the heuristics for finding simple numeric relations and recursing to higher levels give BACON considerable power. Using these two strategies, the system has successfully rediscovered versions of Coulomb's law of electrical attraction, a complex version of Ohm's law, and the ideal gas law. The recursion heuristic has been somewhat modified in BACON.6 to aid the system in dealing with noise. Since more than one functional relation may be found acceptable by the hill-climbing method, the system must be able to store each of the resulting sets of parameters at higher levels of description. However, if a hypothesis is found to be acceptable in one context, but in a later context no analogous hypothesis is found to fit, the hypothesis is rejected and its associated parameters are removed from the higher level store. For example, suppose the laws $Y = 3.0X^2 + 2.0$ and $\log(Y) = 0.5X + 4.0$ both fit the data fairly well when $Z = 1.0$. As a result, the parameter values 3.0, 2.0, 0.5, and 4.0 would be stored at the second level of description for later use. Now suppose that when $Z = 2.0$, only the law $\log(Y) = 0.75X + 6.0$ obeys the data well enough to be accepted. Since it does not appear to be general, the first law relating Y to X would be rejected as a summary of the initial data, and the parameter values 3.0 and 2.0 would be removed. One can imagine more lenient versions of this strategy in which a few exceptions were allowed, but some approach of this type that tests the generality of functional forms would appear to be very useful.

3.2 Discovering Symmetrical Laws

Although the method of varying one term at a time considerably simplifies the task of discovering complex laws, it can require considerable amounts of data to be gathered. One way to avoid this is to employ expectation-driven heuristics to reduce the amount of data required to identify a complex law. For example, the notion of symmetry has played an important role in the history of physics, and

Heuristics for Empirical Discovery

Table 9. Symmetrical laws discovered by BACON

Snell's law of refraction	$\sin \theta_1 / n_1 = \sin \theta_2 / n_2$
Conservation of momentum	$m_1(V_1 - U_1) = -m_2(V_2 - U_2)$
Black's specific heat law	$c_1 M_1(T_1 - F_1) = -c_2 M_2(T_2 - F_2)$

Table 10. Discovering Snell's law of refraction

MEDIUM$_1$	SIN θ_1	MEDIUM$_2$	SIN θ_2	n_2	SIN θ_2/n_2
VACUUM	0.25	WATER	0.33	0.33	1.0
VACUUM	0.25	OIL	0.37	0.37	1.0
VACUUM	0.25	GLASS	0.42	0.42	1.0

one might well use expectations of symmetry to constrain search through the space of laws. Table 9 presents three well-known laws that exhibit symmetry – Snell's law of refraction, conservation of momentum, and Black's heat law.

Although BACON.3 and its successors can discover these laws with just the heuristics we have already described, the inclusion of a new heuristic that postulates symmetry significantly reduces the search required to find the relations. This heuristic applies whenever BACON is asked to run an experiment involving two objects that have the same set of associated variables. The method first varies in turn all terms associated with the first object, and finds an Nth level description of the relationship between these terms. Once the form of this law is known, the heuristic *assumes* that the same function will relate the terms associated with the second object. It then computes the values of these two higher level functions for a number of situations, and checks to see if they are linearly related. If so, the symmetry assumption is verified, and the two terms are combined into the final law.

As an example, consider BACON's discovery of Snell's law of refraction, as summarized in Table 10. The program starts with two objects and two variables associated with each object – the medium though which light passes, and the sine of the angle the light takes. Varying medium$_2$ and holding medium$_1$ and sine θ_1 constant, the system postulates an intrinsic property, n_2, whose values are associated with different media. Of course, the ratio sine θ_2/n_2 has the constant value 1.0. At this point, BACON relates the terms associated with the second object, and decides that it should examine the values of sine θ_1/n_1 and relate them to the former ratio. Upon gathering additional data, the program discovers that the two ratios are identical, or that sine $\theta_1/n_1 =$ sine θ_2/n_2, which is one statement of Snell's law.

The BACON system has discovered two other symmetrical relations – conservation of momentum and Black's specific heat law – following very similar paths. Table 9 presents the full form of the laws; directly observable terms are shown in upper case, while intrinsic properties (discussed in the following section) are shown in lower case. We may have given the impression that the symmetry heuristic eliminates search entirely, but this is not the case. Although the set of hypotheses considered is drastically reduced, it is not always narrowed to a single function. Only one symmetrical hypothesis emerges in Snell's law, since the relation that is found combining the first set of terms involves only one parameter. In discovering both Black's law and conservation of momentum, two parameters occur, so the enhanced version of BACON considers two possible symmetries. For both laws, one of these symmetries is found to satisfy the observed data, while the other is rejected. However, because the system has strong expectations, it can test its hypotheses against much less data than would be necessary using the purely data-driven approach.

In the case of symmetrical laws, we have another example of expectation-driven heuristics and their use in reducing search through the space of possible laws. In rediscovering Snell's law, the data-driven version of BACON.5 required some 40 CPU seconds. However, when the symmetry heuristic was included (along with the similar relations and data reduction heuristics), the system found the same law in only 5 CPU seconds. Even greater savings occurred for Black's heat law, since this involved a total of eight terms. In this case, the data-driven version took 8433 CPU seconds, while the expectation-driven version (using the symmetry heuristic) required only 23 CPU seconds, an improvement of more than two orders of magnitude. Moreover, the symmetry heuristic accomplished this reduction with little loss in generality, since symmetry relations can be found in a wide variety of scientific domains.

3.3 Finding Observational Laws

The numeric heuristics we have considered, together with the method of recursing to higher levels of description, are very useful for finding laws when some of the variables are under experimental control. However, since this approach relies on the ability to vary the values of one term while holding the others constant, it cannot be used to discover relations in purely observational data. Interestingly, a modified version of BACON's first numeric heuristics, which we described in Sect. 2.1, can be be applied in such cases. The modification is a simple one: rather than looking for monotonic trends, one looks at *correlations* between terms. Thus if one found X and Y to be positively correlated, their ratio would be defined as a new term, while if they were negatively correlated, their product would be considered. Since correlations are used, one can apply this revised method to observational data involving many covarying terms. Of course, any pair of terms has some correlation, so one must have some means for directing search through the space of new terms. Our solution is to carry out a beam search, in which only the N highest correlations are used to define new terms. The values of these terms are computed, as well as their correlations with other terms, and the process is repeated. As more complex terms are defined (redundant terms are eliminated), the best correlations approach 1 or -1, until eventually a near linear relation is found and a law is formulated. The system continues until all terms have been incorporated into a law, or until the terms become too complex.

We have implemented this approach to observational discovery, and Table 11 presents a trace of the system discovering the law $XY/WZ = 1$, using a beam size

Table 11. Discovering the law XY/WZ=1 using observational data

The correlation between W and Z is -0.5617
The correlation between W and Y is 0.4704
The correlation between W and X is 0.3161
The correlation between Z and Y is -0.0157
The correlation between Z and X is -0.1234
The correlation between Y and X is -0.5099

Defining XY as the product of X and Y
Defining WZ as the product of W and Z

The correlation between W and XY is 0.8907
The correlation between W and WZ is 0.8907
The correlation between Z and XY is -0.2343
The correlation between Z and WZ is -0.2343
The correlation between Y and XY is 0.6484
The correlation between Y and WZ is 0.6484
The correlation between X and XY is 0.2457
The correlation between X and WZ is 0.2457

Defining XY/W as the ratio of XY and W
Defining WZ/Y as the ratio of WZ and Y

The correlation between W and WZ/Y is 0.3161
The correlation between W and XY/W is -0.5617
The correlation between Z and WZ/Y is -0.1234
The correlation between Y and WZ/Y is -0.5099
The correlation between Y and XY/W is -0.0157
The correlation between X and XY/W is -0.1234
I've found a law: XY/W=1.0Z
I've found a law: WZ/Y=1.0X

---

of two. The program begins by finding the pairwise correlations between the four observable terms X, Y, Z, and W. Since the two highest correlations (in terms of absolute values) occur between W and Z (-0.5617) and between Y and X (-0.5099), these are used as the basis for two new terms. Since both correlations are negative, the two products XY and WZ are defined, and the system computes their values. Next, the correlations between the new terms and the directly observable terms are calculated, and the highest scores are noted. The two highest correlations are between W and XY, and between W and WZ. Since both of these are positive, the products XY/W and WZ/W are defined. However, since the second of these is equivalent to the observable term Z, it is dropped from consideration and the next highest correlation is used. Since the pair Y and XY leads to XY/Y, which equals X, this ratio is rejected and a fourth pair is considered. This time the pair Y and WZ leads to the ratio WZ/Y, which is a genuinely new term. When the third round of correlations is computed using XY/W and WZ/Y, the system finds two relations that exceed its threshold for actual laws. First, it finds the correlation between XY/W and Z to be 1.0, leading to the law XY/W=1.0Z, or XY/ZW=1.0. Second, it finds an identical correlation between WZ/Y and X, producing the law WZ/Y=1.0X, which can also be transformed into XY/ZW=1.0. The current version of the system does not realize that these laws are identical, but it does know that once all known terms have been incorporated into a law, it can halt its search through the space of products and ratios.

We have not incorporated this correlational method into BACON, since that system is so oriented toward dealing with experimental data. However, the method can discover many of the laws found by BACON even without experimental control over the variables involved. For instance, the method discovers Kepler's third law in much the same way as BACON, and it can find the ideal gas law, though it does so at a single level of description. In addition, since the technique uses correlations to direct its search through the space of terms, it is quite robust with respect to with noise. Although this approach cannot arrive at the polynomial relations found by the differencing method, it is a very promising approach to observational discovery that we plan to explore further.

4. Postulating Intrinsic Properties

The heuristics we have examined are appropriate for finding relations between numeric variables, such as distance and current, but they cannot by themselves deal with situations involving *nominal* or symbolic terms. In particular, suppose one's dependent variables are numeric, while the independent terms take on only symbolic values. In this section, we describe a discovery method, first introduced in BACON.4, that deals with such cases. The approach involves postulating a new term, which we call in *intrinsic property*. It also involves inferring a set of numeric values for the new property, associating these values with the observed symbolic values, and retrieving these inferred values when appropriate. Once BACON has associated a set of numeric intrinsic values with a set of nominal values, it can apply its numeric heuristics to discover new laws. We begin with a simple example in which intrinsic properties are required, and then examine a second case that led us to introduce a more conservative strategy for retrieving intrinsic values. After this, we consider the role of symmetry in situations involving intrinsic terms, and propose extensions to the method that handle cases in which multiple intrinsic properties occur.

4.1 Postulating Properties and Inferring Values

We saw earlier that BACON could rediscover Ohm's law when given numeric measures for external resistance (the length of the wire) and current. However, suppose we assume a slightly different situation in which the dependent variable I (the current) is still numeric, but in which the two independent terms - the battery and the wire used in the current - take on only nominal values. For instance, let us take three batteries - A, B, and C - and three wires - X, Y, and Z. These can be combined in different ways to generate different currents, but nothing is known directly about the batteries and wires except their indentities. In this case, BACON could vary the battery and wire and observe the resulting current, but

Table 12. Postulating the property of conductance

BATTERY	WIRE	CURRENT I	conductance c	voltage v
A	X	3.4763	3.4763	1.0
A	Y	4.8763	4.8763	1.0
A	Z	3.0590	3.0590	1.0
B	X	3.9781	3.4763	1.1444
B	Y	5.5803	4.8763	1.1444
B	Z	3.5007	3.0590	1.1444
C	X	5.5629	3.4763	1.6003
C	Y	7.8034	4.8763	1.6003
C	Z	4.8952	3.0590	1.6003

since the independent values are nominal, it would not be able to find a numeric law. Our solution is to let the system "invent" numeric terms that are associated with the batteries and the wires, such as voltage and resistance. We will call such terms *intrinsic properties*, since their values are associated with particular objects or sets of objects.

Let us examine the process of postulating intrinsic properties for our modified electrical experiment. Table 12 presents the currents for nine combinations of batteries and wires. These currents were computed by assuming the voltages $V_A = 4.613$, $V_B = 5.279$, $V_C = 7.382$ for the batteries, and the resistances $R_X = 1.327$, $R_Y = 0.946$, and $V_Z = 1.508$ for the wires. In addition, we assumed that the internal resistance for each battery was negligible. Upon examining the first three rows of the table (when the battery is A), BACON notes that the current I varies as the wire is varied. Since it cannot relate a numeric term to a nominal one, it postulates a new term (let us call it the *conductance c*), and bases its values on those of the current. Given the two numeric terms, any of the numeric discovery methods we have described would immediately find that they are linearly related with a slope of 1.0 and an intercept of zero: Of course, this is hardly surprising, since the values of c were defined to be those of the current I. However, the tautology disappears when BACON considers the next three rows (in which the battery is B). In this case, the system has already encountered the wires X, Y, and Z, so it retrieves their asaociated intrinsic values and compares them to the observed currents. This time BACON's numeric method also finds a linear relation with a zero intercept, but here the slope is 1.1444 rather than 1.0. An analogous law is discovered when the final three rows are examined, this time with 1.6003 as the slope.

Once these three relations have been found, BACON uses the slopes of these lines to search for a relationship at the second level of description. However, the system again finds that it cannot relate a nominal variable (the battery) to a numeric term (the slope). Accordingly, a new, higher level intrinsic property (let us call it the *voltage v*) is created, with its values based on the slope values and associated with the different batteries. Again a tautological linear relation is found, but since no other independent terms exist to be varied, the system cannot move beyond this stage to discover empirically meaningful laws. At this point, BACON halts, having arrived at two intrinsic properties and their values for different objects. The values of the conductance c are associated with individual wires, while the values of the voltage v are associated with particular batteries. In addition, these terms are related to the current by the law $I/vc = 1$. Since the conductance c is the inverse of the resistance r, we can restate this relation as $I = v/r$, which is one form of Ohm's law for electric circuits. Moreover, the values obtained for v and r differ only by a constant factor from the values we used to compute the currents, meaning that BACON has effectively regenerated these values using only nominal values and their associated currents. The constant factor was introduced when BACON used the first set of currents as its values for the conductance, since the introduction of intrinsic properties involves the selection of a measurement scale along which nominal values can be ordered.

Note that intrinsic properties are useful only in cases involving at least *two* independent nominal terms. This is because the first set of dependent values must be used in defining the intrinsic values. Unless one or more additional sets of dependent values are observed, the law incorporating the new property will be tautological and have no predictive power. Thus, this method differs from the numeric techniques we have considered, since the latter can be used to find simple laws relating two variables, while the intrinsic property method applies only to the discovery of complex laws involving three or more terms, and multiple levels of description. Also note that upon achieving predictive power, any law involving an intrinsic property also acquires the ability to make *incorrect* predictions. This suggests a more conservative version of the method, to which we now turn.

4.2 Generalizing Conditions for Retrieval

The strategy described above works well for cases in which intrinsic properties are associated with *single* nominal variables, as conductance is associated with the wire and voltage with the battery. However, one can find cases in which an intrinsic property is instead associated with multiple nominal terms, and to deal with these situations BACON must use a more cautious strategy. As an example, let us consider the friction between two surfaces. Here we have two independent nominal terms, the composition of the first surface and the composition of the second, and one dependent numerical term, the friction observed when the two surfaces are placed in contact. Superficially, this arrangement is very similar to the battery-wire case, and one might expect to be able to postulate an intrinsic property associated with individual surfaces, and to use these values to predict the observed frictions.

Let us step through the strategy described earlier and see how it fares. As before, the system would begin by holding the first surface constant and varying the values of the second surface. Upon noting that the friction is different in each case, BACON would postulate an intrinsic term (let us call it F), and base its values on those of the observed friction. The program would also discover the tautological relationship between F and the friction, and store this information for later use at a higher level of description. BACON would then consider the same values for the second surface, this time using a different value for the first independent term. After observing the friction values, the system would retrieve the intrinsic values that it had associated with the three values of the second surface, and attempt to relate these values of F to the observed frictions. However, in this case, no relation can be discovered, nor can one be found when the first surface is again varied. In this case, associating the intrinsic values with the second surface alone was inappropriate. Instead, these values should be retrieved only when a particular *pair* of surfaces are involved.

In order to deal effectively with cases in which intrinsic values should be associated with sets of terms, BACON employs a more conservative strategy for retrieving intrinsic values. When a property is first postulated, the system assumes that all independent nominal terms are relevant, and so associates the various intrinsic values with a *conjunction* of the nominal values. For instance, given the first three rows of Table 12, BACON associates 3.4763 with both wire X and battery A, 4.8763 with wire Y and battery A, and 3.0590 with wire Z and battery A. When the battery is varied and the wires are reexamined, the system does *not* immediately retrieve the various conductances. However, it *does* attempt to relate the newly observed currents to the original conductances. Upon finding a linear relation, BACON infers that the battery does not affect the conductance, and removes it as a condition for retrieval. When the battery C is considered, the three conductances (now associated only with the wires) are immediately retrieved and related to the observed currents. In the friction example, no linear relation is found when the second set of values is examined, so the values of the first surface are retained as conditions for retrieving the values of F. New conditions are associated with the second set of F values, and still another set with the third. More complex examples are possible in which some nominal terms are relevant while others are not, and BACON's intrinsic property heuristics are general enough to deal with such cases.

The retrieval of intrinsic values under certain conditions can be viewed as a form of expectation-driven discovery, since the system uses knowledge it has gained in one context to aid discovery in a similar yet different context. The main difference is that with the numeric expectation-driven techniques, the *form* of some law is retrieved and used to reduce search, while in the intrinsic property method, a set of *values* are retrieved and used in the discovery process. Also, the numeric methods BACON employs do not require it to generalize the retrieval conditions on the forms before they are used. However, one can imagine a more conservative version of the system that required a particular form of law to prove itself useful in a number of contexts before being used with confidence. This leads us to return our attention to another form of expectation-driven discovery that can also be adapted to laws involving intrinsic properties.

4.3 Symmetry and Intrinsic Properties

We have seen how BACON can use the assumption of symmetry to drastically reduce both its search through the space of laws, and the amount of data it must gather. The notion of symmetry can also be applied to the intrinsic property method, leading to additional computational savings. Let us examine a case where both symmetry and intrinsic terms occur, such as Black's specific heat law. This may be stated as

$$T_f = (c_1 M_1 T_1 + c_2 M_2 T_2)/(c_1 M_1 + c_2 M_2),$$

where T_1 and T_2 are the initial temperatures of two liquids, M_1 and M_2 are the respective masses, c_1 and c_2 are the specific heats, and T_f is the final temperature after the two liquids have reached equilibrium. Specific heat is an intrinsic property associated with the particular (symbolic) type of liquid used, and must be inferred from the directly observable temperatures and masses.

In rediscovering Black's law, BACON varies the initial temperatures and masses, and relates these terms to the resulting final temperature. When it begins to vary the substances used for the first liquid in the experiment, it finds that different substances give laws with the same form but with different coefficients. Accordingly, the system postulates an intrinsic property whose values are based on these differences. When the second liquid is varied and the values of the first liquid are reexamined, BACON finds a linear relation between its first set of intrinsic values and the coefficients found in the new context. As a result, it generalizes the conditions for the retrieval of these intrinsic values, associating them only with the values of the first liquid.

This is the point at which the symmetry assumption comes into play. It is natural to assume that a substance will have the same specific heat, whether it is used as the first liquid in the experiment or as the second liquid. Thus, if the same symbolic values are used for analogous variables, and the program has associated intrinsic values with those symbols in one context, it retrieves them immediately should it require them in the other context. This strategy lets the system avoid postulating an entirely new property in such cases, which would lead it to tautological rather than empirical laws at the higher levels of description. This method works equally well for other symmetric laws, such as Snell's law of refraction, in which the intrinsic term *index of refraction* is inferred, and conservation of momentum, in which the concept of *inertial mass* is generated.

Symmetry plays a different role in the intrinsic property method than in the purely numeric techniques. In the latter, the symmetry assumption lets BACON determine the actual *form* of the law with less search than it would otherwise require. With respect to intrinsic properties, the symmetry assumption simply allows the system to sidestep the generalization process, letting it retrieve intrinsic values in new contexts that would normally require additional observations. Of course, these two applications of symmetry can be used in conjunction, and this is precisely the course BACON follows when it encounters nominal terms in symmetrical situations.

4.4 Extending the Intrinsic Property Method

BACON's intrinsic property heuristics appear to be quite general, and have been used to rediscover Proust's law of definite proportions and a version of Archimedes' law of displacement, as well as the modified version of Ohm's law we have

Heuristics for Empirical Discovery

Table 13. Inferring multiple intrinsic properties

S	T	D	j	m	b
X	A	1	1	1	0
X	B	2	2	1	0
X	C	3	3	1	0
Y	A	4	1	2	2
Y	B	6	2	2	2
Y	C	8	3	2	2
Z	A	4	1	3	1
Z	B	7	2	3	1
Z	C	10	3	3	1

already considered. In addition, we saw that the notion of symmetry could be easily incorporated into the approach, leading to a number of other laws. However, the existing method does have its limitations. For example, it seems odd that BACON's numeric heuristics are able to discover complex functional relations, while the intrinsic property heuristic considers only linear relations with zero intercepts. In fact, as implemented, the intrinsic property method does not require *any* search; it entertains a single hypothesis, and if this fails, the system does not generalize (as in the friction example). Fortunately, the method can be extended to deal with more complex circumstances, and the numeric techniques can be used to direct search through the space of possibilities.

Let us begin with an example that is only slightly more complicated than those we have already considered. Suppose we have two nominal independent terms S and T, along with the single dependent term D, and suppose we observe the values of D shown in Table 13. Since the values in the first three rows differ (when T is varied and S is held constant), we would posit an intrinsic property (say j), and base our initial set of intrinsic values on the observed values of D. When the second set of D values are observed, we find a linear relation between these values and the original set, but this case differs from those we have seen before in having a nonzero intercept. The natural way to deal with this situation is to create a property for the intercept (b) as well as for the slope (m), and to consider both terms when one searches for second level laws. As a result, one would postulate *two* intrinsic properties at the second level of description, basing their values on the values of m and b. This extension of the basic method should work equally well in cases involving quadratic and higher relations, though even more second level intrinsic properties could result in such cases.

In fact, relations involving nonzero intercepts and other complex relations will be found precisely when multiple intrinsic properties are involved. For instance, the data in Table 13 were generated by the law $D = mj + b$, where j is an intrinsic property associated with T, and m and b are independent intrinsic properties associated with S. Since the ability to infer multiple intrinsic properties would seem to be very useful, it is appropriate to consider the circumstances under which this extended method will succeed. The approach appears to work if, at a given level of description at which the nominal term Y is varied first and the nominal term X is varied second, and the dependent term D is affected, there exists a polynomial relation $D = P(i)$, where i is a single intrinsic property associated with Y, and for which the coefficients of the polynomial are intrinsic properties associated with X. For instance, if m and n are intrinsic properties associated with X, and p and q are associated with Y, the method will work for the relations $D = mp$, $D = mp + n$, and even $D = mp^2 + np$. However, the method will fail if the relation $D = mp + nq$ is involved, since it cannot handle interacting sets of intrinsic properties. Also note that the order in which terms are varied can be significant. If the data in Table 13 are rearranged so that S is varied before T, the method will also fail. Given this constraint, future versions of BACON may be forced to examine their data in different orders if they hope to uncover multiple intrinsic properties.

To summarize, we see that BACON's ability to find complex numeric relations can be employed to discover multiple intrinsic properties. In general, any form of numeric law that the system can discover can also be used in assigning intrinsic values. Thus, the differencing method and the hill-climbing method could lead to intrinsic properties based on *transformations* of observable terms, since both can discover laws such as $Y = a \sin^2(X) + b \sin(X) + c$. For example, consider the data in Table 14, in which we again have two nominal terms (S and T) and a single dependent term (D). Upon looking for a relation between the first set of D values and the second set, no polynomial relation is apparent. Since no relation can be found between the directly observable terms, the next natural step would be to examine transformations of the two sets of values, and attempt to relate them.

In this case, a linear relation is found if we examine the *logarithms* of both terms, and a similar relation holds between the first and third sets of values. Based on this success, we would postulate an intrinsic property (i) and base its values on those of D. However, since a transformation of the second set of values was required to discover the relation, our final law will be simplified if we use log(D) for our intrinsic values, rather than the values of D themselves. This leads to a single higher level parameter, which can be expressed as log(D)/i, since we have a zero intercept. This term takes on different values for different values of S, and so leads to a single intrinsic value at the second level of description. The data in Table 14 were computed from the law $D = p^q$, where p is an intrinsic term associated with T, and q is similarly associated with S. The intrinsic values $p_a = 1$, $p_b = 2$, $p_c = 3$ and $q_x = 1$, $q_y = 2$, $q_z = 3$ were employed. Thus we see that by considering transformations, an extended version of BACON would be able to discover

Table 14. Basing intrinsic properties upon transformations

S	T	D	log(D)	i	log(D)/i
X	A	2	0.301	0.301	1
X	B	3	0.477	0.477	1
X	C	4	0.602	0.602	1
Y	A	4	0.602	0.301	2
Y	B	9	0.954	0.477	2
Y	C	16	1.204	0.602	2
Z	A	8	0.903	0.301	3
Z	B	27	1.431	0.477	3
Z	C	64	1.806	0.602	3

Heuristics for Empirical Discovery

intrinsic properties involved in laws of a very different from than we have seen before. Now that we have introduced the notion of intrinsic properties and explored its implications in some detail, let us turn to another discovery method that builds on this concept.

5. Finding Common Divisors

The early versions of BACON were designed with laws from physics in mind, but after BACON.4 had been successfully tested on a number of such laws, we began to look for other applications. In examining the history of early chemistry, we found that BACON's heuristics for finding numeric relations and inferring intrinsic properties were necessary, but not sufficient, to discover many of the empirical laws in this domain. Closer examination revealed that early chemists also employed the notion of *common divisors* for a set of data, leading them to a number of laws that could not be found using the other heuristics in isolation.

For instance, John Dalton's law of multiple proportions (1808) states that if two elements can combine in different ways (leading to different compounds), then the combining weights will always occur in small integer proportions. Thus, 1.3 grams of oxygen combines with 1.0 gram of carbon to form the gas carbon monoxide, while 2.6 grams of oxygen combine with the same amount of carbon to generate carbon dioxide. In 1808, Joseph Gay-Lussac proposed a similar law for volumes, stating that the combining volumes of gases always occur in small integer multiples of one another. In 1815, William Prout hypothesized that the atomic weights of the elements were all multiples of the weight for hydrogen, suggesting that this was the basic building block of nature. Nearly fifty years later, integral values also figured prominently in Stanislao Cannizzaro's redetermination of the atomic weights. At least in the early days of quantitative chemistry, the notion of common divisors played a central role in the search for regularity.

5.1 Detecting Integer Relations

In order to account for these discoveries, we introduced a method (first used in BACON.4 [4, 5]) for noting common divisors in a set of data. This heuristic may be viewed as a special case of the intrinsic property heuristic, since it is applied whenever the latter is applied, but produces useful results only in come cases. Let us consider how BACON used this method to rediscover Dalton's law of multiple proportions. Table 15 presents some data on the manner in which nitrogen combines with oxygen. Three of the independent terms – the first element (in this table always oxygen), the second element (in this table always nitrogen), and the resulting compound – take on nominal values, while the fourth independent term – the weight of the first element used in the reaction – and the single dependent term – the weight of the second element in the reaction – take on numeric values. Upon varying the first weight and observing its effect on the second weight, BACON

Table 15. Determining the combining weights for reactions

ELEMENT$_1$	ELEMENT$_2$	COMPOUND	W$_1$	W$_2$	W$_2$/W$_1$
OXYGEN	NITROGEN	NITRIC OXIDE	1.0	1.14	1.14
OXYGEN	NITROGEN	NITRIC OXIDE	2.0	2.28	1.14
OXYGEN	NITROGEN	NITRIC OXIDE	3.0	3.42	1.14
OXYGEN	NITROGEN	NITROUS OXIDE	1.0	0.57	0.57
OXYGEN	NITROGEN	NITROUS OXIDE	2.0	1.14	0.57
OXYGEN	NITROGEN	NITROUS OXIDE	3.0	1.71	0.57
OXYGEN	NITROGEN	NITROGEN DIOXIDE	1.0	2.28	2.28
OXYGEN	NITROGEN	NITROGEN DIOXIDE	3.0	4.56	2.28
OXYGEN	NITROGEN	NITROGEN DIOXIDE	2.0	6.84	2.28

Table 16. Dalton's law of multiple proportions

ELEMENT$_1$	ELEMENT$_2$	COMPOUND	W$_2$/W$_1$	i	W$_2$/W$_1$i
OXYGEN	NITROGEN	NITRIC OXIDE	1.14	2.0	0.57
OXYGEN	NITROGEN	NITROUS OXIDE	0.57	1.0	0.57
OXYGEN	NITROGEN	NITROGEN DIOXIDE	2.28	4.0	0.57
OXYGEN	CARBON	CARBON MONOXIDE	1.33	1.0	1.33
OXYGEN	CARBON	CARBON DIOXIDE	2.66	2.0	1.33

finds linear relations and defines the ratio W_2/W_1, though different slopes occur for different values of the second element and the compound.

Up to this point, the system has used only its heuristics for finding numeric relations, and the relations it finds are equivalent to those first stated by J.L. Proust (1797) in his law of definite proportions. The constants for the various oxygen-nitrogen reactions are shown in Table 16, along with those for two oxygen-carbon reactions; this table shows BACON's second level summary of the original data. As we have seen, BACON treats such summaries as if they were data, and applies its heuristics to see if any higher level relations can be uncovered. In this case, since the independent terms are nominal and the dependent term is numeric, and since the values of W_2/W_1 are not constant, the program postulates an intrinsic property (let us call it i), and this is the point at which the common divisor detector comes into play. It examines the dependent values of the first three rows and notes that they have the common divisor 0.57. A similar dicovery is made for the carbon reactions, though the divisor is 1.33 in this case.

At this point, BACON diverges somewhat from the course it would normally take in storing intrinsic values. Rather than basing these intrinsic values directly on the dependent values, it divides the latter by the common divisor, giving a set of integers. Thus, the intrinsic value stored for the oxygen-nitrogen-nitric oxide triple would be 2, the value for oxygen-nitrogen-nitrous oxide would be 1, and that for oxygen-nitrogen-nitrogen dioxide would be 4. As a result, the values of the ratio W_2/W_1i become simply the observed common divisors, which are 0.57 for the oxygen-nitrogen pair and 1.33 for the oxygen-carbon pair. Otherwise, events proceed as they normally would. The system initially stores all independent values as con-

Heuristics for Empirical Discovery 47

ditions for retrieval of the integral intrinsic values, and checks to see if these conditions should be generalized. In this case, no generalization can be made, since the values of the compound are never repeated for different values of the elements. Although this makes non-tautological laws impossible at the current level of description, the fact that *different* values occur for the ratio W_2/W_1i make it possible for further discoveries to be made a higher levels. This approach to breaking out of the tautological loop is best illustrated with another example from the history of chemistry.

5.2 Complex Laws Involving Common Divisors

Table 17 presents a slightly different formulation of the standard chemical experiment. In this case we told BACON to vary only one of the elements entering the reaction, along with the resulting compound and the weight of the element used in the reaction. The first two of these terms are nominal, while the third is numeric, as is the single[6] dependent term – the volume V_c of the resulting compound. After gathering these data, BACON employed its numeric heuristics to find linear relations between W_e and V_c. Since these lines always had zero intercepts, we will focus on the slopes, which can be represented as W_e/V_c. Table 17 presents the slopes discovered for a number of element-compound pairs, which were then stored by BACON as second level summaries.

Upon examining these higher level data, the system postulates an intrinsic property (let us call it j), and finds the dependent values to have common divisors. This leads to integers being associated with the various element-compound pairs, such as 2 for hydrogen-water, 3 for hydrogen-ammonia, and 2 for hydrogen-ethylene. These values correspond to the coefficients for the elements in the balanced equation for each compound, though BACON does not interpret them in this

Table 17. BACON's rediscovery of Cannizzaro's law

ELEMENT	COMPOUND	W_e/V_c	integer j	divisor W_e/V_cj
HYDROGEN	WATER	0.0892	2.0	0.0446
HYDROGEN	AMMONIA	0.1338	3.0	0.0446
HYDROGEN	ETHYLENE	0.0892	2.0	0.0446
OXYGEN	NITROUS OXIDE	0.715	1.0	0.715
OXYGEN	SULFUR DIOXYDE	1.430	2.0	0.715
OXYGEN	CARBON DIOXIDE	1.430	2.0	0.715
NITROGEN	NITROUS OXIDE	1.250	2.0	0.625
NITROGEN	AMMONIA	0.625	1.0	0.625
NITROGEN	NITRIC OXIDE	0.625	1.0	0.625

---

[6] In the actual run, BACON was also told to examine two other dependent terms – the weight of the compound and the volume of the element. The program found a number of additional relations involving these variables, including Gay-Lussac's law of combining volumes, but for the sake of brevity we will not focus on them here.

Table 18. BACON's determination of relative atomic weights

ELEMENT	divisor	k	divisor/k
HYDROGEN	0.0446	1.0	0.0446
OXYGEN	0.715	16.0	0.0446
NITROGEN	0.625	14.0	0.0446

fashion. In addition, the term W_e/V_cj takes on the values of the common divisors that were found. As we noted before, these values are different, so that even though BACON cannot generalize the retrieval conditions on its intrinsic values (again because the compounds are never repeated), the potential for higher level discoveries remains. In this case, that potential is fulfilled, as shown in Table 18, which lists the third level summaries that result from BACON's endeavors. Given different values for W_e/V_cj, the program postulates an intrinsic property (k), but a common divisor is again found in these higher level values. Integers are computed and associated with the elements; these integers are equivalent to the relative atomic weights found by Cannizzaro in 1860. Moreover, BACON's statement that these values have a common divisor is equivalent to Prout's hypothesis that all atomic weights are divisible by the weight of hydrogen (though again, it does not interpret its finding in this manner).

5.3 Extending the Common Divisor Method

As with the intrinsic property method, the current version of the common divisor heuristic carries out very little search. It does consider the possibility that the inverses of a set of values will have a common divisor, rather than the values themselves, but one can imagine more sophisticated strategies. At first glance, it seems reasonable to extend the method to handle multiple properties in the same way we proposed for the basic intrinsic property method. However, this extension works only in cases where some relation can be found between two sets of dependent values, and these are precisely the situations where there is no need to look for common divisors. This is because one can generalize the retrieval conditions, and thus find non-tautological laws without resorting to postulating integer values for the intrinsic properties. The two methods are complementary, since the common divisor heuristic may lead to useful results even if the more basic approach fails.

However, the two other extensions we proposed earlier apply equally well to searching for integral relations. If neither the observed values of a dependent term D nor its inverse D^{-1} have a common divisor, then BACON could examine transformations of the term, such as log (D), sin (D), and D^2. Similarly, if multiple dependent terms X and Y are present, the system could consider combinations of these terms, such as XY, X/Y, X^2Y, and so forth. If no divisor was forthcoming, the program could even examine transformations of these terms, such as sin (XY), or even combinations of transformations, such as sin (X) log (Y). Of course, this would lead to vast search spaces, and unless we can find heuristics to direct search through these spaces, the chance of finding useful laws would be small. Fortunately, once a transformation or combination has been proved worthwhile in one context, BACON could immediately try it in analogous contexts, and so reduce search considerably. This is another instantiation of the expectation-driven approach to discovery that we first introduced in BACON.5.

It is interesting to note that, as far as we know, no truly complex common divisors have been found in the history of science. There are two possible explanations for this absence: (1) scientists are very good at selecting useful variables, so that such transformations and combinations are seldom necessary; or (2) such laws are so complex that scientists have simply never discovered them. In either case, we feel that an extended version of the common divisor method should be included in future versions of BACON, and tested on its ability to discover useful concepts and interesting empirical laws.

6. Discussion

In the previous pages we have examined the process of empirical discovery, focusing on a number of heuristics for this domain. We have implemented and tested these heuristics in successive versions of the BACON system, and we have discussed their capabilities and limitations in earlier sections of the paper. We have also suggested some extensions to BACON's discovery methods, such as altering the intrinsic property heuristics so that they consider multiple terms and transformations of directly observable terms. In this section we will also propose some directions for future research, though here we will focus on more global issues that transcend the particular methods that BACON employs. We will address three issues – the role of structural knowledge, the importance of qualitative laws, and the relation between quantitative empirical laws and theoretical explanations. In closing, we consider whether BACON should be classified as an expert system, despite the simplicity and generality of its discovery methods.

6.1 *The Role of Structural Knowledge*

In each of the versions of BACON we have described, the system relied on the programmer to suggest a set of independent and dependent terms that it should examine. Thus, extending the program to select potentially relevant variables in an obvious direction for future research. There is little doubt that research scientists employ domain-specific knowledge in deciding which variables to examine and which experiments to run, and if we hope to extend BACON in this direction, it will also have to accept and manipulate such domain knowledge. However, it would be very desirable to implement these components in a general manner, using a few simple reasoning methods that could operate on many different instances of domain knowledge.

The notion of structural knowledge suggests such a potentially general approach. Given a description of some physical or social situation, one can often reason about potential causes and effects, while having no knowledge of the particular equations governing the situation's behavior. For instance, suppose we have the description of a bridge in terms of the connections between various components. If we believe that forces can only be transmitted through adjacent objects, then we can make immediate inferences about which variables are directly related, and which are unrelated or indirectly related to one another. In addition to simplifying the search through the space of possible laws governing stable entities such as bridges, these inferences will also suggest which experiments to run, since for a given dependent variable, we expect certain terms to be relevant and others to be irrelevant.

The same type of reasoning occurs in economics and econometrics, where scientists begin with certain beliefs about direct connections between socio-economic variables, and use these beliefs to simplify the task of modeling large-scale human behavior. In this case, assuming that there is no direct connection between two variables (such as the unemployment rate and the price of wheat) is equivalent to assuming a zero coefficient in a set of complex simultaneous equations. Once enough such assumptions have been made, the set of equations can be solved and the parameters of the system can be estimated. In some cases, the causal assumptions can be quite general. For example, one naturally believes that a later event can never cause an earlier event, allowing one to rule out entire classes of potential relations. Since economics is an observational science, these inferences cannot be used to aid experimental design, but they can be very useful in directing search through the space of quantitative empirical laws.

BACON has already shown an ability to employ certain kinds of structural knowledge, for the symmetry assumption used in discovering conservation of momentum and other laws can be viewed as an example of such knowledge. The reader will recall that the assumption of symmetry was made in cases involving two analogous objects. The "structure" implicit in this assumption was that no direct causal connections occurred between the observable terms associated with each object. Rather, a single causal connection occurred between two instances of an inferred theoretical terms, one associated with each object; moreover, this theoretical term could be expressed as some combination of an object's associated observable terms. Thus, the task of empirical discovery was reduced to finding the appropriate combination of observable terms, and determining which of the few possible symmetries actually summarized the data. However, the symmetry assumption did more than simply reduce BACON's search through the space of empirical laws. In addition, it led the program to alter its experimental designs so that it gathered much less data, since fewer observations were required to arrive at an acceptable law.

Unfortunately, BACON's use of symmetry was implemented procedurally rather than declaratively, so that it must be restated before we can begin to explore general methods for using structural knowledge to aid the discovery process. Still, the symmetry heuristic will act as a useful example in our attempts to implement more general methods, and it is encouraging to know that the BACON framework has the potential to incorporate such domain knowledge with its data-driven methods. We hope that the combination of data-driven and knowledge-driven discovery methods will lead to a more robust system than would be possible using either method in isolation.

6.2 The Importance of Qualitative Laws

Another approach to determining potentially relevant terms involves the notion of *qualitative* laws. Since qualitative laws are generally formulated before their quantitative counterparts, they are a likely source of knowledge for determining which variables to examine. Let us return to an example from the history of chemistry, and explore the relation between these two types of empirical laws. In an earlier section, we described BACON's rediscovery of Dalton's law of multiple proportions. During its data-gathering process, BACON varied the values of three nominal term – the two elements entering a reaction, and the compound resulting from that reaction. In the run we described, the system was provided not only with the independent terms it should examine, but with their values as well.

Let us examine the sort of knowledge a discovery system might require to design this experiment on its own. Suppose the system had qualitative descriptions of various chemical reactions, such as (reacts inputs (oxygen nitrogen) outputs (nitric-oxide)) and (reacts inputs (oxygen nitrogen) outputs (nitrous-oxide)). Since the arguments of the predicate *reacts* can differ, these suggest obvious independent terms that the system can vary in an experiment. Now suppose that the system knew that only certain elements reacted with one another; using this information, it could limit itself to certain combinations that it knows will give results. Finally, suppose the system had placed certain substances (such as nitric-oxide and nitrous-oxide) into the same *class,* based on similar feature (e.g., both result from reactions involving oxygen and nitrogen). Such a classification scheme, together with knowledge of potential variables and useful combinations of their values, could be used to generate an experimental design like that shown in Table 16.

Of course, if we must provide such domain-specific knowledge to the discovery system, we have not done much better than providing a complete experimental design. However, if the system could discover such qualitative knowledge on its own, and use this information in designing experiments, then this would be significant progress. Since BACON is designed for discovering quantitative empirical laws, one might need an entirely different system that could discover qualitative laws from facts such as the reactions shown above. However, the interaction between BACON and the proposed system would be quite direct, with the new program providing BACON with a basic plan for collecting data. Although the task of finding qualitative laws is interesting in its own right, we are much more interested in the potential for interaction between qualitative and quantitative discovery systems.

6.3 Empirical Laws and Explanations

A third avenue to constraining the search for empirical laws relies on the use of theoretical knowledge or explanations. Given some theory that accounts for a class of phenomena, one can often use this theory to predict those independent terms that will affect a given dependent variable, and in some cases, even predict the *form* of the relation. These predictions can then be tested empirically, providing evidence for the theory if they are borne out. For instance, Dalton's atomic theory can be used to predict and explain both the law of multiple proportions and Gay-Lussac's law of combining volumes, while Newton's theory of gravitation explains both Galileo's law for falling bodies and Kepler's three laws of planetary motion.

However, we encounter the same difficulty using theories to direct the search for empirical laws as we did using qualitative laws for this purpose. If we gave our discovery system detailed knowledge of some domain, we would be effectively building in its discoveries. This would be especially true for the examples given above, since these empirical laws were proposed *before* the theories that were eventually formulated to explain them. In many cases in the history of science, empirical laws were discovered first, and provided the raw material from which theories were constructed. Thus, an obvious direction for future research would be to develop a discovery system that generates such theories; this system would accept BACON's output – empirical laws – as its inputs, and search a space of theories – either structural (like the atomic theory) or mechanistic (like the kinetic theory) – which might explain these laws.

The details of such a theory-building system are far from clear, though some of BACON's current heuristics suggest interesting possibilities. For instance, the notion of common divisors leads naturally to structural models involving component particles, such as the atomic theory. Similarly, the notion of symmetry often seems associated with the conservation of some theoretical quantity, such as heat or momentum. The proposed system might have a small repertoire of theory *types*, each associated with some cue such as the discovery of common divisors or the discovery of a symmetrical law. The particular laws that were found could then be used to instantiate the prototypical theory, leading to a specific theory capable of explaining the empirical laws.

Of course, once such a theory has been forwarded, there is nothing to prevent a BACON-like system from using this knowledge to direct its search for new empirical laws. This would be very similar to BACON's existing expectation-based discovery methods, although the system's expectations would be based on rather more sophisticated grounds in this case. In other words, it may be possible to establish a feedback loop in the discovery process, with BACON finding an initial set of empirical laws using the techniques we have discussed, followed by a theory formation system using these laws to produce explanations, followed in turn by BACON using the resulting theories to find new empirical laws, and so forth. This approach is attractive because it potentially provides the search-reducing power of theory-based discovery without requiring the programmer to build in theoretical knowledge. When combined with the system for finding qualitative laws proposed above, we will have the beginnings of a truly integrated model for the process of scientific discovery.

6.4 Evaluating BACON

There is some question about how to evaluate the BACON systems. Our research goal has never been to model the historical discovery process in detail, though we have turned to the history of science for ideas on discovery methods and for tests of those methods. Neither have we focused on constructing a tool for scientific data analysis that could be used by present-day researchers, though one can imagine extensions of BACON that would be used in this manner. Rather, we have attempted to understand the general principles underlying scientific discovery, in particular the discovery of quantitative empirical laws. With respect to this goal, we feel that we have been quite successful, since we understand considerably more about this process than we did at the outset of our research some years ago. Moreover, the principles and methods we have uncovered appear both simple and general, criteria usually considered desirable for scientific theories.

Some colleagues have suggested that BACON may be viewed as an expert system for the domain of empirical discovery. In fact, our concern with generality and simplicity was largely a reaction against the traditional expert system approach of building in considerable domain knowledge of great specificity. Still, BACON does share certain characteristics with expert systems, and we should examine this relationship, however briefly. In particular, expert systems can be viewed as moving through potentially very large search spaces; however, their motion through these spaces is constrained by knowledge of the domain, so that very few states are actually visited.

BACON can also be viewed as moving through a large search space, in this case a space of empirical laws and theoretical concepts. On close examination, we found that BACON actually carried out very little search, since its heuristics were generally powerful enough to lead to the optimum concepts and laws. Most of these heuristics were data-driven, so that if different data were observed, the system would follow quite different paths and discover quite distinct laws. However, this is no different from an expert system like DENDRAL [12], which follows different paths when given different input. Thus, on this dimension, BACON may profitably be viewed as an expert system concerned with empirical discovery. However, this does not detract from either the generality or the simplicity of its methods, and we plan to continue using these criteria in directing our future work on discovery.

Fortunately, the generality and simplicity of BACON's heuristics have not detracted from the system's power, and it has shown itself capable of finding laws that were very significant when first discovered centuries ago. It remains to be seen whether the most recent versions of the system, with their ability to deal with noise, can aid modern-day scientists in discovering new empirical laws, and this is another obvious direction for future work. However, based only on the historical examples covered in the previous pages, we may conclude that BACON has led to significant improvement in our understanding of empirical discovery, and we fully expect that it will lead to deeper insights in the years to come.

References

1. Langley P: BACON.1: A general discovery system. Proceedings of the Second National Conference of the Canadian Society for Computational Studies of Intelligence, 1978, pp 173-180
2. Langley P: Descriptive Discovery Processes: Experiments in Baconian Science. Ph.D. Th., Department of Psychology, Carnegie-Mellon University, 1979
3. Langley P: Data-driven discovery of physical laws. Cognitive Science 5, 1981, 31-54
4. Bradshaw G, Langley P, Simon HA: BACON.4: The discovery of intrinsic properties. Proceedings of the Third National Conference of the Canadian Society for Computational Studies of Intelligence, 1980, pp 19-25
5. Langley P, Bradshaw G, Simon HA: Rediscovering chemistry with the BACON system. In Machine Learning: An Artificial Intelligence Approach, Michalski RS, Carbonell JG, Mitchell TM, (eds), Tioga Press, Palo Alto, CA, 1983
6. Langley P, Bradshaw G, Simon HA: BACON.5: The discovery of conservation laws. Proceedings of the Seventh International Joint Conference on Artificial Intelligence, 1981, pp 121-126
7. Langley P, Bradshaw G, Simon HA: Data-driven and expectation-driven discovery of empirical laws. Proceedings of the Fourth National Conference of the Canadian Society for Computational Studies of Intelligence, 1982, pp 137-143
8. Langley P, Bradshaw G, Zytkow J, Simon HA: Three facets of scientific discovery. Proceedings of the Eighth International Joint Conference on Artificial Intelligence, 1983, pp 465-468
9. Langley P, Zytkow J, Simon HA, Bradshaw GL: The search for regularity: Four aspects of scientific discovery. In Machine Learning, Volume 2, Michalski RS, Carbonell JG, Mitchell TM, (eds), Tioga Press, Palo Alto, CA, 1984
10. Gerwin DG: "Information processing, data inferences, and scientific generalization." Behavioral Science 19, 1974, 314-325
11. Collins JS: A regression analysis program incorporating heuristic term: selection. In Machine Intelligence 2, Dale E, Michie D, (ed), American Elsevier, New York, 1968
12. Feigenbaum EA, Buchanan BG, Lederberg J: On generality and problem solving: A case study using the DENDRAL program. In Machine Intelligence 6, Edinburgh University Press, Edinburgh, 1971

Transfer of Training in Procedural Learning
A Matter of Conjectures and Refutations?

Stellan Ohlsson[1]

Abstract

Heuristics learning is defined as the process of discovering rules for how to apply problem solving operators. An analysis of transfer of training with respect to problem solving heuristics results in two transfer mechanisms; one based on the interplay between conjectures and refutations, and one based on the partitioning of a goal into independently realizable parts or subgoals. First, rules called *proposers* produce suggestions about which operator(s) should be considered in the current situation, while other rules – called *censors* – refute those suggestions which previous experience has shown to be bad. A system which can learn proposers and censors can grow by the successive attenuation of the conditions on the proposers and through the successive addition of censors. In the long run, such a system will apply each problem solving operator when and only when it is appropriate. Second, *subgoaling* rules encode knowledge of which parts of a goal description can be attained separately. Such rules can be learned by noticing the successive transformations of the current state during problem solving; each step which makes the current state more similar to the goal state defines a potential future subgoal. Subgoaling rules learned while solving one task can facilitate the solution to another task, if the tasks share at least one subgoal. A computer program is written on the basis of this theory, and shown to be able to transfer within a simple task domain.

Introduction

The information processing approach to learning differentiates several categories of learning, some new and some old. Recent research has concentrated on the acquisition of intellectual skills, usually called "procedural learning". The topic of the present paper is *heuristics learning,* a type of procedural learning which occurs when a problem solver has settled on a representation for a task, but does not yet know a strategy for how to process that representation. He/she/it then has to proceed by trial and error, creating problem solving rules on the basis of accumulating experience. The pioneering work in the simulation of heuristics learning is the study of Anzai and Simon (1979), who modeled a think-aloud protocol from a human subject with a program capable of discovering strategies for the Tower of Hanoi puzzle. The ACT theory of John Anderson (Anderson, 1983; 1986) is currently the most widely applied theory of human acquisition of cognitive skills. The collections of articles edited by Michalski, Carbonell, and Mitchell (1983; 1986) and by Klahr, Langley, and Neches (1987) summarize most of current research into computer implementation of learning processes.

In the present paper, heuristics learning will be discussed with special refer-

---

[1] Learning Research and Development Center, University of Pittsburgh, Pittsburgh, PA 15260

ence to the problem of transfer of training. First, a method which is incapable of transfer is presented, and the contrast between its behavior and human behavior is used to highlight five important characteristics of human learning. The problem of transfer of training is analyzed, and a theory stated which shows how transfer can be achieved in a problem solving system which is organized in terms of (a) conjectures and refutations, and (b) goal-subgoal decomposition. A computer program built on the analysis is described and a sample of its performance shown. The theory is then compared to previous work on procedural learning. A final section summarizes the strong and the weak points of the theory.

Problem solving will here be conceptualized as in the theory of Newell and Simon (1972). In brief, problem solving is search through a *problem space*. A problem space is defined through an ordered triple, containing the *initial state* of a problem (e.g., the "givens"), a list of *operators* by which the problem can be processed (e.g., legal moves, valid theorems, etc.) and a *goal-state* (i.e., a specification of what counts as an answer to the problem). Problem solving proceeds through the successive application of operators to the problem, creating a sequence of knowledge-states – a *solution path* – leading from the initial state to the goal-state. A *heuristic* is a rule which specifies, for a particular operator, the class of knowledge-states in which that operator should be applied. A collection of heuristics is a *strategy*. The strategy of an expert problem solver determines with a high degree of selectivity which operator should be applied in each knowledge-state, while a newcomer to a particular task domain has to proceed through *unselective search*, i.e., systematic trial and error.

The notion of heuristic search through a problem space is often extended with the notion of a *goal-hierarchy*. A goal is a symbol-structure which describes a desired state of affairs. Clearly, what one is trying to achieve has, or ought to have, implications for what actions one performs. Thus, goals should be part of the heuristics which control the application of operators during problem solving. However, the concept of a goal can be taken one step further. The top-goal for a problem solving effort can be *decomposed* into a set of "parts" or *subgoals*. Each subgoal, in turn, is decomposed, etc. Such successive decomposition generates a hierarchy of goals and subgoals. Each subgoal defines a subproblem of the original problem (or, more accurately, of the problem defined by the goal immediately above it in the hierarchy). Since the subproblems are "smaller" in some sense than the original problem they ought to be easier to solve. Thus, a goal-hierarchy replaces a "big", possibly very difficult problem with a set of "smaller", hopefully easy problems. The first problem solving system to use goal-subgoal decomposition in an essential way was GPS (Ernst & Newell, 1969; Newell & Simon, 1963; 1972). The idea figures prominently in current research on problem solving and procedural learning.

Given the theory summarized in the previous two paragraphs, it is natural to represent a problem solving strategy as a *production system* (Davies and King, 1976; Hunt and Poltrock, 1974; Young, 1979). A production system language is a formalism in which procedures are represented as collections of condition-action rules called *productions*. The left-hand side of a production specifies under what conditions the rule is to apply; its right-hand side specifies what actions are performed when it does apply (or "fires"). All productions refer to a common store of currently available information, the *working memory*. The conditions are tests on the content of working memory, and the actions usually change that content in some way. The *interpreter* decides which rule to apply, and executes its actions. Information processing proceeds through a series of *cycles*, each cycle involving the selection and execution of some production rule.

Both problem spaces and production systems will be discussed in more depth in the section on the implementation of the current theory. The brief introduction given here gives sufficient background to the theoretical section.

The Ariadne Algorithm vs. Human Learning

The problem of heuristics learning yields to an universal algorithm. Suppose that we have a problem solver which embodies some exhaustive search procedure such as depth-first or breadth-first search.

Add to such a system the following learning mechanism:

For any step taken during search, if it led from a state S_1 to a state S_2 through the operator Q, then create the two rules

$$P1: (GOAL\ S_2) \rightarrow (GOAL\ S_1)$$

$$P2: (GOAL\ S_2)\ S_1 \rightarrow (DO\ Q)$$

Assume that the problem solver keeps searching until the goal state has been reached, applying the above mechanism at each step. Any future attempt to solve the same problem will succeed without any search. The backward chaining rules like **P1** will generate a plan, a sequence of goals connecting the goal state with the initial state. The plan, once completed, will be executed by the forward working rules like **P2**. This learning method will eliminate search in a single pass over a problem.

I propose to call this method the *Ariadne Algorithm*, after the ancient story of the girl who figured out that one can find her way out of a labyrinth by unwinding a thread as she goes in.

The Ariadne Algorithm creates and stores a pair of rules like **P1** and **P2** above for each knowledge state visited; if the initial trial and error search generated N states, it creates 2N rules. The algorithm is unselective; it works by memorizing each step in the solution path. The Ariadne Algorithm can thus serve as a yardstick for the selectivity of other learning methods, in the same way that exhaustive search algorithms (e.g. depth-first search) serve as yardsticks by which the selectivity of search methods can be measured.

The Ariadne Alorithm obviously represents a primitive form of learning. It does not allow improvement with extended practice. Once a plan for a particular problem has been found, it is used in all future attempts to solve that problem.

Shorter solutions to that problem cannot be found. This contrasts with human learning, which is characterized by *gradual improvement* which continues even after a "correct" solution has been found.

Similarly, the Ariadne Algorithm does not allow *transfer of training*. The rules learned while solving one problem can only be used in future attempts to solve that very same problem. If they are applied to another problem, search will be re-introduced as search through the goal-tree. This again contrasts with human learning.

It is thus obvious that the Aridne Algorithm is different from human learning. Humans continue to improve their performance over long periods of practice, and they readily transfer what they have learned to other problems within the same domain (although transfer across domains is more difficult; see Hovland, 1951).

However, the Ariadne Algorithm also has the following further characteristics: Learning is error-free. Errors are only made during the initial pass over a problem. On all future solution attempts, the correct solution path is generated without any errors. This contrasts with human learning which is *error-ridden*. Errors are ubiquitous, and they disappear gradually.

Also, the Ariadne Algorithm needs only a single pass over a problem in order to learn how to solve it. Humans, on the other hand, usually need repeated trails before a solution path is mastered; human learning is *repetition-based*. In a labyrinth-learning contest, the Ariadne Algorithm would beat humans easily if trials to perfect performance was used as measure.

Finally, since the rules learned by the Ariadne Algorithm are local to a particular problem, the outcome of the learning process is independent of the exact sequence of practice problems encountered. The solution path for a particular problem is not dependent on which other problems have been solved. This is not true of humans, as is shown by research on *Einstellung* and other similar effects (Luchins, 1942). Human learning is *sequence dependent*.

Each of the characteristics of human procedural learning mentioned here – gradual improvement which continues even after the correct solution has been discovered, transfer of training, errors, need for repeated trials, sequence dependence – might have a distinct cause. Each characteristic might be independent of the others in such a way that one could construct learning systems which have any four of these properties, but not the fifth. It is more interesting, however, to try to see these five characteristics as a cluster of related surface symptoms, produced by a single underlying cause. The work reported in this paper is based on the hypothesis that being the victim of errors, the need for repetitions, and sequence dependence is the *price* a learning system has to pay for its ability to improve and to transfer what it learns. Thus, a good learning theory should explain improvement and transfer through a mechanism which also yields, as a byproduct, an explanation of those three weaknesses of the learning system.

A Theory of Transfer

Transfer of training can be said to occur when a problem solver applies knowledge gained while solving one set of problems - the practice problems - during the solution of one or more problems in a different set - the target. For transfer to occur, what is learned during practice must be processed in such a way that it becomes applicable to the target. Focusing on a particular problem solving operator Q, what is learned is a heuristic which governs the use of Q. The problem of transfer is then the problem of generating, out of the experience accumulated during practice, a heuristic which will apply the operator Q appropriately on the target problems.

More formally, the problem of transfer can be stated as follows. Suppose we have a way of enumerating all specific problems in some task domain D; suppose there are N such problems. Let n be the index which varies over this enumeration. Let U(n) be the set of states relevant to problem n, i.e., U(n) is the state space for problem n. The total set of states (or situations) relevant to the task domain D - call this set U - can be defined as the union of all U(n), where n varies from 1 to N. Next, let G(Q) be the set of states or situations in which the application of the operator Q is appropriate, i.e., in which Q has a good effect. (In general, a good outcome is one which brings the problem solver closer to the current goal.) Clearly, G(Q) is a subset of U. The set G(Q) is circumscribed by some conditions $C_1, C_2, ..., C_j$. If a situation satisfies these conditions, it is a member of G(Q), otherwise not. If the problem solver had complete insight into the structure of the task domain, he/she would obviously create the heuristic

$$\textbf{P3: } C_1, C_2, ..., C_j \rightarrow (DO\ Q).$$

The operator Q would then be applied in all and only those situations in which it is, in fact, appropriate. Thus, the heuristic **P3** represents the goal or the ideal output of a transfer mechanism[2]. Having worked a few practice problems through trial and error, the problem solver has had some experience of applying Q in different situations. In some cases Q would have had a good effect; in others, a bad effect. The knowledge gained from practice can be represented as a sample S* of situations in U. Some members of S* fall inside G(Q), others outside, as illustrated in Fig. 1.

The question is what conclusion to draw about the application of the operator Q, given a particular sample S*. A transfer method computes a function g such that

$$g(S^*) = G(Q)$$

---

[2] At this point, I am finessing the problem by assuming that there is a single operator which is appropriate in each state, so that there is no need to choose between rival operators. This simplification will be abandoned shortly.

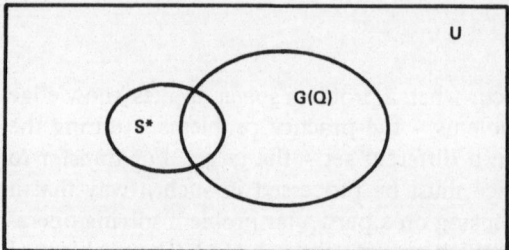

Fig. 1. The relationship of previous experience in the shape of a sample S* of instances to the universe U of situations, and the set G(Q) of situations in which operator Q is appropriate.

for any S* and any G(Q). The transfer function g computes the boundary of G(Q) on the basis of available experience.

This formulation makes clear that in order to design a transfer mechanism, we must first have a general characterization of G(Q) (or, equivalently, of $C_1, C_2, ..., C_j$); we must know what it is that g is supposed to compute. Having defined what the output of g is to be, we then have to define some method by which that output can be computed. These two parts of the transfer problem – to define the output of the transfer mechanism, and to design a method of computing it – will be treated in the two following subsections.

Defining the Target Procedure

The purpose of this subsection is to provide a general description of G(Q), i.e., of the set of states in which a given operator Q has a good effect; or, equivalently, of the conjunction of conditions $C_1, C_2, ..., C_j$, which circumscribe that set.

Intuitively, there seems to be no reason to expect such a characterization of G(Q) to be possible. Task domains differ from each other in structure and content; within a domain, operators have different functions. There seems to be no reason to expect any regularities to hold on which a general characterization of G(Q) could be based. In short, it is not obvious that the problem of transfer of training *has* a general solution.

When a formal object resists direct definition, it is often useful to approach it indirectly, by finding some easy-to-compute *approximation* to it, which is then improved by various *corrections*. Instead of trying to define G(Q) directly, it might be worthwhile to define some other set which approximates it as closely as possible, and then see what corrections can be found.

It is important that such an *approximation set* includes all of G(Q). There should be no situations in G(Q) which are not also members of the approximation set. This point rests on the fact that there are two kinds of errors which can occur. First, consider a situation S_1, outside G(Q). If Q is applied in S_1, it will, *ex hypothesis*, produce a bad outcome. Noticing the bad result, the problem solver can correct his/her mistake. Therefore, it is not a serious difficulty if the approximation set contains areas of U *outside* G(Q). Second, consider a situation S_2 inside G(Q). If Q is applied in S_2, a good outcome will result. However, if Q is *not* applied, the problem solver has no information about this good outcome. Unless Q is tried in S_2, the problem solver may never discover that this step is good. Each situation in G(Q) in which Q is never tried represents a good step which the system will be incapable of learning. In short, this type of error sets a limit on what can be learned. To avoid such errors, the approximation set should be a superset of G(Q).

What supersets of G(Q), other than the universe U, can be considered as approximation sets? One alternative is to focus on the set of situations in which Q is applicable. An operator usually cannot be applied in each and every situation; there are some conditions which have to be satified. Therefore, the applicability set is smaller than U. Obviously, the applicability set for the operator Q will be a superset of G(Q). The applicability set has the advantage of being known *a priori*, since its definition is part of the operator itself.

In the present theory, a different alternative has been chosen in the hope to achieve a better approximation to G(Q). The conditions $C_1, C_2, ..., C_j$, which define G(Q) include both the necessary and sufficient conditions for Q to have good effect. One easy-to-describe set is the set circumscribed by the necessary conditions only. Call it N(Q). Obviously, N(Q) is a superset of G(Q). How good the approximation is will depend on the properties of U. If there is a set of conditions which is both necessary and sufficient for Q to have a good result, then N(Q) is equal to G(Q). How different N(Q) is from the applicability set for Q also depends on U. If there are regularities in the problem space, i.e., there are some properties which are common to all states in G(Q), then N(Q) is more narrow than the applicability set. If there are no such regularities, then N(Q) is equal to the applicability set. Thus, the difference between G(Q) and N(Q) is a measure of how much structure there is in the task domain.

Let us call the necessary conditions for Q to have a good result $N_1, N_2, ..., N_j$. We can now let the use of Q be controlled in part by the heuristic

P4: $N_1, N_2, ..., N_j \rightarrow$ (SUGGEST Q).

Such a heuristic can be called a *proposer*, because it proposes that Q might be the right thing to do in any situation fulfilling the conditions $N_1, N_2, ..., N_j$. The expression "(SUGGEST Q)" is a *conjecture*.

The proposer **P4** is an approximation to the desired heuristic **P3**. It errs by suggesting Q in situations in which the latter does not, in fact, have a good effect. The nature of the corrections needed is therefore clear; they should reject the operator in those situations which fall "between" the boundaries of N(Q) and G(Q). Such rules would have the general form

P5: (SUGGEST Q) S $\rightarrow$ (REJECT Q),

where S is a description of a situation (or of a class of situations). Such a rule can be called a *censor*, because it refutes the suggestion made by the proposer. It

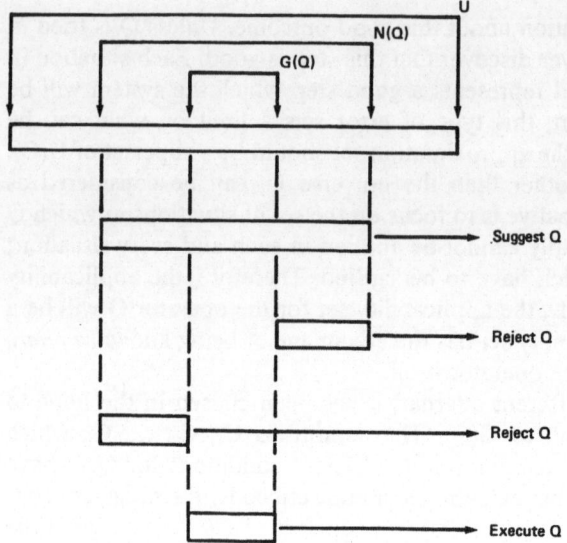

Fig. 2. The set of situations in which an operator Q is executed can be defined collectively by a proposer plus a set of censors

shrinks the set of situations in which Q will be *executed* (without changing the set of situations in which the operator will be *considered*), and thereby improve the approximation. The expression "(REJECT Q)" is a *refutation* of the conjecture that Q is the right thing to do.

To complete the performance organization, we add the following rule of execution:

P6: (SUGGEST Q) absent(REJECT Q) → (DO Q).

Rule **P6** says that the operator Q will only be executed in a particular situation if it is suggested in that situation and if no censors reject it in that situation. The proposer and the censors collectively define the set of situations in which Q will be executed, as Fig. 2 illustrates.

A problem solving system which has its performance organized as in Fig. 2 will work as follows. A situation is entered; all proposers which have their conditions satisfied "fire" and create conjectures about which operator to execute. If no proposer "fires", the situation is dealt with through trial and error (i.e., random selection of an applicable operator). If there are some conjectures, the censors go to work on them, refuting those which are known to be bad. If a single conjecture survives, it is executed. If more than one conjecture services, some principle of conflict resolution must be applied.

Thus, the present use of the principle of conjectures and refutations is different from that of Bratko and Niblett (1979). In the present case, what is conjectured is a single step along a solution path, rather than entire solution paths. Informal observations of human problem solvers suggest that processes which deal with entire solution paths as units are not psychologically plausible.

It is important to be clear about what has and what has not been archieved so far. The task of a transfer mechanism is to compute the boundary of G(Q) for an operator Q, on the basis of some sample S* of applications of that operator. Fig. 2 shows how G(Q) can be defined collectively by a proposer and a set of censors. In other words, Fig. 2 shows a general characterization of G(Q), i.e., of what a transfer mechanism is supposed to produce. How proposers and censors could be *aquired* has not been discussed yet. This is the issue for the next subsection. Of course, the point of characterizing G(Q) in the above way is to facilitate the design of the aquisition process.

The Acquisition Method

The purpose of this subsection is to discuss how the function g can be computed. The formula

$$g(S^*) = G(Q)$$

presents the act of generalization as a computation which is performed once and for all at a particular moment in time, and which halts, i.e., which "knows" when the desired heuristic has been found. Viewed in this way, it is doubtful whether g is computable. There seems to be no reason to expect an arbitrary sample S* to contain enough information to compute the boundary of G(Q), and, in addition, to prove that the boundary has been found. However, if the goal is to erect a psychological theory, there is no reason why g should be a halting process. In real life, the effort of making the most of the previous experience never stops. There is no mental state corresponding to certain knowledge that a particular problem solving strategy is "finished"; there is always more to learn. The acquisition process designed here will be a non-terminating process which runs as long as new problem solving steps are taken. It will produce the desired heuristic **P3** in the limit only, but a each point in time, there is a set of rules which is the best approximation so far to the desired heuristic.

How could a proposer like **P4** be acquired? The acquisition process proposed here is based on the fact that the set of necessary conditions for an event to happen is, by definition, unique. In other words, the conditions N_1, N_2, ..., N_j will recur in every situation in which Q has a good result. This means that those conditions can be found by comparing such situations. When a situation is first encountered in which Q has a good effect, a proposer rule is created which has a description of that situation as its condition. At that moment, the proposer is maximally restricted; it suggests Q in a single situation only. The next time trial and error generates a situation in which Q has a good effect, the conditions in the proposer are compared to the new situation. Those conditions which are not true of the new situation cannot be among the necessary conditions for Q to have a good outcome, and are therefore deleted from the proposer. The result is that the conditions of the proposer are weakened; Q will now be considered in a wider set of situations. Each time a new situation is encountered in which Q has a good effect the conditions on the proposer for Q are revised. In the long run, only the necessary conditions $N_1, N_2, \ldots N_j$ will remain.

The acquisition of censors is also straightforward. Suppose that a problem solver has been in a situation S, and found that Q has a bad effect in S. In order to prevent the same mistake from recurring again, he/she could then create a censor which says that when in S, reject any suggestion to execute Q. The censor will thus subtract, as it were, a situation from the area between N(Q) and G(Q).

In principle, one could create a separate censor for every situation encountered in which Q was found to have a bad effect. In order to lower the number of rules to be created, and to increase the power of the censors, some operation of minimal abstraction (e.g., a conservative replacement of constants with variables) should be applied to the censors. Each censor will then "cut out" a small area between the boundaries of N(Q) and G(Q), as shown in Fig. 2.

To summarize, according to the theory presented here, heuristics learning proceeds through two counterbalancing processes. The first begins with a maximally restricted proposer, which is successively attenuated through the deletion of conditions found to be unnecessary for a good outcome. Thus, for each operator, the set of situations in which it is considered grows steadily wider. This will eventually lead to errors. The second process will then set in, successively correcting the proposer by the creation of censors. For each operator, the set of censors will gradually cover more and more of the bad cases, so the set of situations in which the corresponding operator will be executed shrinks. As both these processes proceed, the proportion of situations in which the problem solver will have to fall back on trial and error search will diminish. In the limit there will be no trial and error search and each operator will be applied in, and only in, situations in which it is appropriate.

The properties of the learning processes generated by this kind of system will be considered in the next subsection.

Strategies and Goal Hierarchies

The theory stated above is a theory about learning to use a particular problem solving operator. However, in most problems more than one operator has to be applied in the course of problem solving. A strategy is a collection of heuristics for applying all the operators in a particular problem space.

The present theory handles the learning of a problem solving strategy by the obvious means of regarding it as the learning of the appropriate heuristics for each of the relevant operators. In other words, the theory makes the simplifying assumption – almost certainly false with respect to human learning – that the rules learned by a problem solver for how to apply operator X are unaffected by whatever rules that the problem solver has already learned for how to apply some other operator Y. Since the ensemble of operators which belongs to a problem space represent rival alternatives for action, such independence is implausible. However, it is a reasonable simplification at the current state of learning theory.

Relating the theory of heuristics learning presented above to the notion of a goal-hierarchy uncovers a difficulty. Goals should direct action during problem solving. However, the obvious device of including the relevant goal in the problem solving heuristics causes difficulties for the notion of transfer. If a specific goal-description is included in the conditions of the proposers and cencors learned whole solving a problem, *the new rules will only apply whenever that particular goal is active,* which directly prevents transfer of training.

The important implication of this observation is that a heuristic learning system which is build on the idea of goal hierarchies must have some way of transferring goals, i.e., of making goals acquired with respect to one task relevant to some other task as well; unless the goal is relevant for that other task, the heuristics learned cannot be relevant for that other task.

A solution to this problem can be constructed by combining goal-subgoal decomposition with the idea of "shared components". As a top-goal is decomposed into smaller and smaller "parts", those "parts" are likely to become more and more general, less and less specific to the situation at hand. For instance, the general goal of "making coffee" might be analyzed into the subgoal of "heating the water", which is clearly a goal which might be relevant in many different contexts. The goal of getting hot water, in turn, may become decomposed into the goal of "turn on the stove", which, obviously, is a subgoal with even wider application.

In other words, the present theory makes the simplifying assumption that transfer of training from one task to another presupposes that the two tasks share at least one subgoal. Transfer occurs because the solution to the second problem can make use of the heuristics learned for how to archieve that subgoal. This is probably too simple a picture of how the sharing of heuristic knowledge between two tasks occurs, but it is a reasonable simplification at the present time.

Qualitative Predictions

In the present subsection, some qualitative properties of learning processes generated by the theory presented in the previous subsections are discussed informally. The previous subsection showed how the transfer mechanism defined there can improve its solutions and transfer insights from one problem to another. In a previous section, it was argued that the price a learning system has to pay for the ability to improve and to transfer involves errors, gradual learning, and dependence on the sequence of practical problems. It will now be shown how these three characteristics are explained by the assumptions of the present theory. (Quantitative predictions are discussed in the next subsection.)

It is obvious from the way the conjecture-refutation system works that errors is a necessary feature of its learning behavior. It is the occurrence of errors, i.e., the application of inappropriate operators, which trigger the acquisition of censors.

But the theory also makes a more detailed prediction. It predicts that there will be, for each operator, two kinds of errors, and that they will be differently distributed over time. Initially, the problem solver will err by being too restrictive. He/she will not "see" that a particular operator is appropriate in a particular situation, because the conditions of its proposer are still too restrictive to include that situation. Later, when the conditions of the proposer have been attenuated, but before enough censors have been collected, the problem sover will err mainly by applying operators in situations in which they are inappropriate; thus he/she will now appear "rash" instead.

The present theory accounts for the need for repeated learning trials in the following way. First, the initial construction of a proposer for an operator Q must await a positive instance of the use of that operator. Second, the attenuation of the conditions on the proposer msutmust await repeated successful applications of Q. Third, the acquisition of censors must await errors, i.e., it cannot happen until some attenuation of conditions has happened *and* the attenuated proposer has fired inappropriately. In short, learning is gradual because one change builds on another. This contrasts with learning theories in which learning is gradual because new problem solving rules have strengths which are *postulated* to increase gradually.

The heuristics acquired by the mechanism proposed here are dependent upon the exact sequence of practice problems encountered. The theory predicts that learning will be faster with more varied experience. The more varied the problems (within some domain), the faster the deletion of accidental conditions on the proposers; the sooner errors will begin to occur, which in turn speeds up the creation of censors.

Conversely, the theory explains the *Einstellung* effect. If the learning sequence contains a set of problems with limited variability, the deletion of conditions on the proposers will only proceed to a certain point. Confronted with a new type of problem, the proposers will be too restricted, and the problem solver will either proceed as with the practice problems, if possible, or else fall back on trial and error.

In summary, the effort to define a system capable of improvement and of transfer of training has resulted in a system which necessarily makes errors, learns by repeated trials, and is influenced by the sequence of practice problems.

Implementing the Theory

A theory like the one presented in the previous section does not readily yield quantitative predictions. It would be extremely difficult to derive, say, the shape of the learning curve analytically from the principle of conjectures and refutations. For this reason, the theory has been embedded in a computer program from which learning curves and other quantitative results can be derived through computer runs. (An earlier version of the program was described in Ohlsson, 1982).

The program, called the *Universal Puzzle Learner* or UPL for short, can be said to consist of two parts. First, there is a domain-independent part which performs various general functions needed in problem solving, such as back-up, management of the goal-stack, memory retrieval, etc. This part will be discussed below under the heading *performance organization*. Second, there are the *learning mechanisms* which create the task-specific heuristic rules that the program learns. These two parts work on a task description in the form of a problem space (Newell and Simon, 1972).

Before presenting the details of the program itself, the programming language in which UPL has been implemented will be described. After that each of the parts mentioned above will be described in a separate subsection. Then follows a subsection presenting some computational results.

The PSS Programming Language

Much work in Artificial Intelligence and computer simulation has been carried out within a principle known as

> The Production System Hypothesis. Information processing procedures are best represented as *production systems*, i.e., collections of condition-action rules.

This hypothesis has given rise to a class of programming languages, known as *production system languages*. Davis and King (1976) and Young (1979) have discussed the various types of production system languages and their uses. The collection of articles by Klahr, Langley, and Neches (1987) contains examples of recent research using production systems to model cognitive development and learning.

The basic features shared by all production system languages are the following. Structurally, a production system consist of three parts: a set of productions, a working memory, and an interpreter. The *productions* are condition-action rules, i.e., they consist of a set of tests or "conditions", sometimes referred to as the "left-hand side" of the production, and one or more *primitive operations* to be carried out, sometimes called the "right-hand side" of the production. The tests in the left-hand sides of the production rules are applied to the contents of the *working memory*, which is a data-structure that contains the currently available (or currently attended) information. A production for which all tests in the left-hand side are true is said to be *satisfied*. The agent which investigates whether the tests in the left-hand sides are true is the *interpreter*. Satisfied rules are executed by the interpreter, i.e., the primitive operations in their right-hand sides are carried out.

Functionally, production system languages share a basic mode of operation. The interpreter operates in *cycles*. At the beginning of each cycle, the interpreter compares the production rules against the current contents of working memory in order to find those rules which are currently satisfied. The comparison takes the form of *pattern-matching*. The conditions of the production rules are used as patterns, and the interpreter identifies which, if any, elements in the working memory are substitution instances of them. If a substitution instance can be found, the test is regarded as true, otherwise not.

Next, the set of satisfied productions is pruned through some *conflict resolution* algorithm. Those productions which remain after conflict resolution are evoked or "fired", i.e., the primitive operations in their right-hand sides are executed. The operations perform computations on the working memory, changing its contents in some way. The interpreter then begins a new cycle; etc. The system continues to run until either a state is reached in which no rule is satisfied, or an explicit halt-signal is encountered. In short, production system interpreters work in a match-resolve-evoke cycle.

Within this general framework, many different kinds of production systems are possible. Languages may differ with respect to the structure of the working memory, whether working memory is subject to forgetting or not, how the matching of rules against memory content is done, what scheme is used for conflict resolution, which primitive operations are available, etc. (Langley, Ohlsson, Thibadeau, and Walter, 1984).

PSS (Ohlsson, 1979) was originally designed to be a vehicle for computer simulation of verbal reasoning processes (Ohlsson, 1984), but has also been used for the simulation of cognitive development (Nason, 1986), and for the implementation of the UPL learning system (Ohlsson, 1982; 1983). There are three features of this language which are central to the UPL system, namely ranged variables, sequence-variables, and the possibility of structuring production memory into distinct subsets.

The pattern matchers of most production system languages recognize *unrestricted variables,* i.e., variables which can be bound to any distinct expression or sub-expression in working memory. For instance, the pattern

(object X),

where X is an unrestricted variable, will match against any expression beginning with the word "object", followed by some other expression, e.g.,

(object $table_1$),

in which case the variable X is bound to the simple expression "$table_1$", or

(object ($table_1$ color green size small)),

in which case X is bound to the complex expression "($table_1$ color green size small)".

The pattern matcher of PSS recognizes unrestricted variables, but is in addition capable of handling *typed variables,* which have a specified ranged of expressions to which they can be bound. For instance, it is possible to define the typed variables <table>, <color>, and <size> in the following way:

<table> ::= $table_1$, $table_2$
<color> ::= green, blue
<size> ::= small, big.

The pattern

$$(\text{<table> <color> <size>})$$

will now match, for instance, against the expression

(table$_1$ green small)

with "<table>" bound to "table$_1$", "<color>" to "green", and "size>" bound to "small".

The typed variables can be defined hierarchically in PSS, i.e., one variable can be defined in terms of complex patterns which themselves contain ranged variables. For instance, a variable "<description>" could be defined through

$$\text{<description>} ::= (\text{<object> <property1> <property2>})$$
$$\text{<object>} ::= \text{<table> <chair>}$$
$$\text{<property>} ::= \text{<color> <size>}.$$

The ranged variable definitions thus constitute a sematic or conceptual memory in the form of a BNF grammar which is executed as the pattern-matcher compares patterns to the contents of working memory.

A second feature of the PSS pattern-matcher is that it can handle *sequence variables*. A sequence variable is a from of abstraction similar to the three dots of informal mathematics:

$$N_1, N_2, \ldots$$

Such a variable stands for any sequence of expressions. For instance, if "<sequence>" is a sequence variable, the pattern

(operators <sequence>)

will match against any list of possible operators (including the empty sequence), e.g.,

(operators LIFT, TURN, MOVE, BREAK).

Notice that the pattern

$$\text{(operators X <sequence>)}$$

will bind "X" to the first operator (i.e., LIFT in the above example), and "<sequence>" to the remaining operators. Sequence variables allow very abstract patterns to be written as conditions for production rules. Sequence variables can be used in the definition of ranged variables.

The final feature of the PSS language to be mentioned here is the *structured production memory*. In many production systems, the set of production rules form a homogeneous set. Each production rule has a chance to be considered on each cycle. But PSS allows the user to compartmentalize production memory into distinct rule sets. There is at all times exactly one such set that is considered the current rule set. The interpreter considers the rules in that set before it considers any other rules. The construction of rule sets is entirely unconstrained. A set can have a single rule, or it can have any number of rules. The same production can appear in several different rule sets. One rule set can be included in another.

A rule set is being selected as the current rule set through a PSS primitive operation called GOTO, which takes the name of a rule set as input. Its effect is that the named set becomes the current rule set on the next cycle. This operation can occur in the right-hand sides of productions. Thus, control is passed from rule set to rule set as a consequence of the firing of productions.

Performance Organization

The performance organization of the UPL program is based on a principle known as

> *The Problem Space Hypothesis*. Information processing activities take place in *problem spaces*, i.e., structures which consist of (a) a *notation* in which the problem can be described; the description of the problem-as-given is called the *initial knowledge-state;* (b) a set of problem solving actions or *operators* which can be applied to formulas in that notation; and (c) and a *goal-state*, or termination criterion, which specifies when the problem has been solved.

The Problem Space Hypothesis was first proposed as a basic principle of information processing by Newell and Simon (1972).

The Problem Space Hypothesis implies that information processing in general and problem solving in particular takes the form of *search* through the space of possibilities, until a knowledge-state is encountered which satisfies the termination criterion.

A corollary of this principle is that problem solvers differ mainly with respect to how *selective* the search is that they carry out. Novice problem solvers who do not have any good strategy for solving a particular type of problem will have to proceed by some type of unselective search, such as breadth-first or depth-first search. The more knowledgeable problem solver, on the other hand, is in possession of *heuristics,* i.e., strategic rules which allow him to search the problem space

INITIALIZE	Retrieves and reinstates a problem space; encodes the current problem.
LOOK-AHEAD	Performs a one-step look-ahead to see whether any operator can bridge the gap between the current state and the current goal.
GENERATE	Generates the set of as yet untried legal moves for the current state.
RESOLVE	Takes a set of legal operators and selects one operator to be executed.
EXECUTE	Executes a selected operator, thus generating a new state.
EVALUATE	Evaluates a new state; more specifically, notices loops, and computes whether the distance to the current goal was increased or decreased as a result of the last step.
STACK	Checks whether the current state satisfies any goal on the current goal-stack, and revises the stack accordingly.
BACK-UP	Backs up the state immediately preceding the current state.
RESTART	Back up to the initial state.
CLEANUP	Ends a problem solving step by deleting data from working memory which will not be used again.

Fig. 3. General problem solving capabilities of UPL

more selectively. Thus, the Problem Space Hypothesis implies that the problem solving expertise resides in selective heuristics.

The UPL program has depth-first search with random ordering of operators as its default problem solving method. In other words, when the program does not have any task-specific heuristics to guide its behavior, it will simply choose at random one of the available operators that has not yet been tried in the current knowledge-state.

More specifically, the task-independent part of the UPL program consists of a number of *modules* of "subroutines". Each module is a rule set in the PSS sense (see previous subsection). Each module contains a handful of productions which carry out some general problem solving function. Different versions of the program differ slightly in how they are organized, but they all have the modules shown in Fig. 3.

The ten problem solving functions in Fig. 3 are encoded in a task-independent way, i.e., they operate on arbitrary list-structures. They make no assumptions about the syntax of the representation used to encode the task the system is operating on. Thus, they can apply to any problem space. If UPL is run with only these modules in operation, it will behave as a depth-first problem solver with a one-step look-ahead and random ordering of steps.

The above functions are encoded in a total of 137 production rules. The smallest rule set (RESOLVE) contains 7 rules, while the biggest (EXECUTE) contains 20 rules. The average number of rules in a module is 14. The condition sides of the productions typically contain a small number of conditions. Only 28 rules (21%) have more than four conditions. The action sides of the production rules are also small; only 22 (16%) have more than three primitive operations in their right-hand sides. A single operation is typically to insert or delete a single working memory

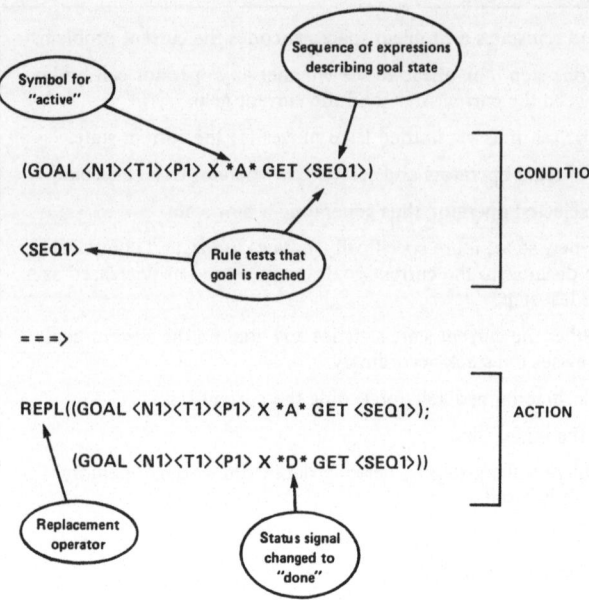

Fig. 4. An example of a PSS production rule. The function of the rule is to indentify a knowledge-state which satisfies the current goal, and change the status of that goal from "active" to "done". The symbols "*A*" and "*D*" are status signals. The symbol "<SEQ1>" is a PSS sequence variable (see text for explanation). The variables "<N_1>", "<T1>" < "<P1>", and "X" bind to parameters which describe the number of the goal, its type, its place in the goal-tree, etc.

expression. As examples of the types of rules included in the program, Fig. 4 contains an example taken from the STACK module.

Task-specific heuristics are kept in three different modules, each representing a particular *rule type*. UPL has three different types of task-specific heuristics, namely *proposers, censors,* and *subgoaling rules.* Proposers are rules which suggest which operator apply in the current situation. Censors are rules which veto the suggestions by the proposers. These two types of heuristics correspond to the proposers and censors as discussed in a previous section. In addition to these two types of heuristics UPL is equipped with the capacity to set itself new goals. This is the function of the subgoaling rules.

Each type of heuristic is kept in a separate module which knows how to interact with the task-independent modules. The modules are called PROPOSE, CENSOR, and SUBGOAL. When UPL is started up, those three modules are empty. It is the task of the learning mechanisms to fill them with relevant rules. As learning accumulates, problem solving behavior becomes increasingly under the control of the learned rules, and the system less often falls back on its general depth-first search method.

A *problem solving cycle* proceeds as follows. First, the PROPOSE module is called. The proposer rules (if any) then have a chance to make suggestions about which step to take in the current state. If no proposer has anything to say about the current state, control is passed to the SUBGOAL module, in order to break down the current goal into component subgoals. If this succeeds, control goes back to PROPOSE. Thus, control goes back and forth between these two modules until either some proposal is made, or no further analysis of the state is possible. If no proposal can be made, control goes to the LOOK-AHEAD module, which looks through all available operators to see if any of them can accomplish the current goal in a single application. (This is done in a task-independent fashion). If LOOK-AHEAD does not return anything, control passes on to the GENERATE module, which will find all applicable operators for the current state. The output from the first phase is thus one or more operators which can be applied to the current state.

Second, control goes to che CENSOR module, where the censors (if any) have a change to veto the proposals made in the first phase. The operators which servive the scrutiny are then passed on to RESOLVE, which resolves the conflict between them. (In the version of the program reported here, RESOLVE selects one of the surviving operators at random.) The output from the second phase is thus a single operator. Third, the EXECUTE module takes the selected operator and performs the computations described in its definition. This is where the problem solving step is actually taken, and a new knowledge-state is generated.

Fourth, the EVALUATE module performs tests on the new state in order to decide (a) if the state has already been visited, (b) whether the new state satisfies any of the goals on the current goal-stack, and (c) whether the distance to the current goal has been increased or decreased. The output of the fourth phase is thus a description of the value of the newly generated state.

Fifth, depending upon the evaluation of the new state, control is passed either to the STACK module, which revised the goal-stack, the CLEAN-UP module which designates the newly generated states as the current state and prepares for the next problem solving cycle, the BACK-UP module, which returns to the previous state, or the RESTART module, which causes the program to start over.

The above description gives the basic outline of how problem solving performance is organized in UPL. The following further details are worth noticing.

If the output from the first phase is empty, i.e., no operator is applicable, then the state is recorded as a dead-end, and control is passed to the BACK-UP module.

If UPL finds that *all* steps leading out from a particular knowledge-state are "bad" in the sense that they lead further away from the current goal, *one of those steps will be taken away*. In other words, the system is reluctant to back up, and will only do so if all legal steps lead into dead-ends or into loops. In the cases where a step leads further away from the goal, the system prefers to take that step rather than to back up. This feature forces the system to explore some bad steps, and thus allows it to discover any unsuspected advantages they may have. It allows the system to "climb down" from a local maximum in the state space.

The default problem solving strategy of UPL is depth-first search. However, the system does not save all visited states. At any one time, the system only keeps in working memory four knowledge-states: the initial state, the state in which the current goal was set, the current state, and the state immediately preceding the current state. One of the implications of this sparse path memory is that the system cannot back up twice. If a back-up to the immediately preceding state occurs, the system does not remember what *its* immediately preceding state is. Therefore, a second back-up cannot be made. The system then restarts from the initial state.

UPL takes as input a problem space and a problem. The problem space is defined, first, by a notation in the form of the ranged variables (see previous subsection on the PSS matching options) which describe the objects, properties, relations, etc., which are relevant to the domain, and, second, by a list of operators. Each operator is defined by three lists of expressions: the list of input expressions, the list of expressions added by the operator to the working memory, and the list of expressions deleted from memory. The productions in the INITIALIZE module defines the variables, and the EXECUTE module contains general interpretative productions which can read an operator definition and apply the operator to a knowledge-state.

A problem is presented to the program in the form of two knowledge-states, the initial state and the goal state. The INITIALIZE module sets up the first as the current knowledge-state, and translates the second into the top-goal of the system. Thus, given a problem space, any pair of states in that space constitutes a recognizable problem.

Learning Mechanisms

The learning mechanisms of UPL are designed according to two principles of learning. The first is common to much of the work on machine learning and computer simulation of learning which as been done over the past ten years. We can call it the

> *Additive Learning Hypothesis.* Acquisition of new procedures in a production system is done through the addition of new production rules to the existing set of rules (without revision of the former).

Indeed, one of the reasons for adopting the Production System Hypothesis is that the modular organization of a production system allows extension of a program without extensive revision of already existing procedures.

The learning in UPL is also in accordance with another principle, which is relatively less common. I will call it the

> *Hypothesis of Learning While Doing.* It is possible to create useful problem solving heuristics on the basis of the information available *while* solving a problem, i.e., without knowledge of the complete solution path.

For workers in the field of Artificial Intelligence, this principle may be of less interest. In an A.I. system, it does not matter whether the learning occurs while doing the problem, or after the entire solution path has been found. However, for researchers in the field of simulation, building learning systems according to this principle is essential, since it is obvious that human beings change their problem solving behavior as they go along.

The Hypothesis of Learning While Doing implies that there are three issues that have to be settled for each learning mechanism:

- The first issue in constructing a learning mechanism is how to recognize a *learning opportunity*. When, during problem solving, should the system pause to create new rules? Under what conditions should the system try to create a new rule? What are the characteristics of a situation which contains some useful experience which can be encoded in a new rule?
- A second issue is what from the *learning outcome* is going to take. What kind of addition to existing procedures should be made in any particular learning opportunity? As described previously, UPL encodes task-specific heuristics in three types of rules, proposers, censors, and subgoaling rules. For each rule type, there is a learning mechanism which is responsible for creating that type of rule. A learning outcome is thus always the addition of a rule of either of these three types.
- Finally, the third issue is by what *learning algorithm* the learning outcome is to be constructed. Given that we have recognized a learning opportunity, how can we identify in that situation which information should go into the learning outcome? What is the computation to be performed in order to create the new rule?

The three issues will be discussed with respect to each of the three learning mechanisms.

A. Learning Proposers

Learning opportunity for proposers: Proposers are created whenever a good step is taken, i.e., a step which brings the system closer to its current goal.

Learning outcome: Proposer rules have the general form:

GOAL SITUATION → suggest OPERATOR

Example of proposer: If you want to subtract two numbers, and you are currently attending to column C, and N_2 is the bottom digit in C, and N_1 is smaller than N_2, then consider shifting your attention to the column to the left of C.

Learning algorithm: The GOAL is the current goal, the SITUATION is the state immediately preceding the current knowledge-state, and the OPERATOR is the action that lead to the current state. In short, proposers are acquired by a simple process of remembering problem solving steps which had a good outcome.

B. Learning Censors

Learning opportunity for censors: A censor rule is created when the system makes a bad step, i.e., a step which (a) leads further away from the goal, (b) leads into a loop, or (c) leads into a dead-end state.

Learning outcome: Censors have the general form:

GOAL SITUATION OPERATOR → reject OPERATOR

Example of censor: If you want to drive to the airport, and you are in the right-hand lane, and there is a fast car coming up from behind in the left-hand lane, and you are contemplating shifting into that lane, then reject shifting lanes.

Learning algorithm: The GOAL is the current goal, the SITUATION is the state immediately preceding the current knowledge-state, and the OPERATOR is the action that lead to the current state.

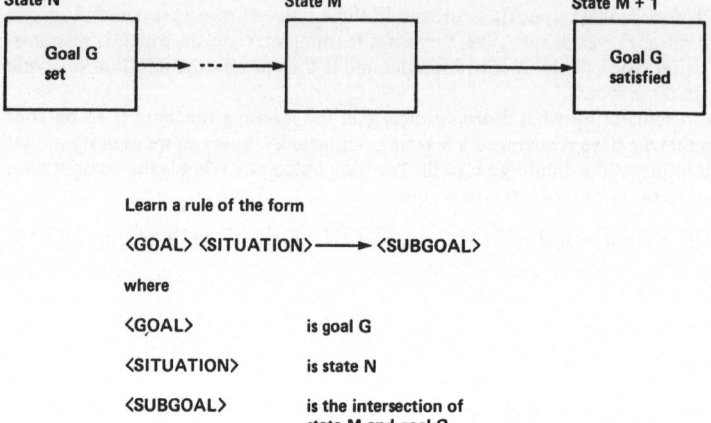

Fig. 5. New subgoals are being constructed while searching for the solution to a problem

C. Learning Subgoals

Learning opportunity for subgoaling rules: A subgoaling rule is created whenever the current goal becomes satisfied.
Learning outcome: A subgoaling rule has the general form:

$$\text{GOAL SITUATION} \rightarrow \text{set SUBGOAL}$$

Example of outcome: If you want to get disks D_1, D_2, and D_3 on Peg3, and they are all on Peg1, then set the goal to get D_2 and D_3 on Peg3.
Learning algorithm: GOAL is the goal satisfied by the current state, the SITUATION is the knowledge-state in which GOAL was set, and SUBGOAL consists of the commonalities between GOAL and the knowledge-state immediately preceding the current state. This algorithm is explained graphically in Fig. 5.

The learning mechanisms have been implemented in the form of 16 production rules which are kept in three distinct rule sets or learning modules, one for each rule type (GOOD, BAD, and SUBGOAL). Whenever a learning opportunity is identified, the appropriate learning productions are evoked, and a new rule created.

There are two features to be noticed about these learning mechanisms. First, the EVALUATE module described in the previous subsection has a central role in the learning of UPL, because the evaluation of the new state determines which type of learning opportunity we are dealing with. If the evaluation is good, a proposer is going to be created; if bad, a censor. If a goal was satisfied, then a subgoaling rule will be created. If none of these events occurs, then there is no learning opportunity. Thus, the problem solving activity and the learning activity are both directed in the same way. No extra machinery is needed to trigger the learning mechanisms, over and above the machinery that is needed for problem solving itself.

Second, notice that the explicit goal-expressions which UPL entertains have a central role in its learning. The evaluation of a state is essentially a judgment whether or not the last step brought the system closer to the goal or not. This means that the goal is part of the evaluation which, in turn, guides the learning process. The ability to set new subgoals is therefore central to the learning of the system, since new goals brings new evaluations of states, and therefore new learning opportunities.

The learning algorithms above are described in such a way that they create completely *opportunity-specific* rules. A proposer will mention a particular situation, a particular goal, etc. These rules could only be evoked again if exactly the same circumstances were encountered again.

To give the acquired rules more power, they have to be *generalized*. In UPL, this happens in the following way. A generalization algorithm has been defined which takes two expressions as input, and returns the revisions of the first expression which would be needed if it were to have the second expression as one of its substitution instances. In other words, the first argument to the generalization algorithm is generalized until it "covers" the second argument. The algorithm has been described in Ohlsson (1983).

Whenever a new rule is created, this generalization algorithm is used in order to see if the new rule is not already "included in" or "covered by" any of the existing rules. The new rule is compared to each of the previously learned rules of its type. Each existing is paired with the new rule, and the pair passed to the generalization algorithm. The generalization is done by replacing constants with variables and/or by deleting conditions on rules.

If a generalization can be found, then the generalization is stored. If no generalization can be found, then the specific rule is stored, possibly to be generalized when feature rules are created. Thus, each rule of a particular type serves as a "location" for the accumulation of heuristic knowledge. Only when no existing rule can be generalized in such a way that it covers the new experience, does the new experience lead to the creation of a totally new rule. This generalization step is applied to all three types of learned rules.

Computational Results

UPL has been applied to several puzzle-like tasks which are used in psychological research on problem solving, including the Tower of Hanoi Puzzle, the Water Jar Puzzle, the Missionaries and Cannibals Puzzle, and a new, very simple puzzle called the Tiles and Squares Puzzle.

Figure 6 shows learning curves for the program on three of these tasks. It is capable of improving its performance on tasks like these.

A transfer experiment was run on the Tiles and Squares Puzzle in the following way. Seven different Tiles and Squares Problems were selected. Four of these were used as practice problems, and three as target problems. The program was given practice in the form of blocks of four trials, one trial on each the four practice

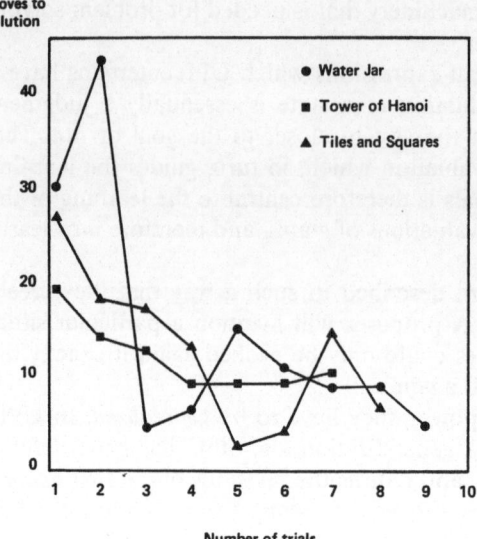

Fig. 6. Improvement curves for UPL on three different problems

problems. The practice problems were presented in a different random order in each practice block. Before the first practice block, and after each block, the learning mechanisms were switched off, and the system run on the three target problems. Thus, the system was never in a position to learn anything while doing the target problems. The target problems serve only as a tool for assessing whether the heuristics acquired while doing the practice problems can be transferred to a new set of problems or not.

Figure 7 shows the results of the transfer experiment. Each point along the curve represents the average steps to solution over the three target problems, after each block of four practice trails. As we see, the system improves its performance on the target problems, thus proving that the system can transfer what it has learned.

There are four aspects of the computational results which deserve to be mentioned here. First, UPL learns slowly. No version of UPL has been able to generate learning curves which follow a power law, as the typical learning curve of a human learner does (Newell & Rosenbloom 1981). The reasons for this is principled. UPL learns by accumulating experience. Its learning has to wait, as it were, for some experience to be generated before it can produce dramatic changes in the problem solving procedure. Therefore, rate of change is slow in the beginning, and increases when there is a larger store of experience to draw upon. It is difficult to see any way in which this aspect of UPL's learning could be changed within the framework outlined here.

Second, the learning curves of UPL have "bumps" in them. In other words, as learning progresses, there are temporary set-backs in performance. Inspection of runs reveals that these set-backs coincide with the setting of a new goal. Again the reason for this aspect of UPL's performance is principled. Suppose that the system

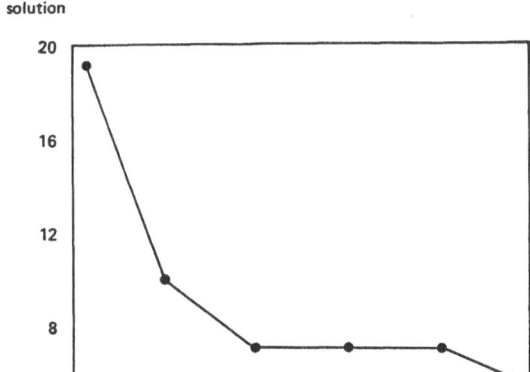

Fig. 7. Transfer curve for UPL on the Tiles and Squares puzzle

has created a new subgoaling rule, which sets the goal G. Suppose that this rule fires in some situation S, setting G as the current goal. Since this is the first time this rule fires, the *system has never entertained the goal G before, and it therefore has no heuristics for how to work towards it*. Recall that a problem to UPL is an ordered pair of states from the problem space, an initial state and a goal state. When a new goal is set, the system sets itself a new problem, with the current state as the initial state and the new goal as the goal state. If this problem has never been set before, the system now has to learn how to solve this type of problem. Unless very general heuristics are already available, the system may have to fall back on depth-first search to solve the new subproblem *even though the subproblem is part of a problem for which the solution is already known*. In other words, setting a new goal is to disrupt performance temporarily on that segment of the solution path which is controlled by that goal. This is desirable because it allows the system to discover shorter solutions to subproblems: the re-introduction of search for a segment of the solution path allows the system to experiment with steps that are ruled out by the heuristics learned so far, and thus allows it to discover possibly shorter paths than those already identified as leading to the solution.

Again, it seems unlikely that this aspect of the behavior of UPL could be changed within the basic framework. It seems necessary that a new goal will cause unselective search-behavior to reappear unless it is so similar to previously used goals that already existing heuristics apply to it.

Third, we may ask what effects on the learning behavior of UPL are caused by the severe limitations on its path memory. Recall that UPL can only keep in working memory representations of four knowledge-states: the initial state, the state in which the current goal was set, the current state, and the state immediately preceding the current state.

The runs show that this limitation on memory affects learning on some tasks, but not on others. The main aspect of the problem space that affects this is whether it contains many-step loops or not. The limitation on memory prevents the program from recognizing that it has entered an already visited knowledge-state. Thus, it can keep going in circles for ever, without reaching the goal-state. In problem spaces which do not contain such loops the program performs well. Thus, the memory limitation interacts with the structure of the problem space to give a selective effect. Whether human problem solvers have more trouble with problem spaces which contain many-step loops than with spaces which do not contain such loops is not known at the present time.

The final aspect of UPL's performance worth mentioning here is that it adapts what we might call its learning "style" to the structure of the task domain. In the Tower of Hanoi problem, where a very regular goal-structure is possible, the program learns mainly by acquiring subgoaling rules. It discovers the recursive analysis of the top goal, and its final procedure for the task is based on this subgoaling structure. In the Missionaries and Cannibals Puzzle, however, no such subgoaling structure is available. Indeed, it is even difficult to state any general heuristics for how to solve this problem. In consequence, the UPL program learns mainly by acquiring censors in this domain, i.e., it focuses on how to avoid mistakes. In the Tiles and Squares puzzle, which has a very simple perfect solution consisting of two proposing rules, the UPL program learns mainly by acquiring those proposers. (See Ohlsson, 1983, for more details of these results.) Thus, the learning mechanisms outlined above are adaptive in the sense that they are sensitive to the structure of the problem space which the program is working in. This sensitivity has not been explicitly programmed into the system, but is a consquence of how the different parts of the program interact.

Relationship to Previous Work

Computer programs that learn from experience are not yet common and programs which are intended as models of human learning are even more rare. The purpose of this section is to make brief comparisons between UPL and five other computer systems: SAGE, LEX, GPS, XAPS3, and GRAPES.

SAGE: Discrimination Learning

The SAGE system constructed by Langley (1982; 1983; 1985) is a heuristic learning system which has been applied to a variety of artificial tasks. It starts out with maximally general heuristics for applying its problem solving operators. The initial conditions on those heuristics are just the applicability conditions for the operators. This means that every operator will be considered in every state in which it is logically possible to apply it (i.e., essentially every state in which the appropriate arguments for the operator exist). As long as the result of applying an operator is positive, no learning occurs. When a negative result appears, the system compares the negative instance with some state in which the operator was applied with a positive result, and tries to identify the crucial difference between them. That difference is added as a new condition to the heuristic which suggests that operator. In this way, the system learns to discriminate states in which an operator is appropriate from states in which it is inappropriate.

The SAGE system is similar to UPL in that both assume that to learn a strategy for a task is to learn the heuristics for when to apply each of the operators which are involved in solving that task. There are three main differences. First, SAGE begins with maximally general conditions on the heuristics. These conditions are hand-crafted by the programmer. UPL constructs maximally specific rules based on its (first) application of each operator. Learning proceeds by first generalizing these and then constraining them again when experience shows that they are overgeneralized. Taken as a model of human learning[3], SAGE predicts that the *only* type of error humans ever make in problem solving are over-generalization errors, while UPL makes the more complicated prediction about the distribution of different kinds of errors over time which was discussed in a previous section.

Second, SAGE encodes the outcomes of learning into new versions of the rule being learned, while UPL encodes learning outcomes into new rules, where the heuristic learned is represented by the total *set* of rules working together. The main effect of this is that in UPL a *component* of a heuristic, i.e., a single rule in the set, can be generalized independently of the other components. For instance, a censor rule can be generalized, making its censorship more generally applicable, without affecting the proposers. In the SAGE system, learning has only a single "direction": towards more and more constrained application of operators. In the UPL system, the learning process consists of alternating generalization and discrimination steps.

Third, SAGE does not learn to break down a top-goal into subgoals. It is purely a system for discovering the conditions on heuristics.

LEX: Version Spaces

The LEX system created by Mitchell and coworkers (Mitchell, 1977; Mitchell, Utgoff, Nudel & Banerji, 1981; Mitchell, Utgoff & Banerji, 1982) discovers heuristics for when to apply various transformations of integrals. Like UPL, LEX represents a heuristic with a *set* of rules, rather than a single rule. LEX is build on the idea that one should consider the entire space of possible "versions" of a rule, given some specification of the language which is available for expressing the heuristics. More precisely, this space can be represented by two versions (or groups of versions) of the rule being learned, one which represents the most *general* version of the rule which is consistent with all currently available instances and one which

---

[3] No strong claims for SAGE as a model of human learning has been made.

represents the most *specific* version which is consistent with all available instances. Any application of an operator which has a positive result is used to generalize the most specific version; any application which has a negative result is used to constrain the most general version. If these two processes result in one and the same version, then that must be the correct form of the rule; if the two never co-incide, the correct form of the rule is garanteed to lie "in between" the two versions. No claims have been made for the LEX system as a model of human learning.

There are three main differences between LEX and UPL. First, LEX learns from a complete solution path, while UPL is a learn-while-doing system which learns even before the first complete path has been discovered i.e., in the generation of the experiences which will be the basis for further learning. Second, although LEX represents a heuristic by a set of rules, each rule is a version of the heuristic sought; in UPL, the single rules are *components* of the heuristic. Third, LEX does not discover subgoals.

Comments on UPL, SAGE, and LEX

The UPL, SAGE, and LEX systems share a family resemblance. Each of these systems assume that to learn a strategy for a task is to learn heuristics for when to apply each of the operators which are involved in solving that task. Each of these systems learn by using its experience of applying some operator to make stepwise improvements in some representation of the heuristic for that operator. The main difference between them is the representation of a heuristic. In SAGE, a heuristic for an operator Q is, in principle, represented by a single rule which is the most general rule consistent with past experience of applying Q. Consequently, learning takes the form of constraining that rule. In LEX, the heuristic is, in principle, represented by two rules, one which is the most general rule consistent with past experience and one which is the most constrained rule consistent with past experience. Consequently, learning takes the form of either constraining the former or generalizing the latter. In UPL, a heuristic is represented by a set of proposers and a set of censors. Consequently, learning takes the form of constructing either new proposers or new censors.

Intuitively, these three representations and their associated learning mechanism are equivalent, i.e., capable of learning the same heuristics. To formally establish such a thesis would require a lengthy investigation which cannot be attempted here. Obviously, the *path* to learning some particular heuristic will be very different for each of these systems.

Both SAGE and LEX are *strategy acquisition systems*. They start out without any strategy for a particular task, and create heuristics for how to solve that task. The notion of a goal-hierarchy does not play a central role in either system. In contrast, the notion of a goal-hierarchy is central to the three systems to be considered next. The first system is a problem solver, the second and third are strategy improvement systems.

GPS: Subgoal Discovery

The General Problem Solver (GPS) created by Allen Newell and Herbert Simon (Ernst & Newell, 1969; Newell & Simon, 1963; 1972) was the first A. I. system which made essential use of a goal hierarchy. GPS was not a learning system, i.e., it would go through exactly the same sequence of computations if applied several times to the same task. However, its mode of problem solving is such that it discovers the correct break down of the top-goal into subgoals as it goes. In principle, it could be turned into a learning system if extended with some mechanism for saving the results of one run and making use of them in another. The main interest here is in its method for discovering the appropriate subgoals.

GPS discovers subgoals as part of its problem solving activity. Its problem solving strategy is based on the notion of a *difference* between a current state and a desired state. Its main strategic knowledge is encoded in a difference-operator table, i.e., a set of rules for which operator is relevant for reducing which type of difference. Given a problem, i.e., a current state and a desired state, GPS computes the difference between the two states and consults the difference-operator table for which operator should be applied. If that operator can be applied in the current state, it is applied and the problem is solved. If it cannot be applied, it must be because one or more of its applicability conditions are not satisfied in the current state. GPS then sets itself the subgoal to achieve a state in which the applicability conditions are satisfied. In other words, the (instantiation of the) applicability conditions for the relevant operator becomes the subgoal. The problem solving cycle now repeats itself: the difference between the new goal and the current state is computed and the difference-operator table consulted, etc. In this manner, a sequence of subgoals is discovered.

The UPL system also discovers subgoals while solving problems. The are two main differences. First, since it is the applicability conditions for operators which constitute the new subgoals in GPS, the system must be able to retrieve and inspect its operator definitions. In UPL, it is a (part of a) state which becomes the new subgoal, so it does not have to inspect its operator definitions, but only its state descriptions. Second, UPL reacts to the creation of a new subgoal by creating a rule for it, so that the subgoals need to be rediscovered when the same task is encountered a second time. Nevertheless, the two systems share a family resemblance. Both use the available operators to compute which "parts" of a given top-goal can be achieved independently of the others. Inspecting the operator definitions and inspecting the effects on state descriptions of applying the operators can be seen as two different procedures for computing what the implications of a set of operators are for the break down of the top-goal.

XAPS3: Chunking a Goal-Hierarchy

The XAPS3 system created by Rosenbloom and Newell (1986) is a strategy improvement system which assumes that there already exists a goal-hierarchy for a task. It contains a mechanism for "flattening" the goal-hierarchy. The basic idea is the following. Suppose a system sets itself the (sub)goal G' in state S', and, that it keeps working on the problem until it reaches state S" in which the goal G' is satisfied, due to the result R. Whatever the computations being performed along the path from S' to S", if the same problem is encountered again, it can be solved more efficiently with the help of a rule which simply asserts the result R in state S'. Thus, the subgoal G' need not be set and whatever computations were carried out under its control can be avoided, thus speeding up the executions of the strategy for that task. XAPS3 has been applied to simple laboratory reaction time tasks, with excellent fit to data from human subjects.

The learning process in UPL is exactly the opposite of the one which is carried out by XAPS3: the former creates subgoals, the latter gets rid of them. UPL learns how to "unpack" a top-goal into its independently achievable parts, thus creating a goal-hierarchy, while XAPS3 takes a goal-hierarchy as input and learns how to avoid setting subgoals in particular situations. Since human beings discover subgoals as well as automatize their cognitive skills, poth processes are presumably going on in the human mind. The obvious question whether the hierarchy expansion processes in UPL could work productively together with the hierarchy contraction processes in XAPS3 cannot be answered here.

GRAPES: Knowledge Compilation

The ACT* theory developed by John Anderson has been implemented in two programming systems, the *ACT* simulation (Anderson, 1983) and the *GRAPES* simulation (Anderson, 1986; Anderson, Sauers, & Farrel, 1985). GRAPES has mainly been applied to the domain of Lisp programming. The basis of GRAPES is a problem solving system which is driven by a goal hierarchy. At any one time, a single goal is active and only problem solving heuristics which are relevant to that goal can be operative. The system improves its performance with the help of a complex learning mechanism known as *knowledge compilation*. The first process in knowledge compilation is *proceduralization* which creates special-purpose rules out of more general ones by incorporating situation-specific information into a new version of a rule. The second process in knowledge compilation is *composition* which takes (at least) two problem solving rules and creates a single rule which achieves the effect of both.

Proceduralization can improve performance by replacing computation-intensive interpretation of declarative structures with new problem solving rules, and composition can speed up performance by creating "bigger" rules which accomplish more of the required problem solving in a single step. In the GRAPES system, knowledge compilation works on rules which include tests on the current goal in their conditions, and the setting of subgoals in their actions. Thus, knowledge compilation can affect the goal-hierarchy which the system is working with. One possible outcome is to get rid of some subgoals, i.e., to flatten the goal-hierarchy. In a recent analysis Anderson (1986) has shown how knowledge compilation can mimick the effects of generalization and discrimination. It therefore appears that knowledge compilation can both achieve strategy acquisition, strategy improvement, and revision of goal hierarchies.

There are two main differences between the GRAPES and UPL systems. First, GRAPES treats subgoaling rules in the same way as other problem solving rules. It has no special learning mechanism which discovers subgoals. It is not clear from the published accounts how GRAPES would recover from an incorrect subgoaling rule. Second, UPL does not have any step-chunking mechanism like the composition mechanism. Once UPL has discovered a minimal solution path for a problem, it cannot improve further, while GRAPES, like XAPS3, automatizes the execution of that path by combining successive steps along the path into single steps.

Discussion

It may seem self-evident that the construction of a learning mechanism should begin with a specification of what its output ought to be. But such specifications are seldom given, even when learning is discussed in formal terms. For example, Vere (1978) presents a mechanism which takes a set of particular rules as input and delivers a (smaller) set of more general rules as output. The process by which this is done is given an abstract specification in terms of set theory. But its output, i.e., the general rules themselves, are only characterized as able to "cause any transformation" caused by the particular rules and "containing all the common features" of the particular rules. This characterization does not show why we should want to create those generalizations. Why should we expect them to be useful? How do we know that they are not harmful? This type of criticism applies to much of current work on learning, both in psychology and the field of Artificial Intelligence.

In the present work, the goal of a mechanism for heuristics learning is taken to be the creation of a heuristic which applies a problem solving operator in all and only those situations in which that operator is appropriate. Direct characterization of the set of situations in which an operator is appropriate would be difficult. However, an approximation is possible if performance is organized in terms of conjectures and refutations. In such a system, an operator is controlled by a proposer which suggests the operator whenever the necessary conditions for its success are satisfied, plus a set of censors which refute the suggestion when previous experience supply reasons against it. Once the end-product of learning is characterized in this way, designing the appropriate acquisition mechanism becomes tractable.

The strong point of the present theory is that it explains the positive and the negative aspects – the strength and the weaknesses – of human learning by the same mechanism. If transfer of training is achieved as described previously, errors are unavoidable, and learning is necessarily gradual and influenced by the order of presentation of practice problems. A theory which explains deficiencies as unavoidable side-effects of advantages is to be preferred to one which postulates independent causes for them.

However, the results from the computer simulations show that the theory in its current form is a first approximation only. The main difficulty is that its initial learning is slow. The basic cause of this phenomeon is that several instances of successful application of an operator have to be encountered before significant learning can occur. Thus, a fair amount of problem solving activity has to be carried out before there is any improvement in performance.

This predicament is not unique to the present theory. Any theory which relies on comparisons between instances which have to be created through the activity of the system itself will encounter the same difficulty. The straight-forward prediction from such a theory is that there will be little or no change while instances are being collected, and that rapid change will set in only after enough instances have been encountered. This tension between the empirically observed rapid initial learning of humans and the need to collect instances to learn from seems to be inherent in the very idea of an inductive or experience-based learning mechanism which learns while doing.

This conclusion raises the question to what extent human *are* inductive learners. Are practice effects in procedural learning adequately covered by a theory which assumes that new procedures are created on the basis of experience only, i.e., executed problem solving steps and their evaluations? The weakness in this type of learning is that it leaves out the role of *knowledge* in learning. It seems intuitively obvious that the (declarative) knowledge of the objects, properties, and relations which are involved in a task domain should have some influence on the acquisition of strategies for that domain. A beginning of a theory for such *rational learning* – as opposed to the *empirical learning* which has been discussed in the present work – has been made and published elsewhere (Ohlsson, 1986, 1987). To make UPL into a powerful learning system, rational learning mechanisms need to be added to the system.

A different type of extension centers on the use of goals. The reader may wonder about the lack of symmetry in the treatment of operators and goals. Operators are handled through a balance between conjectures and refutations; why is this performance organization not used to cover the goals as well?

UPL in its present form has no method for recovering from a faulty or mistaken subgoal. Once a subgoaling rule has been created, it cannot be deleted. Once a subgoaling rule has fired during a solution attempt, and the new goal has been set, the new goal controls behavior until it has been satisfied. This is clearly an unsatisfactory situation. It is tempting to believe that the conjecture-refutation principle can be extended to goals.

The main difficulty with such an extension is to identify the conditions under which a goal should be abandoned. Looking at a particular solution attempt, if a goal has not been reached within some number of steps, then one can suspect that it is not a fruitful goal to pursue with respect to the current problem. However, such a limit on the amount of effort that should be spent on a goal before abandoning it must clearly be a function of the particular task that the system is working on. It is reasonable to expect to spend more effort on subgoals in a complex task than in a simple one. At the present time it is not clear how to formally define such a dependency.

It is even more difficult to give an answer to the question of when a particular subgoal should be judged as mistaken *in general*. When should a subgoaling rule be deleted, or a censor for a particular subgoal be created? By what criteria can a subgoal be identified as misleading in *any* context? The question of how to recover from mistaken subgoals will be a major concern for learning systems which can set themselves new goals.

The backbone of the present theory is the principle of conjectures and refutations, i.e., the idea that performance is organized in terms of proposers and censors. The property of production systems which make them a natural formalism for such an organization is that they consist of independent modules, the so-called production rules. This fact allows proposers and censors to function as independent and counterbalancing forces, communicating through the working memory. Also, it allows proposers and censors to be acquired independently of each other.

This observation suggests that the principle of conjectures and refutations should be applicable to other systems which consist of independent (but communicating) units. Going up one organizational level from the mind of an individual thinker to say, a group of scientists, we find the theory that a scientific discipline develops through conjectures and refutations already well established in the philosophy of science. Indeed, the very phrase "conjectures and refutations" is, as the reader has no doubt noticed, taken from the philosophy of Popper (1969). But the account by Toulmin (1972), in which biological evolution is taken as a metaphor for conceptual evolution assigns a very similar structure to scientific development, as does the philosophy by Lakatos (1976).

In summary, the principle of conjectures and refutations describes a type of performance organization which allows systems at different organizational levels to make the most out of previous experience in the service of future action.

References

Anderson JR (1983). The architecture of cognition. Cambridge, MA: Harvard University Press

Anderson JR (1986). Knowledge compilation: The general learning mechanism. In Michalski RS, Carbonell JG, Mitchell TM (eds.), Machine learning: An artificial intelligence approach (Vol II). Los Altos, CA: Kaufmann

Anderson JR, Farreli R, Sauers R (1985). Learning to program in LISP. Cognitive Science, 8, 87–129

Anzai Y, Simon HA (1979). The theory of learning by doing. Psychological Review, 124–140

Bratko I, Nisblett T (1979). Conjectures and refutations in a framework for chess endgame knowledge. In Michie D (ed.), Expert systems in the micro-electronic age. Edinburgh: The University Press

Davis R, King J (1976). An overview of production systems. In Elcock EW, Michie M (eds.), Machine Intelligence (Vol 8). New York: Wiley

Ernst GW, Newell A (1969). GPS: A case study in generality and problem solving. New York: Academic Press

Hovland CI (1951). Human learning and retention. In Stevens SS (ed.), Handbook of experimental psychology. New York: Wiley

Hunt EB, Poltrock SE (1974). The mechanics of thought. In Kantowit BH (ed.), Human information processing. New York: Wiley

Klahr D, Langley P, Neches R (eds.) (1987). Production system models of learning and development. Cambridge, MA: MIT Press

Lakatos I (1976). Proofs and refutations. Cambridge, MA: The University Press

Langley P (1982). Strategy acquisition governed by experimentation. Proceedings of the European Conference on Artificial Intelligence, Paris

Langley P (1983). Learning search strategies through discrimination. International Journal of Man-Machine Studies, 18, 513–541

Langley P (1985). Learning to search: From weak methods to domain-specific heuristics. Cognitive Science, 9, 217–260

Langley P, Ohlsson S, Thibadeau R, Walter R (1984). Cognitive architectures and principles of behavior. Proceedings of the Sixth Conference of the Cognitive Science Society, Boulder, Colorado

Luchins AS (1942). Mechanization in problem solving: The effect of Einstellung. Psychological Monographs, 248

Michalski RS, Carbonell JG, Mitchell TM (eds.). (1983). Machine learning. Palo Alto, CA: Tioga

Michalski RS, Carbonell JG, Mitchell TM (eds.) (1986). Machine Learning (Vol II). Los Altos, CA: Kaufmann

Mitchell TM (1977). Version spaces: A candidate elimination approach to rule learning. Proceedings of the Fifth International Joint Conference on Artificial Intelligence, pp 305–310

Mitchell TM, Utgoff PE, Banerji R (1983). Learning by experimentation: Acquiring and refining problem-solving heuristics. In Michalski RS, Carbonell JG, Mitchell TM (eds.), Machine learning: An artificial intelligence approach. Palo Alto, CA: Tioga, pp 163–190

Mitchell TM, Utgoff PE, Nudel B, Banerji R (1981). Learning problem-solving heuristics through practice. Proceedings of the International Joint Conference on Artificial Intelligence, Vancouver

Nason R (1986). A production system analysis of young childrens' number development between the ages of two to eight years. Unpublished doctoral disseretation, Deakin University, Victoria, Australia

Newell A, Rosenbloom P (1981). Mechanisms of skill acquisistion and the law of practice. In Anderson JR (ed), Cognitive skills and their acquisition. Hillsdale, NJ: Erlbaum

Newell A, Simon HA (1963). GPS: A program that simulates human thought. In Feigenbaum EA, Feldman D (eds.), Computers and thought. New York: McGraw-Hill

Newell A, Simon HA (1972). Human problem solving. Englewood Cliffs, NJ: Prentice-Hall

Ohlsson S (1979). PSS3 reference manual (Report #4). Working Papers from the Cognitive Seminar, Department of Psychology, University of Stockholm

Ohlsson S (1982). On the automated learning of problem solving rules. In Trapp R (ed.), Cybernetics and systems research. Amsterdam: North-Holland

Ohlsson S (1983). A constrained mechanism for procedural learning. Proceedings of the Eighth International Joint Conference on Artificial Intelligence pp 426–428. Karlsruhe

Ohlsson S (1984). Induced strategy shifts in spatial reasoning. Acta Psychologica, 57, pp 47–67

Ohlsson S (1986). Rational learning and intelligent tutoring systems. Proceedings of the Tenth World Computer Congress. Dublin, Ireland

Ohlsson S (1987). Truth vs. appropriateness. In Klahr D, Langley P, Neches R (eds.), Adaptive production system models of learning and development

Popper KR (1969). Conjectures and refutations. London: Routledge and Kegan Paul

Rosenbloom PS, Newell A (1986). The chunking of goal hierarchies: A generalized model of practice. In Michalski RS, Carbonell JG, Mitchell TM (eds.), Machine learning: An artificial intelligence approach (Vol II). Los Altos, CA: Kaufmann

Toulmin S (1972). Human understanding (Vol 1). Oxford: Clarendon Press

Vere SA (1978). Inductive learning of relational productions. In Waterman DA, Hayes-Roth F (eds.), Pattern-directed inference systems. New York: Academic Press

Young RM (1979). Production systems for modeling human cognition. In Michie D (ed.), Expert systems in the micro-electronic age. Edinburgh: The University Press

Conceptual Knowledge Acquisition in Search

Larry Rendell[1]

This paper concerns effective and efficient concept learning in difficult situations, when the data are uncertain and learning must be incremental. The probabilistic learning system PLS is outlined, and some ideas and principles underlying it are developed. PLS1 was the first AI system to use probabilistic conceptual clustering, and to exhibit optimal learning. A new system PLS0 may permit tractable induction of structure and relations using "second order" clustering.

This tutorial paper analyzes PLS in terms of some machine learning issues. It is generally agreed that for significant results with nontrivial tasks, domain-specific knowledge is indispensable. Its mechanized acquisition is one of the most important problems in AI, the solution of which could, for example, relieve the knowledge acquisition bottleneck. In computer systems, domain-specific knowledge is usually generalized: abstract rules controlling the task are designed to apply equally to many similar data or situations sharing common descriptions. Abstract knowledge has sometimes been learned mechanically from data having a relatively low measure of abstraction. This paper contends that automated learning or knowledge acquisition is generally feasible.

These are issues of generalization or induction. To compare degrees of induction, we define the term *conceptual knowledge;* this quantity may help to develop systems and to clarify research goals. As an example of research clarification, consider that domain-specificity in the ultimate, task-oriented knowledge structures does not preclude acquisition of that knowledge using *mediating* structures which are less abstract, and which may facilitate the acquisition. With this viewpoint, a spectrum of conceptual knowledge results: data have none, mediating structures acquire some, and the ultimate, task-oriented form has maximum conceptual knowledge. The acquisition of conceptual knowledge is induction.

The concepts and methods developed in this paper domain independent. The task of search has been selected for a combination of appropriate characteristics: this domain is sufficiently complex, yet it permits a relatively uncomplicated data base; moreover system training may be automated. Consequently, our effort can focus on concerns of effective and efficient knowledge acquisition.

The learning system PLS unifies several approaches and perspectives: observation of success probability, regionalization of feature space, accommodation of feature interaction, analysis using information theory, efficiency in information extraction, stability with criticized parallelism, refinement of inductive inference, and comparisons with cognitive psychology. The attempt has been to synthesize viewpoints and enunciate principles, and to implement ideas and demonstrate effectiveness.

One conclusion is that efficient and effective learning demands both symbolic structuring and also statistical methods (for noise immunity). Another conclusion is that knowledge acquisition should be both data-determined and model-driven. Finally, knowledge layering may make difficult problems tractable (such as the problem of new terms or constructive induction).

Author's Note

This paper is a minor revision of [Re 83e], which describes machine learning research on probabilistic, incremental, and otherwise difficult induction or concept formation. The early experiments involved the task of incremental learning in the uncertain domain of problem solving and game

---

[1] Department of Computer Science, University of Illinois at Urbana-Champaign, Urbana, Illinois 61801

playing. The goal of a learning system for such tasks is the induction of a concept such as "shortest solution" or "forced win". Because of their inherent complexity, such concepts must, in practice, be inexact or uncertain.

This real-world difficulty leads to a broader view of induction: Rather than a representation suitable for learning, we consider the classical, logic representation of a concept (e.g. [Mi 82, Mc 83]) to be just a final stage or external expression of deeper processes. Our view is that the underlying processes are probabilistic and layered.

Some of these ideas are developed in this minor revision of the early summary [Re 83e] of work on uncertain and incremental concept formation done up to 1983. This included probabilistic conceptual clustering [Re 77] and second order (layered) clustering [Re 85b]. For further development and recent perspectives, see [Re 86a, Re 87].

1. Introduction

Many AI systems comprise at least two major components: a *performance* element for the primary task or problem domain, and a *higher level* system by which control of this task is promoted, using suitable knowledge structures and appropriate means for modifying them [Di 82]. This more abstract component may be designed to facilitate human alteration of the control structures, or it may permit autonomous adaptation (in which case it is a *learning element* [Bu 78]). Certain elaborations, properties, and principles of this model form the subject of the present tutorial paper.

This introduction is divided into three sections. The first outlines the broad context, and the second section narrows the context. This narrowing is designed to simplify, but not to restrict: what is narrowed is the problem domain; the higher level system remains general.

Our research goal is to help discover essential properties of effective knowledge representation and acquisition; these are related to the higher level system, particularly if it can learn. With emerging principles, design for individual applications can become reliable and standardized. Hence the main thrust of this paper is toward development of "laws" of knowledge acquisition for task performance. This suggests effective and efficient *performance,* but also implies effective and efficient knowledge *acquisition*. An examination of these emerging principles is begun in the third section of this introduction (and is developed in later parts of the paper). To advance such a goal, however, requires some background.

1.1 Perspective

Although it is only three decades old, artificial intelligence has already exhibited a pattern common to science: periods of fairly stable development in research, alternating with stages of more abrupt reorganization in paradigm [Ku 61]. Discovery reforms.

This is actually a simplified picture, since different streams of research are in progress concurrently, each with a somewhat independent cycle of growth. Nevertheless there have been identifiable, sometimes major, shifts in emphasis and areas of greatest advancement. A well known example in AI of this pattern of gradual evolution then restructuring involved two seemingly opposed representations of knowledge: a declarative formulation using mechanized logic, being challenged by a procedural approach using programmed advice. The eventual outcome was a synthesis of the two approaches and a better understanding of important issues.

In the early sixties the combination of mathematical logic and computing power spawned work on automatic deduction (theorem proving), in which knowledge is expressed as statements in the predicate calculus. The set of assertions deducible in these systems is complete and precise, and the data base of facts is easily modified. However, without guidance by an informed strategy of some kind, exponential growth of valid but irrelevant statements overwhelms any system. About 1970, an alternative was pursued in which suggested courses of action appropriate to the domain being represented were embedded in procedures of a program. While this approach is often efficient and easy to understand, the knowledge structures are difficult to alter.

The resolution of these two approaches may now seem rather obvious (as it usually does with hindsight): When knowledge is being *used* it becomes procedural;[2] when it is being *improved,* it is declarative. Successful systems now separate knowledge structures from the program in order to facilitate their evaluation and modification. Moreover, this organization admits not only representation of facts, but also expression of knowledge about how to use the facts. This heuristic knowledge for task control is essentially both procedural (implicit) *and* declarative (explicit): procedural during task performance, and declarative during knowledge acquisition.

One way to view this duality is to separate structures and procedures into two layers. One layer is the primary task, such as playing checkers or analyzing chemicals. In such a domain, knowledge is required for basic relationships and operations, e.g., to make a checkers move [Sa63] or to enumerate causes of a peak in a mass spectrum [BF78]. (This knowledge may be embedded in procedures of a program, or supplied as rules to be interpreted.) The upper layer exists to improve control of the primary task, i.e. to learn a heuristic which will avoid the combinatorial explosion of unguided search at the lower level. (This upper level program may ease interaction with a human who does most of the work to generate heuristics [DL82], or it may be fully automated [Bu78].) In any case, knowledge is coded into a convenient structure (e.g. a vector of weights for features in checkers, or a set of rules for assessing hypothetical interpretations in chemical analysis).

Depending on the level at which they are viewed, these knowledge structures have one of two dominant *aspects*. At the upper level they embody, collect and refine knowledge about the particular domain; at this point they are declarative, and knowledge is explicit. At the lower level the structures control the task; then they are procedural, and their knowledge is implicit.

Heuristic knowledge is highly *specific* to the particular task being performed. Frequently this domain-specific knowledge is the form of condition-action rules or productions. (This conforms to the two-layer framework: some fixed program

---

[2] More accurately: when knowledge is being utilized, it *partly* controls some procedure. The control may take various forms, such as a simple parameter vector, or a complex set of condition-action rules.

interprets the stored heuristic structures (the production rules); some other program or user updates this same modular knowledge.) Expert systems using the representation can rival human performance in some domains (see the review articles [Da 77, Du 83]).

These successful systems generally use a knowledge base for control which is expressed in a highly abstract form. For example a typical condition-action rule in Dendral [BF 78] includes a condition "If there are two peaks ..." Many situations fit this description. An abstract rule in checkers might be "If a man is threatened and another piece can be moved safely to prevent the jump, then block the threat". This advice does not specify an exact location for any of the men involved; it also disregards any irrelevant pieces (cf. [BM 80]). Abstract rules controlling such a task are designed to apply equally to many similar data or situations sharing common descriptions.

Note that abstraction and specialization take place simultaneously. The abstract knowledge in the Dendral example is obviously much different from that in the checkers one. That is, high level knowledge is bound up with domain-specificity. If the abstract knowledge is autonomously generated or modified by the upper element, the result is *machine learning;* in our case, it is intelligent generalization or *induction*.

The knowledge paradigm for task control is related to the theme of learning, which has had its own evolution. Around 1960 machine learning was very active and successful (see the historical sketch in [CMM 83]). Then, after optimistic expectations were not realized, much of the AI effort focused elsewhere. However, advances in induction such as version spaces [Mi 77, Mi 83] and formal frameworks (e.g. [Mi 82, Mc 83, Re 86]) suggest a fuller knowledge paradigm: *domain-specific knowledge is essential, but it can be acquired autonomously*.

When used for control of the primary task, knowledge is generalized; it is attuned and compressed. The "upper layer" system component acquires and refines knowledge for fast guidance of the "lower level" performance element (see Fig. 1). Knowledge is inferred from less general cases, then abstracted toward a relevant and concise form. This difficult task has often been done by a human, but in some cases, abstract knowledge has been attained autonomously from information having a relatively low measure of abstraction (and with reasonable efficiency). An extension of this argument is that full knowledge acquisition, from primitive data, may be feasible.

Mechanization of inductive learning is equivalent to conceptual knowledge acquisition, perhaps the main problem in AI. For example the greatest difficulty with current knowledge based systems is acquisition. Pointing out several applications, Michalski [Mc 83] explains the centrality of induction.

In summary: As a result of both gradual and acute advances in AI, several issues are clearer. Heuristic knowledge has *both a procedural and a declarative aspect*. It is procedural when the task performance program uses it; it is declarative when the "upper level" program improves it. Knowledge tuning is facilitated if the structures are *separable* from both programs. Since heuristic knowledge is usually compact, compared with data at the task level, adapting this knowledge generally involves *induction,* or creation of *conceptual knowledge*. If the upper layer system that acquires knowledge is autonomous, it is a *learning element*.

These ideas underlie the perspective of our current research, which studies principles for effective and efficient representation and learning.

1.2 Scope

This tutorial paper examines the acquisition of conceptual knowledge. Although appropriate knowledge is normally generalized (abstract rules apply equally to many similar situations), data from which this knowledge might be acquired are specific (individual but unimportant differences obscure and confound generalization). Between the particular, massive data, and the ultimate, compressed information, intermediate knowledge structures can facilitate learning. Because these *mediating structures* are important, the learning model of Buchanan et al [Bu 78] will be elaborated in Part 2 to highlight them. To measure the extent of their abstraction, elementary information theory will be used to define *conceptual knowledge*.

With the formalization of this term, objectives and means will become more distinct. During use, ultimate knowledge is abstract and peculiar to an individual task, while in acquisition, intermediate knowledge may be in a different form and still be utilized to infer a concise and appropriate representation. Domain-specificity does not require a high level of abstraction (high conceptual knowledge) *during* learning.

A related issue is that of *cognitive economy* or concise efficacy [LHK 79, Ro 76]. Mediating structures should be cognitively economical but should not compress data too much. These and other aspects of conceptual knowledge and mediating structures will be introduced in Sect. 1.3, developed in Part 2, and used throughout the paper to aid understanding and design of a general learning system. Particularly important is a scheme for mechanized acquisition of complete conceptual knowledge directly from primitive data (outlined in Part 5 and further examined in [Re 85b]).

Since the problem of inducing conceptual knowledge is complex, the primary task domain of search has been selected for a combination of appropriate characteristics [Ba 82, Ni 71]. This domain permits a relatively uncomplicated knowledge base for control (simpler than that for a typical expert system), yet search allows extensive investigation of learning (since arbitrarily difficult problems can be tackled). Moreover, heuristic search allows automated training. The result is that effort can focus on central concerns such as effective and efficient knowledge acquisition.

The ideas developed in this paper are domain independent. Since the task domain is used primarily to develop and study general principles of knowledge structuring and acquisition, search becomes a paradigmatic example for controlled investigation of learning.

Using this domain for development, a scheme for acquisition of conceptual knowledge has been created which synthesizes several approaches and perspectives. These include: observation of success probability, creation of utility concepts, regionalization of feature space, accommodation of feature interaction, analysis using information theory, efficiency in information extraction, stability with criticized parallelism, refinement of inductive inference, and comparisons with cognitive psychology.

Some superficially disparate views are united. For example evaluation functions implicitly represent both concepts and strategies. Observation of data can result in structured knowledge through a process that is both data-directed and model-determined. (Some of the ideas are explored in Part 2 and others are developed throughout the paper.)

Based on these ideas, a working system (PLS) has been implemented which is general, successful and extensible. One domain of this learning system is state-space problems and games. Here PLS generalizes experience to other problem instances or games; the system acquires knowledge and forms concepts under conditions of noise (most methods cannot handle incorrect data, although some recent learning systems have been modeled on PLS). Moreover, few attempts have been made to learn directly from very elementary data ([EG 82, Qu 83, Re 85b], and Part 5 of this paper are exceptions). Part 3 describes the approach that led to consistent solution of the fifteen puzzle and the discovery of locally optimal feature weights (a result not otherwise obtained). PLS can be applied to other problems involving classification (such as concept formation and expert systems).

The design and programming of PLS are in varying stages of development. Some aspects have been well tested and found successful, e.g. concept formation under uncertainty and optimization of linear evaluation functions. Other schemes have been designed to generalize the approach; these include nonlinear feature composition (Sect. 3.3), accuracy improvement (Part 4), and the feature formation project (Part 5). Their testing is incomplete yet encouraging.

Some material in this paper has appeared elsewhere in a different form, and some material is new. The knowledge issues discussed in Part 2 are also examined in [Re 83d]. PLS1, the original learning system for state space problems, is detailed in [Re 83a], and some of Part 3 of this paper is a condensed version. Included in Part 3 are extensions involving nonlinearity [Re 83b] and games [Re 84], along with elaboration of some knowledge issues; these extensions have not been circulated previously. Part 4 is an extension of [Re 83c]. (Results related to Part 4 appear in [Re 85a]; developments arising from Parts 2 and 5 are reported in [Re 85b, Re 86b, Re 87].)

Some parts of this paper can be read out of order. Part 6 can related aspects of cognition provides a different context for various aspects of the system. Depending on the reader's interests, this discussion of cognition can augment other parts of the paper (cross-references are given). Part 2 provides a more direct foundation for the system. It examines interrelationships of knowledge representation, content, meaning, structuring, and complexity.

1.3 Principles

In this paper, we shall study the acquisition of conceptual knowledge in search. Its basic mechanism is straightforward: trees are built using states as nodes and pre-specified operators as links. (State space and game playing formalisms are detailed in Appendix A.) Just about any problem can be cast as a search problem. On the other hand, interesting problems are very difficult (e.g. even the spaces of the fifteen puzzle and checkers have about 10^{13} and 10^{18} states respectively), so the required induction is considerable. Most important, a search task allows an uncomplicated data base and automated training, and these simplifications of the primary task permit concentration on the learning element.

Samuel's checker player [Sa 63, Sa 67] is probably the best known learning system for a search domain. It used two different kinds of structures to direct search. One was fixed, a user-defined set of *features,* functions measuring various aspects of a board position (such as piece advantage, center control, etc.). The other structure facilitated composition of features into a single *evaluation function* H with which to appraise the overall utility of the board configuration. In the original system [Sa 63], features were merged simply as a linear combination to give the heuristic $H = \mathbf{b} \cdot \mathbf{f}$, where $\mathbf{f}$ is the feature vector, and $\mathbf{b}$ is a vector of coefficients. This $\mathbf{b}$ is variable knowledge structure for control; it embodies information about the relative importance of the features, (it was what was learned in [Sa 63]).

A number of aspects of Samuel's approach can be studied. Some relate to the conceptual separation of such a system into a performance element (knowledge use) and a learning element (knowledge acquisition). Here the performance element (PE) searches in *state space* for desirable board configurations or states (see Appendix A). But the learning element (LE) also searches, in rule or *hypothesis space* [Di 82, Mi 82, Re 86a], for a useful vector $\mathbf{b}$ of feature coefficients with which to guide the PE.[3] During task performance, $\mathbf{b}$ is a structure for control; during learning, it is a structure in which to encapsulate knowledge.

Using an evaluation function is one way to specify a plan or stategy. It is fully general [FY 74] unless constrained in some way (for example a linear combination of features is restrictive). As described in Part 2, an *explicitly* expressed strategy can be produced automatically by observing behavior governed through *implicit* knowledge represented in H. In a layered, fully automated learning system, features would be created first, next an evaluation function would be formed from them, and finally a plan could be extracted. (This increasing structure in knowledge manifestation may follow ontological and phylogenetic development – see Part 6.)

Another aspect of the checker player (and many other systems – e.g. [Be 77, Be 79, CK 86, Do 66, Gas 79, MR 70, Re 83a, Re 83b, SB 68, SF 71]) is the evaluation function as a composition of features. Features are high level, abstract constructs, typically containing most of the conceptual knowledge (this is explained in Part 2). Hence, if $H = \mathbf{b} \cdot \mathbf{f}$, adjustment of the coefficient vector $\mathbf{b}$ is of limited value, not only because feature combination is then restricted in generality, but also because prior knowledge is supplied in the features themselves. Nevertheless, even this lessor learning has been accomplished only infrequently (e.g. [Re 83a, Sa 63]). Attempts at the much more difficult problem of feature formation are rare ([EG 82, Qu 83, Re 85b], and Part 5 here).

---

[3] In state space, the states of a problem or game are represented in full detail. In contrast, states are normally described for the LE in terms of the more abstract feature vector $\mathbf{f}$. This involves "feature space." Still another space is "problem space", the set of possible training problems. See Appendix B and also [Di 82, SL 74].

Of the two knowledge structures discussed so far, the feature vector **f** and the coefficient vector **b**, both are active or relevant in performance and learning. Samuel's scheme used another knowledge structure, to bridge the gap between the data — nodes from the search tree (i.e. in state space) mapped to feature space (using **f**) — and the desired result **b** (a point in hypothesis space). A *mediating* structure recorded observations during play of a game for the purpose of improving **b**. Knowledge was gathered from individual states encountered, this information being compressed into running counts indicating whether individual coefficients in **b** produced evaluations agreeing with better estimates from lookahead.

For our present purposes, the details of this scheme are not so important as certain of its tactics and properties. In the running counts, *every* expanded node contributed to assess *every* feature in **f**. This was a stochastic process, so that any misleading data did not have an overwhelming effect, but rather swayed the assessments temporarily; in contrast, typical data lent support to predominating tendencies.

These properties of Samuel's highly successful learning system suggest principles for efficacy anf efficiency. Some of these seem to be loosely expressible as follows.

(1) *An appropriate knowledge structure between the elementary data and the evaluation function facilitates learning.* The data are massive, the heuristic is very concise, and the structure that records statistics *mediates* the required information compression.
(2) *Efficient and effective learning depends on good use of data.* Samuel's checker player converged quickly. Every datum contributed, so learning was fast and error resilient.
(3) *Induction, confidence, models, and data are bound up together, and good learning methods extract knowledge combining all available resources.* Statistical methods such as curve fitting and clustering effect induction. They accomplish *mutual data support,* i.e. greater assurance developing as a by-product of the generalization process itself. (This is one of the themes of this paper.)

Several of these characteristics are shared by Samuel's systems and PLS, such as knowledge mediation, statistical observation, and feature clustering. The original system PLS1 can be considered a refinement of Samuel's signature tables (which essentially clustered feature space areas of uniform task utility). PLS1 uses a basic structure called the *cumulative region set,* a partition of feature space. In each region, a feature volume is associated with a goal-oriented quantity called the *utility* for the intended task. An example of utility is the probability of a state's contributing to a win. Learning proceeds incrementally: utility estimates are gradually revised and the feature space partition is refined. Accuracy and differentiation improve as knowledge accumulates.

The cumulative region set has various advantages. First, it is a flexible representation that allows easy differentiation. This representation has independent members (regions coding localized utilities) that permit a critic to assess them (Part 4 of this paper), yet can determine an evaluation function having feature interaction (Sect. 3.3). The cumulative region set is a mediating structure.

Another advantage of the region set is that it embodies probabilistic goal orientation (through utility) and discrimination (through feature space refinement). Our mediating structure models aspects of cognition (Part 6).

Finally, the cumulative region set may be used even if data are low level. When features are replaced by "primitives", cumulative regions can become the basic building block for conceptual knowledge acquisition without any prior knowledge except objects and operations defining the primary task.[4] This allows mechanized construction of features themselves, an important but difficult problem of "new terms" [Di 82], toward which only moderate progress has been made.

Part 5 of this paper argues that this problem is computationally feasible. The scheme involves mutual data support, now manifest as a complex kind of clustering. A hierarchy of knowledge structures mediates a sequence of subprocesses. These have a common foundation and build one upon another: the basis is the cumulative region set (now in primitive space). Beginning with this structure, conceptual knowledge is acquired gradually, first extracting relevant subpatterns, then coalescing these units increasingly organized wholes. This layered approach is a "divide and conquer" technique. Organization is gradually imposed on statistical observation, to form a system which is both data-directed and model-determined (Usually one *or* the other is implemented.)

Development of these ideas is based on concepts examined in Part 2 of this paper.

2. Knowledge: Orientation and Issues

This part provides a foundation for the paper, examining knowledge representation, acquisition, and use. Among the issues discussed are the power of selected structures, the measurement of acquired knowledge, and the efficiency of associated learning. Viewpoints include evaluation as utility classification, and knowledge as information compression. Although the context is search problems, the ideas are general. To begin, components for knowledge acquisition are organized for subsequent development and analysis.

2.1 A Framework for Acquiring Knowledge

Often the purpose of gaining knowledge is to accomplish some task more effectively or more efficiently. It is these twin performance criteria that are of interest in AI, since the theoretical solution of a problem is usually known. For example to prove a theorem or to win a game it is only necessary to consider all possible alter-

---

[4] Either high level features or else fundamental measurements are used, depending on the amount of prior knowledge given the system. Features in checkers (such as center control, mobility, etc.) have much conceptual knowledge, whereas primitives (the contents of the 32 legal squares on the board) have little or no conceptual knowledge.

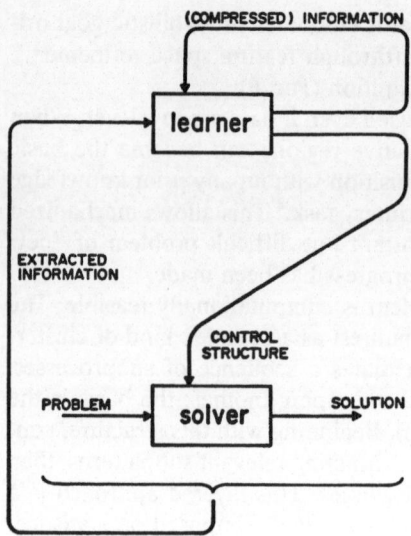

Fig. 1. A simple learning system (LS) for problem solving. Low level data from the solver are fed to the learning element to improve the control structure, which embodies abstract knowledge expressed in a concise form. Between the data and the control structure may be mediating knowledge structures that facilitate the generalization. In these structures, compressed information is retained, modified, and accumulated

atives and choose the best (just enumerate and test).[5] Of course the trouble is that for any interesting problem, exhaustive search results in an exponential explosion. Some heuristic, plan or strategy is necessary to limit exploration. This immediately raises some fundamental questions:

(i) How should information for search be *represented*? That is, what form should the rules take that are to govern search in state space?

(ii) How can this knowledge be *acquired* and *improved*? Since the purpose of capturing knowledge is to discover appropriate rules for the primary task, this can also be considered as a problem of search (see [Mi 82]). How should the search in rule or hypothesis space be conducted?

In an important paper on learning systems, Buchanan et al [Bu 78] developed a standard model designed to create, use, and modify knowledge stored in an abstract structure. They give several examples such as Samuel's classic checker player. Here we adopt this general model, which is exemplified in Fig. 1.

The components of a *learning system* (LS) are:[6]

(1) an *algorithm schema* for some primary task, the *performance element* PE;
(2) some separable *control structure* S for the PE;
(3) the *critic,* whose role is "[to analyze] the current abilities of the performance

---

[5] For the reader unfamiliar with state space search, Appendix A provides definitions and brief examples.

[6] For now we consider a learning system to be singly layered. Buchanan et al allow a system to be multilayered, which we shall discuss later.

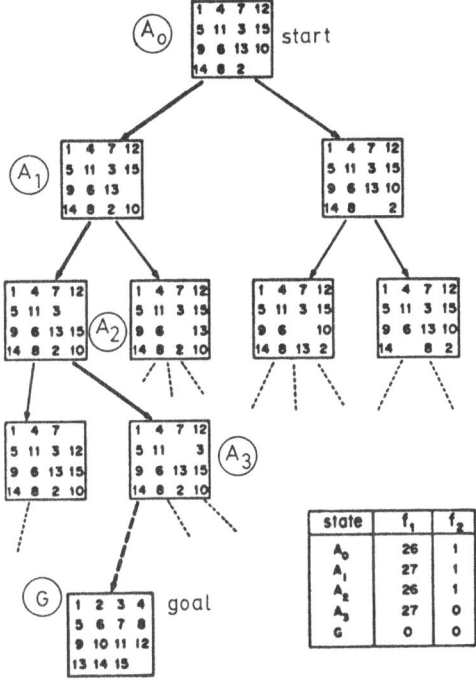

Fig. 2. Fifteen puzzle illustration. A move of the puzzle corresponds to a link in the search tree. With breadth-first search (a small part of which is shown), a solution (heavy lines) is eventually obtained. In order to develop a heuristic, features can be defined, such as f_1 (sum of distances of tiles from home) and f_2 (number of pair reversals). Notice that the "7" and "3" are reversed in nodes A_0 through A_2; this would eventually block progress. In (f_1, f_2) feature space, vectors close to the origin are generally better (i.e. both features are "penalties" – see inset table)

element," PE[S] by *assessment* of the overall effectiveness of S, and sometimes by *localization* of credit within S;

(4) the *learning element* LE, designed to improve S according to recommendations of the critic;[7]

(5) a *blackboard* on which to store S and other information between activations of algorithms.

This synthesis allows a clearer examination of the original questions (i) and (ii): A standard form is to be selected for the structure S. An instance of S is to be "plugged into" the performance element PE to complete and control it. S is not only a control structure for the PE, but also a knowledge structure manipulated by the LE. The evolution of this structure depends on repeated information transfer between the PE, the critic, and the LE, using the blackboard. The process of perfecting S is complex: PE performance data influence the decisions made by the LE, and these in turn affect the direction of the PE.

---

[7] Instead of a feature vector, many alternative knowledge structures are possible such as a set of productions or condition-action rules. Different kinds of knowledge representation are described in Ch. III of [AIH 82].

If the PE is a problem solver or game player, probably the simplest choice for the control structure S is a coefficient vector $\mathbf{b}$ for an evaluation function $H = \mathbf{b}.\mathbf{x}$, where $\mathbf{x}$ is the value of feature vector $\mathbf{f}(A)$ describing the problem configuration or game state A (and where $\mathbf{b}.\mathbf{x} = b_1 x_1 + b_2 x_2 + \ldots + b_n x_n$ is the dot or inner product). The vector $\mathbf{f}$ is itself a knowledge structure, a fact that will be examined later. An example of a useful feature vector for the fifteen puzzle is shown in Fig. 2. (See Appendix A for a description of this puzzle.) In Fig. 2 the vector $\mathbf{f}$ has two features: the obviously effective $f_1 =$ the sum of city block distances of the tiles to their home positions, and another penalty (i.e. feature for which a larger value is bad) $f_2 =$ the number of reversals (adjacent tiles being in their correct positions except switched). For checkers, $\mathbf{f}$ might instead include piece advantage, control of center, mobility, and so on [Sa 63]. The weight or coefficient vector $\mathbf{b}$ expresses the relative importance of the features.[8]

At this point, our two questions (i) and (ii) have been interpreted to some extent for search. Some aspects are undetermined, e.g., the kind of control structure to use.

2.2 Limitation and Power in Structures

An important criterion for the choice of a knowledge structure is its power of expression. The knowledge structure should not inhibit control of the primary task. (Implicit in Question (i) about representation is the desire to avoid system limitation.) The simple weight vector $\mathbf{b}$ as described permits only a linear combination $\mathbf{b}.\mathbf{f}$ of features, whereas the relationship between the value of a state and its characteristics is often more complex.

There may be interaction among features. One feature, f_0, say, might represent game progression. Depending on this pivotal measure f_0, certain other features might play greater or lesser roles (e.g. center control is not critical in an end game). For proper expression of the worth of a state, this situation entails interaction with f_0. In other words, the linear combination $\mathbf{b}.\mathbf{f}$ is inadequate, and a more expressive structure must be used. In general, feature interaction is prevalent [Sa 67, Be 77].

Nonlinear capability can be provided, but one might still question whether an evaluation function formed from features is enough anyway. Is not an elaborate plan, say one constructed from a set of condition-action rules, more powerful in terms of the range of strategies that can be created? The answer is that any plan can be represented with a sufficiently expressive feature vector [FY 74].

This can be illustrated by considering Fig. 3 (a), where a solution path is transformed into a path in feature space, called the "feature trace" (of a solution) [Re 82].[9] A complete strategy or plan is reflected in some collection of feature

---

[8] Instead of a feature vector, many alternative knowledge structures are possible, such as set of productions or condition-action rules. Different kinds of knowledge representation are described in Ch. III of [AIH 82].

[9] Since the feature trace preserves order of nodes in a solution, this mapping is a homomorphism. Because a single feature space image can result from many similar problem solutions, the homo-

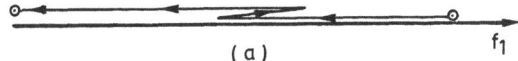
(a) f_1

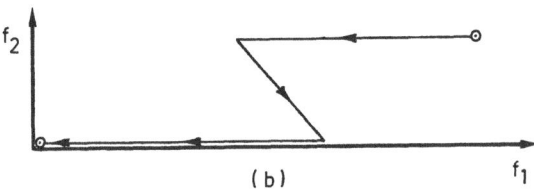
f_2 (b) f_1

Fig. 3. Feature traces of solutions. These might be used to help generalize a macro-operator or plan. f_1 and f_2 are the distance and reversal scores for the fifteen puzzle. In the one-dimensional f_1 space (a) solutions sometimes trace strange paths. However they appear normal in the (f_1, f_2) space (b), where the distance score is temporarily worsened to unclog a reversal. Bundles of feature traces reflect a strategy or plan, such as "Temporarily worsen the distance score if a reversal can be removed." Irregular solution paths followed in feature space (e.g. a) become unsurprising when enough appropriate features are present (e.g. b)

traces. For example the plan "Make a move so as to bring some tile closer to home" corresponds to a (large) set of traces like the one in Fig. 3 (a). As long as enough discriminating features are incorporated, any strategy can be represented by an appropriate evaluation function, which will in turn determine the feature traces.

Sophisticating a plan may require additional features. For example, adding "If there are any reversals, get rid of them" to the naive original advice can be expressed with f_2 of Fig. 3 (b). Encompassing a grand strategy, many plans can coexist in feature space; each in analogous to a distinct *category* of feature traces. Consequently, the feature space representation provides one direction in answering Question (i) posed earlier.

Nevertheless one important difference between an evaluation function and a strategy is that the former represents knowledge *implicitly,* while the latter is *explicit*. If behavior governed through an evaluation function is observed, a strategy can be induced (cf. [FHN72, Ge83, Sac74]). Since feature traces are generalized, they could form part of a scheme designed ultimately to create plans. In a layered, fully automated learning system having a little prior knowledge, first features would be created, then the evaluation function would be formed from them, and finally a plan could be extracted (see Part 5). This increasing structure in knowledge manifestation may follow phylogenetic and ontological development (see Part 6).

To summarize: in theory an evaluation function is a fully general means to specify any plan (and a plan can be learned from the "less intelligent" function). Our present concern is to learn an evaluation function, and we shall see that this is essentially a problem of classification and concept formation.

(Footnote 9 continued) morphism is actually a surjection, i.e. an epimorphism [Gi76]. Thus feature traces condense information, although to a lesser degree than a complete strategy.

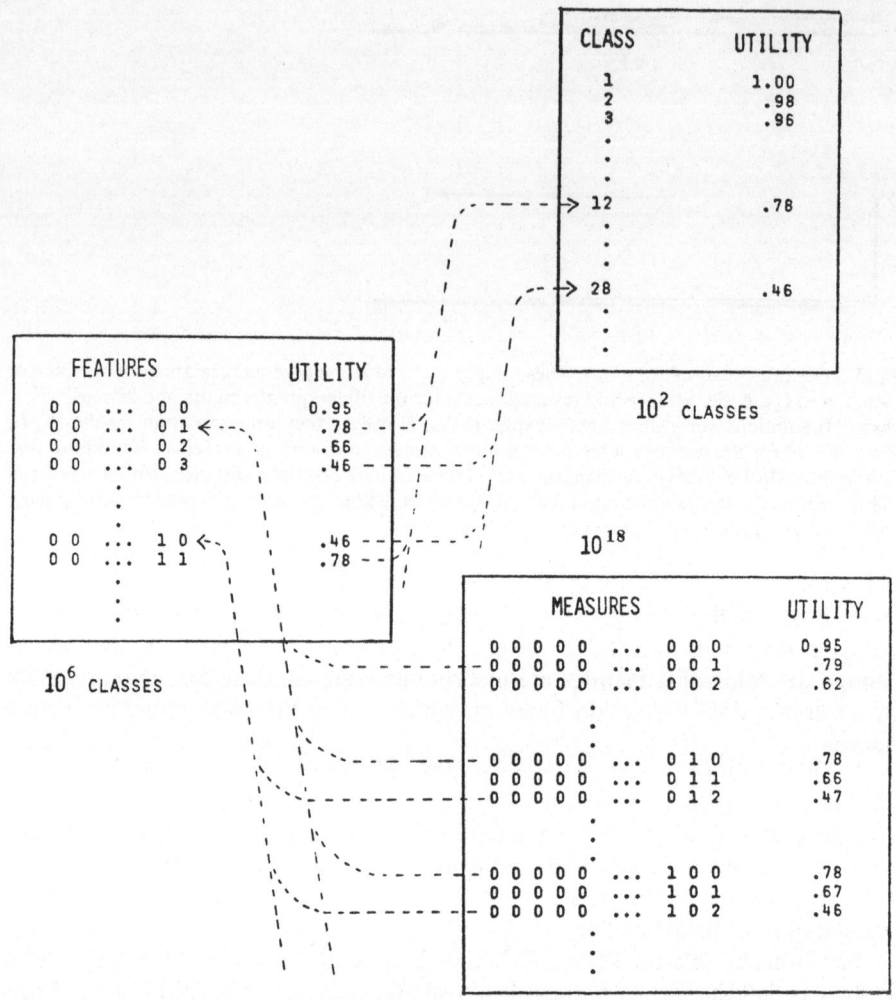

Fig. 4. Levels of conceptual knowledge in search. Primitive data (bottom-most table) represent fully detailed knowledge (little or no abstraction); such data are massive and infeasible to gather. At the other extreme (top-most), very concise descriptions exhibit maximal information compression; this information is hard to learn. Intermediate representations (center table) facilitate learning: features discriminate utility well and bear a nearly monotonic relationship with it, but a relatively mild interaction amongst each other. At the top level, complex concepts classify individual table entries from the lowest level. As an intermediate aid, features facilitate concise and orderly description (concept formation). Features are mediating concepts

2.3 Evaluation as Classification

Figure 4 relates classification to concepts. A class C can be defined by *extension* as an exhaustive set explicitly listing individual members of the class (lowest level). Usually, however, a class is defined by *intension,* as a list of properties shared by individuals in C. Then membership is expressed as a proposition, e.g., $x \in C$ if x satisfies $2 \le f_1(x) \le 7$ and $0 \le f_2(x) \le 3$. The requirement for class membership is called a *concept* (this term is used especially if the same class arises often; then its description (the concept) is frequently useful). In our example, C is described as a conjunction of feature ranges (a rectangle r in two dimensional feature space). If a concept r_1 is satisfied by more members x than another concept r_2 (i.e. if the volume of r_1 is greater), r_1 could be said to be more abstract (cf. [Di 82]).

How do classes and concepts relate to evaluation functions? Theoretically, an evaluation function can be expressed at a very low level. The set of situations at or close to the level of the data could be represented as a table listing the node description or *primitive* vector along with its corresponding worth or *utility* value for the task (Fig. 4).[10]

The primitives might be detailed, for example the contents of *individual* squares in the fifteen puzzle or checkers. A complete (and accurate) table based on primitives would enable perfect choice of a node to expand, but the quantities are immense. For checkers, roughly 10^{18} table entries would be required.

Consider instead an abstract heuristic, the topmost level of Fig. 4. How many utility classes are required for perfect state evaluation, i.e. how many categories are needed for sufficient resolution of the worth of a state? Since optimal solution (shortest path length and fewest nodes developed) for a state space problem requires only knowledge of path length remaining to the goal [HNR 68, Ni 71, Ni 80], the number of classes need be just the maximum of the shortest solution for any problem instance. For a game, half the number of moves in a long contest might be sufficient. (These numbers are roughly 75 for the fifteen puzzle and about the same for checkers.)

Although prior knowledge of solution length is not feasible in interesting cases, practical evaluation functions might be expected to follow a similar pattern. To test this assertion, an experiment with the best heuristic known for the fifteen puzzle [Re 77, Re 81, Re 83a] was conducted. Figure 5 shows the relationship of performance to the number of classes when the evaluation function was arbitrarily rounded. Notice that the required number of utility classes roughly agrees with theory.

In the construction of a concise heuristic for checkers, the number of utility classes is reduced from about $10^{18} \simeq 2^{60}$ to $2^6 \simeq 10^2$. The *information* at level I is $\log_2 N_I$, where N_I is the number of classes at level I. The *information compression* between level I and level J is $\log_2(N_J/N_I)$ [Wa 69a, Wa 72]. The compression in our checkers example is huge: about 52 bits.

Let us consider the intermediate feature level in Fig. 4 from the viewpoint of information compression. Typically, the number of classes at the feature level (i.e. the feature space volume) is about 2^{20} for checkers [Sa 63]. Computing the information compression throughout, we find that most of it occurs by the middle (feature) level, while the remainder occurs in the evaluation function as a particular

---

[10] Various interpretations of the utility are possible. In a state space problem the utility might be the path lenght remaining to the goal [HNR 68, Ni 71, Ni 80] or some probability of usefulness [Re 83a, SB 68, SF 71]. For a game the utility could be the probability of a win, perhaps averaged over experience with many good opponents [Gd 77, Pe 83, Re 84]. Pattern recognition techniques use similar probabilities [Ba 71, DK 82].

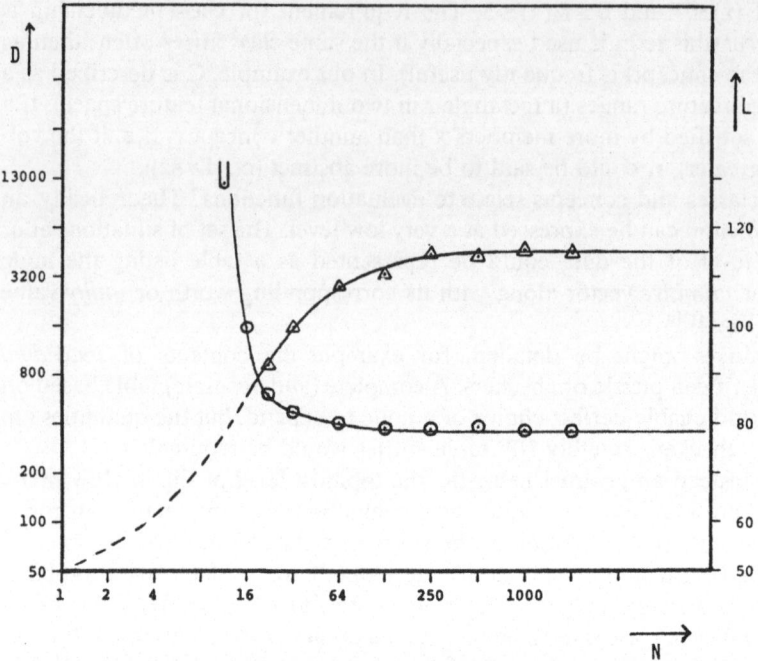

Fig. 5. Discretizing an evaluation function. When utility values are forced into discrete categories by arbitrary rounding, the evaluation function becomes a classifier. The performance (D and L) depends on the number of categories N, because N affects the accuracy of classification. D is the average number of states expanded before solution and L is the average solution length, for a random sample of 32 fifteen puzzles. Unlike D, L improves with smaller N since the heuristic is imperfect and lower N means search is more nearly breadth-first

combination of features. Other examples, such as the fifteen puzzle with its typical features, exhibit similar compression – often about 80%. Most of the information compression is in the features themselves. Further, these calculations do not account for the fact that the relationship between utility and features is much more regular than the relationship between utility and primitive descriptions (see [Re 85b, Re 86a]). This explains why the composition of a heuristic from features is unimpressive: learning systems should be able to *create* the features from primitives.

Because there is such a gap between low level primitives and abstract features, perhaps there should be multiple levels between primitives and features. (Watanabe [Wa 72] has found that uniform reduction is most effective.) Multiple layers will be discussed in Part 5 of this paper.

Question (ii) posed earlier about knowledge acquisition (Sect. 2.1) can be rephrased: "How can appropriate classification be realized?" Does it help to know the amount of information compression in a layered approach?

2.4 Structuring Conceptual Knowledge

If features typically represent most of the information compression between the data and the most concise expression, we might say that features contain a lot of knowledge. We define the *conceptual knowledge* present at a level to be the information compression required to form the classes at that level, from the most primitive classes (the raw data). (But see [Re 86a] for a refinement of this idea.) An evaluation function that compresses information just to the point at which performance begins to suffer (Fig. 5) could be said to capture maximum conceptual knowledge, while data represent none and features often about 80%. Referring to Question (ii) about knowledge acquisition, we can say that our learning system will be designed to acquire conceptual knowledge (by compressing and inducing information from data).

This view of learning also relates to Question (i) about appropriate knowledge representation. The compression of information requires a structure for development, retention, and revision of conceptual knowledge. From the classification standpoint, any utility category is associated with a description, rule, or condition to be satisfied for membership (Fig. 4). In the case of low level data, the description is the disjunction of a large number or primitive vectors. At higher description levels, the utility membership rule r is more concise: in general this rule r is paired with its utility u: r entails u. A node is good (fairly good, bad, etc. – as many descriptions as there are classes) providing it has certain attributes.

Concise expression is conceptual knowledge. Conceptual knowledge implies not only information compression, but also rational ordering. As indicated in Fig. 4, an exhaustive listing of primitive vectors has haphazard utility values (i.e. the utility surface in primitive space is extremely irregular). Features begin to impose regularity: an arrangement based on feature values recorders elements from the low level table into locally uniform utility categories (i.e. features are surjections – their range is smaller than their domain – and the utility surface in feature space is fairly smooth: consider for example the two illustrative features for the fifteen puzzle). The high level evaluation function merges features to construct a meaningful global organization of the smaller utility clusters.

Conceptual knowledge implies conceptualization. Features represent rational components of concepts. The evaluation function codes complete concepts. Features associate partially formed concepts with values that relate to the task domain. The evaluation function operates on these intermediate values to produce a sensible worth or utility value. The evaluation function maps a description r into its task utility u (Fig. 4). Meaningful classification, rational ordering, concept attainment, and effective use are all interrelated.

A convenient representation for a concept description is a hyperrectangle r. The actual PLS1 knowledge structure is a set of feature space "regions" (r, u, e), where u is r's utility, and e is the error in u (see Fig. 6). Each region (r, u, e) of a set $\{(r, u, e)\}$ can be considered as a "sub-concept" with description r, or, alternatively, the whole set can be considered as a (step-)function that indicates the degree or probability with which an object is part of the ultimately desired concept (e.g., "winning").

As we shall see, the region set helps answer Question (i) posed in Sect. 2.1 concerning effective knowledge representation. This knowledge structure will also help answer Question (ii) about effective acquisition and improvement of knowledge. Regions become blackboard structures (Sect. 2.1) for the learning system (Part 3). During learning, a region (r, u, e) is modified in two basic ways. Its utility u can be revised, and the region itself can be refined (split) as r is differentiated. Using regions in a context of statistical observation facilitates noise management and incremental modification.

The region set is useful in many domains, whenever the worth of something is measurable and contingent on some description. For example an expert system could incorporate this structure to learn appropriate conditions for firing production rules. In heuristic search, the region set can be used directly to give a discrete evaluation function, or indirectly to determine a smoothed function.

2.5 Performance Measurement of Acquired Knowledge

In our search context the results of learning are easily observable. Task *performance* can be defined in several ways [Ni 71, Ni 80], but throughout this paper two simple measures will be used. One gauges efficiency: the number D of nodes developed before the goal is reached; the other reflects efficacy: the length L of the solution (in a problem) or of the win (in a game). To improve the accuracy of these quantities, they will be measured not just for a single training problem, but rather for a set. Depending on purpose, the set will be selected completely randomly or else with a difficulty constraint. The quantities D and L will be compared for different control structures (region sets) and learning methods (ways of using the region sets).

Two factors affect performance. One is the completeness of classification or refinement of the region set: Are the utility classes sufficiently differentiated? The other concern is accuracy: To what extent are the categories correct? As an illustration, suppose that the final knowledge structures for performance include a feature vector **f** and a weight vector **b**. Classification would be incomplete if **f** did not discriminate fully, or if its coefficient vector **b** had inappropriate zeroes.

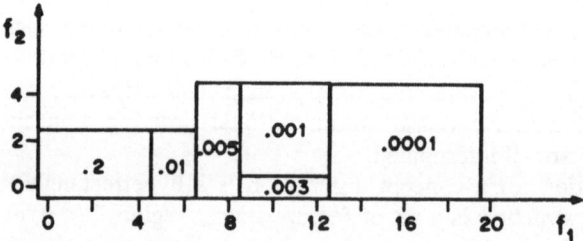

Fig. 6. The region set, a partition of feature space with associated information. Shown are rectangles r and their utilities u. Equivalently, r is a candidate component of the desired concept, and u is the probability that r is included in the concept. If the pair (r, u) is extended to the triple (r, u, e), the error factor e indicates inverse confidence in u, and is useful for weighting contributions of regions during learning (e.g. in revising u, and in curve fitting)

We can consider an example of each of these factors underlying performance. As an example of the first factor, the vector (f_1, f_2) for the fifteen puzzle (where the features are as in Fig. 2) misses reversals if $\mathbf{b} = (-1,0)$. In other words, the heuristic function $H = -f_1$ classifies poorer states with reversals as having the same utility as good states without this blockage (and so some node expansions are wasted, worsening D; or reaching the goal is delayed, worsening L).

As an example of the second factor in performance, consider that the optimal coefficient vector is $(-1, -4)$, and if $\mathbf{b}$ is instead $(-1, -8)$, this is a case of inaccurate categorization since the effect of a high f_2 value is overestimated (and again the incorrect classification results in worse D or L). Sect. 3.4 will show the optimization of coefficients for similar features. Investigations of the effect of error on performance can be found in, e.g., [Gas 79, Har 74, HDP 80, Pe 83].

Summarizing: We might predict improved performance if classification has been refined, but its error is usually unknown without performance feedback. Accuracy can be determined through performance measures such as number of nodes developed D and solution length L. Classification and performance have a causal relationship. We can conclude retroactively that conceptual knowledge has improved if the performance has improved.

These considerations relate to Question (ii) of Sect. 2.1. Now we can clarify the meaning of the "acquisition" and the "improvement" of knowledge. Knowledge is greater if it leads to effective and efficient search (measured through L and D respectively).

Let us consider efficiency, not of the search in state space for a solution or win, but rather of search in hypothesis space for a good evaluation function.

2.6 Efficiency of Knowledge Acquisition

First consider the formation of an evaluation function from its constituent features. In Sect. 2.3 we saw that when the features are initially known, the problem is much easier, since typically about 80% of the conceptual knowledge resides in the features. Despite this advantage, creation of a good evaluation function is still difficult to mechanize with reasonable efficiency [Re 83, Sa 63]. The task is particularly hard if nonlinearity is allowed (but see [Re 83b, Sa 67] and Sect. 3.3 here).

Traditional optimization methods can be used to find the best coefficient vector $\mathbf{b}$ for feature vector $\mathbf{f}$ in the evaluation function $H = \mathbf{b} \cdot \mathbf{f}$ [Re 81]. For example, we could minimize the number of nodes developed D as a function of feature values. Since the variance in D is typically high, a statistical technique would be chosen, such as fitting second degree polynomials in the coefficient space. This *response curve fitting,* though, is computationally expensive. One reason is that too many nodes must be developed (i.e. D is too high for typical coefficient vectors $\mathbf{b}$). Even if the approximate location of the optimal $\mathbf{b}$ is known, the process is still inefficient (see [Re 81]).

Experiments have shown that the learning system of Part 3 is superior. Intuitively it is clear why this is so. For each attempt to solve a training problem, the optimization technique obtains just a single number (D) and disposes of everything else. In contrast to this brute force "generate-and-test" method, a good learning system extracts more information from each search.

Good use of information is the key to success in heuristic formation. Consider the problem again as utility classification or conceptual knowledge acquisition (Sect. 2.3 and Fig. 4). At the primitive level, a table of utilities could theoretically be constructed for every individual state. But operating solely with this detail, a rote learning system would never gather much knowledge in practice. Furthermore, patterns among table entries (conceptual knowledge) would never be discovered.

In contrast, the ability to assign many states to a single, meaningful class is of double importance. First, during evaluation, states which have not been encountered can be judged since they are similar to other members of the class. Secondly, during learning, similar data help the formation ot utility classes and concepts.

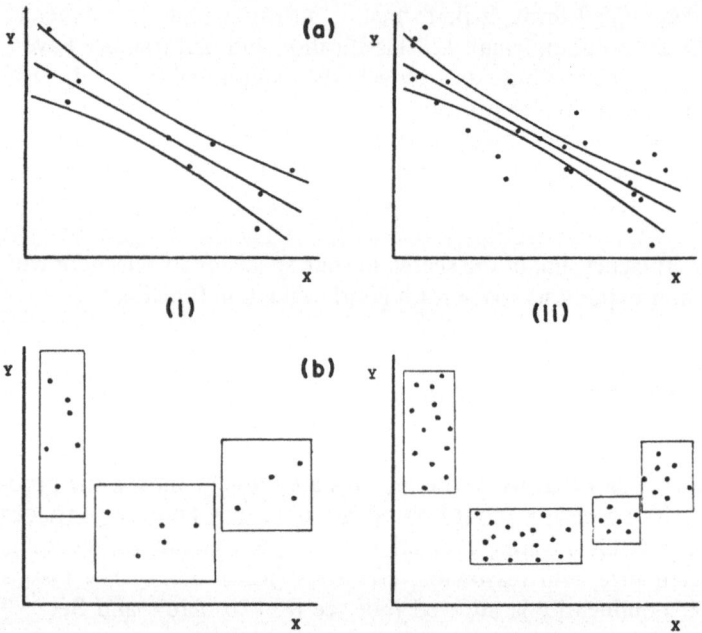

Fig. 7. Mutual data support in statistical methods. Suppose an independent variable X (e.g. some feature) bears some relationship to a dependent variable Y (e.g. the utility). If the relationship is known to be linear, a straight line can be fitted as shown in (a). If the correct model is not known, clustering can be used (b). This second method assumes no prior knowledge about the form of the relationship. As part of the clustering process, a concept emerges in which enclosed points are "similar" (they have comparable Y values). In either case, data combine to induce a generalization. Given a value of X, Y (X) can be interpolated. (Compare Fig. 6.)

For both (a) and (b), the number of data influence our confidence. With just a few points (i), the error in Y may be large. As the number N of points increases (ii), the estimate becomes more accurate. (The error is indicated by the curves in (a) and by the vertical extent of rectangles in (b). The error varies as $1/\sqrt{N}$ in either case).

Large N can also refine our knowledge: a greater number of independent variables may become active (not illustrated), or more clusters of Y values may result (e.g. b ii more refined than b i). Data support each other, to determine characteristics of a cluster (b) or to provide coefficients in a model (a). As data coalesce, greater assurance and increased organization occur *simultaneously*

This class formation, itself, is doubly beneficial: as data coalesce, generalizations are made (classes are hypothesized); at the same time, increasingly greater assurance is possible (utility values of classes are backed by more data). This *mutual data support* is a characteristic of statistical techniques. *Curve fitting* (regression) takes advantage of regularity in the relationships between dependent variable (here, utility) and independent variables (the features). As Fig. 7 shows, the data are conformed by a (linear) model; this inductive learning is feasible because of inherent smoothness in the utility-feature relationships. (The same regularity permits valid interpolation during subsequent node evaluation.) If the proper model is unknown, *cluster analysis* can be substituted in place of curve fitting (Fig. 7b).

Techniques such as utility clustering may be contrasted with a brute force method of generating a control structure and then testing it. In terms of our questions about how knowledge should be acquired (Sect. 2.1), automated search for good control structures should be efficient. Part 3 will detail the use of statistical approaches and Part 5 will discuss these and other means of mutual data support for tractable feature formation.

2.7 Summary of Knowledge Analysis

While domain specific knowledge is indispensable, it can be acquired from specific cases. To help design learning systems, we quantify acquired knowledge: we define *conceptual knowledge* as the amount of information compression compared with primitive data.

In our context of heuristic search in problems and games, the acquisition of conceptual knowledge is the learning of a strategy, plan, or evaluation function. The compression of information is based on similar *utility,* a goal-oriented quantity, the probability of task usefulness.

Utility classes are specified by a set of concept-utility pairs (the *region set*). This structure can be used as a discrete evaluation function, or it can generate a smooth evaluation function.

Features represent partially constructed concepts and formative utilities. Typically, features contain about 80% of the conceptual knowledge, so if the features are known initially, the creation of an evaluation function is much easier. Domain specific conceptual knowledge may be learned if features are given, and perhaps even if they are not (see Part 5).

In a learning system, the task *performance element* (here problem or game search) communicates with the *learning element* through the *blackboard* containing the *control structure*. One control structure is the evaluation function (which is theoretically equivalent to a plan or strategy, and which can generate one).

The blackboard may also contain *mediating structures* (e.g. region sets) which efficiently determine the control structure. If these various ingredients are not too limited, they promote general learning systems for many domains.

Knowledge structures and learning algorithms should be designed for efficiency and accuracy in uncertain conditions. Efficiency is improved when data are clustered for *mutual support*. Learning based on statistical techniques helps accuracy and noise immunity.

3. The Basic Probabilistic Learning System (PLS1)

PLS1 is applicable to tasks of classifications or concept learning. Like systems such as ID3 [Qu83] and AQ [Mc80], PLS1 must be given a set of "well behaved" features (see [Re86a]). Unlike other systems, PLS1 is capable of optimal incremental learning in uncertain domains. (Some recent systems, such as [LR86], are basically similar to the clustering of PLS1.) PLS1 effectively and efficiently learns effective and efficient performance.

As described earlier, concept learning or classification is essentially the same problem as learning an evaluation function in search. The most broadly effective and efficient way to learn is to permit uncertainty; then a concept is preceded and determined by a probabilistic "proto-concept." Similarly, in learning an evaluation function, the concept is "task-utility" which is inherently uncertain. In a general system the two problems of concept learning and evaluation learning merge into a single common approach. These and related ideas are pursued in [Re86a, Re87].

This part of the present paper describes the fundamental PLS1 scheme for acquiring knowledge in problem solving and game playing. First the system is examined in the context of state space problem solving (here the experimental results are substantial). A later section extends the method to games (this has been implemented but testing is incomplete). The result is a uniform approach applicable to either domain. In either case, learning can take place after completion of training searches (like [SLM82]), or alternatively, learning can occur during search (like [Sa63, Sa67]).

The requirements are a set of predefined features, along with a measure of the desired purpose, some goal-oriented quantity called the *utility*.[11] Here utility is solution (or win) density in feature space, i.e. the probability that a node might be useful given its feature values (see Fig. 8). Hence the system is a *probability learning system* (PLS).[12]

Since PLS1 computes statistics (measuring feature-contingent probabilities), it is data driven yet intensitive to noise (contrary to popular belief [DM83]). The stochastic aspect of PLS1 may be compared with that of Samuel's learning systems [Sa63, Sa67]. Moreover, the "region" of PLS1 may be seen as an extension of Samuel's signature table approach. The region was outlined in Part 2 as PLS1's basic knowledge structure; its analysis continues in this part.

---

[11] Classification by utility was examined in Section 2.3; utility is seen as a goal oriented quantity in Section 6.1.

In the basic system PLS1, features should not interact heavily, although recent extensions have been designed for feature interactions (discussed in Section 3.3 and Part 4). The ultimate goal is to construct features automatically (Part 5).

[12] The acronym PLS refers to any or all of the system. The basic component, described in this part of the paper, is PLS1. Part 4 describes a higher layer of learning using parallelism, PLS2. The feature formation system (Part 5) is named PLS0.

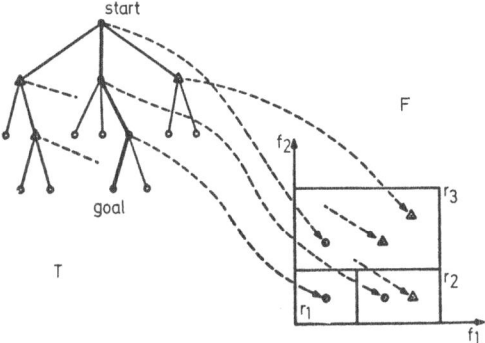

Fig. 8. In search, utility or success probability becomes localized penetrance. This statistic discriminates node quality based on features. Shown are a very small hypothetical search tree T and two dimensional feature space F. Developed nodes from T are mapped into F. The Doran and Michie penetrance of T is $3/6 = 0.5$, whereas localization in F via the (here arbitrary and rectangular) partition gives three elementary penetrance values: $p(r_1, T) = 1/1 = 1.0$, $p(r_2, T) = 1/2 = 0.5$, and $p(r_3, T) = 1/3 = 0.3$. Elementary penetrance from real search trees can be used as a basis for a probabilistic heuristic (an evaluation function)

3.1 The Mediating Knowledge Structure

As described in Sect. 2.1 and illustrated in Fig. 1, a learning system for problem solving extracts some control structure for guiding search. One design decision is the choice of this structure; another is the form of any knowledge structure(s) for determining it.

Perhaps the simplest control structure is a coefficient vector **b** for a given, fixed feature vector **f**. These two complementary structures determine an evaluation function $H = \mathbf{b} \cdot \mathbf{f}$ (see Sect. 2.2). In search performance, what data arise that might be used to find and improve **b**? Given these data, what additional knowledge structures can be utilized to help form **b**? And how can information be extracted from task performance (from solver experience)? The most basic PLS1 approach is described in the following.[13]

Suppose a problem instance is attempted, resulting in a corresponding search tree T. As originally defined by Doran and Michie [Do 66], the *penetrance* was length of the solution path in T divided by the number total of nodes developed. Since T depends on the heuristic H guiding the search that produced it, untreated penetrance is not a good absolute measure from which to determine **b**. (Fig. 9 shows the drastic effect of H.) T is also dependent on the difficulty of the problem solved.

In PLS1, however, these difficulties are lessened or eliminated, in two ways. First, the penetrance is localized to finite volumes r in feature space (see Fig. 6).

---

[13] A further question is the scales of the features. This is a minor consideration for our main purpose: the development of principles of efficient learning. To a large extent nominal, tree-structured, and linear or interval scales are interconvertible. Although PLS1 can handle other scales, here we assume a linear one. This facilitates curve fitting and other mutual data support.

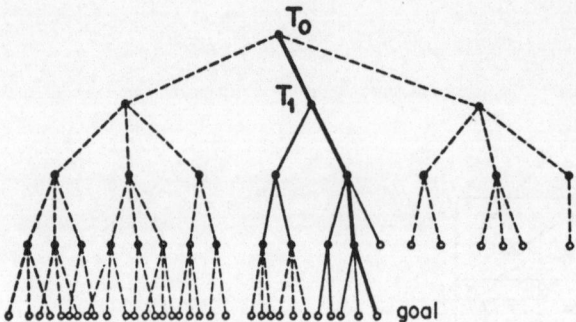

Fig. 9. Variation of elementary penetrance or success probability with search quality. A constant evaluation function might result in the breadth-first search tree T_0 (solid and broken lines), while a good heuristic might give T_1 (solid lines only). If, for example, the rectangular volume r is the whole feature space, then $p(r, T_0) = 4/24 = 0.17$, whereas $p(r, T_1) = 4/6 = 0.67$. Relative to breadth-first search, a good heuristic H causes an upward bias in penetrance since good search implies few wasted nodes (i.e. a high proportion of them contribute to a solution). When r is some portion of feature space, this bias pattern continues, although its extent depends on obscure properties of H and of the domain

Secondly, raw statistics obtained from search trees are modified to remove biases. Moreover, to improve sampling, a *set P* of training problems is presented, resulting in a set of search trees $T(H, P)$.

If the total count $t(r, H\ T)$ is the number of nodes mapping into feature volume r, and the good count $g(r, H, T)$ is the number of these also on the solution path of one of the search trees in T then the *elementary penetrance* $p(r, H, T) = g(r, H, T) / t(r, H, T)$. Fig. 8 shows a simple example.

This localization captures underlying relationships between feature values and utility p (success probability). This is important since we ultimately want a discriminator of utility to construct a revised heuristic, an improvement of H.[14]

An obstacle remains however: The biasing effect of H (Fig. 9) interferes with the direct use of localized elementary penetrance as a predictor of absolute utility. This obstacle cannot be avoided by using unguided (breadth-first) search: On the one hand, no difficult problems could then be solved in practice (and so no useful information would be obtained). On the other hand, easy instances might not be representative. This might seem like an impossible problem: Information is available from solving only if the training problems are simple enough, or if the search is informed enough, and yet either biases the penetrance.[15]

---

[14] Doran and Michie used penetrance was a measure of overall search performance, but also they considered is as a basis for improving the evaluation function [Do 66]. This did not involve localizing penetrance in feature space, although Michie and Ross discussed "regionalization" in a different context [MR 70]. The present approach of associating utility with rectangles is similar to Samuel's signature tables, both in the regionalization aspect and in the stochastic one. Other researches have suggested or used probability for a heuristic function [Gas 79, Pe 83, SB 68, SF 71].

[15] This raises the question of chosing appropriate training instances for a given heuristic. As Appendix B explains, PLS1 is automated not only from the point of view of selecting individual states, but also the system can operate without intervention of the user, to choose its own problem instances [CR 84].

To approach this difficulty, consider that an ideal approach would be to measure p(r, H, T) when T includes all problem instances (or at least a very large random subset or them), and when H is a constant function (giving breadth-first, unbiased, and admissible search). The result would be the *true penentrance* $\bar{p}(r)$. (Perhaps the best choice for the rectangles r would be all individual feature space points.) True penetrance would make a perfect evaluation function — perfect in the sense that the probability of success would always be maximized by using $\bar{p}(r)$ as utility.

This is ideal that PLS1 attempts to approach. From the elementary penetrance data, a normalized value $\hat{p}(r)$ is derived. The system tries to normalize or remove the biases introduced by the practical necessity of using easy training problems P or a nontrivial heuristic H. Thus $\hat{p}(r)$ is the estimated probability of a state A being in a breadth-first solution of a random problem instance, given that A maps into r. (This is a conditional probability; see [Re86b]).

To house the true penetrance (unconditional probability) estimate $\hat{p}$ of the feature space volume $\hat{r}$, a *region* R is defined to be the quintuple (r, c, $\hat{p}$, e, **b**). The second element **c** is the prototype or *centroid*, a representative of r. The final two elements relate to $\hat{p}$: e is the *error factor*, an inverse measure of the reliability of $\hat{p}$, and **b** is a coefficient vector, explained later. A set of these regions, the *cumulative region set R*, forms both the control structure used by the problem solver and also the knowledge structure improved by the learning element (see Figs. 11 and 15). As explained in the next section, this set accumulates information over several iterations; its regions are incrementally resolved into smaller units just adequate to express known relationships. The result is an effective economy, a distillation of experience. The cumulative region set is a refinement of Samuel's signature tables [Sa67] which did not alter data categories automatically. (This "cognitive economy" is discussed in Sect. 6.2.)

A region set can also be considered as a set of "sub-concepts", each representing a conjunction of feature ranges (given by r) having a common worth or utility (Sects. 2.3, 2.4). Here the utility is the true penetrance estimate $\hat{p}(r)$. It can be blurred to some extent without degrading performance (see Fig. 5). For example, as shown in Fig. 10, the error factor e of a region R=(r, c, $\hat{p}$, e, **b**) determines a range of true penetrances [$\hat{p}$/e, $\hat{p}$e], a utility or probability class. The requirement

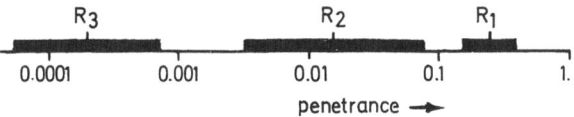

Fig. 10. Utility bands of three hypothetical regions. The error factor e of a region R is used to indicate the likely range in which the true penetrance really falls. If the true penetrance estimate of R is $\hat{p}$ and its error is e, then the band has lower and upper limits of $\hat{p}$/e and $\hat{p} \times$ e. For example, if R=(r, c, .011, 5.0, **b**), the band is [.0022, .055]

(Footnote 15 continued) Another mode of solver operation is described in Section 3.5, which does not require that search trees contain a solution.

for membership is satisfaction of the predicate r (a node must map into rectangle r to be assigned utility $\hat{p}$). If the error bands of two regions coincide, or overlap enough, class membership could then be given by a *set* of rectangles, i.e. a disjunction of a set of conjunctions of feature ranges. This is equivalent to a disjunction of logical formulas in conjunctive normal form implying the utility class; hence the region representation is fully expressive (cf. [Ni71, Ch.6]).

During knowledge acquisition, a region $R = (r, c, \hat{p}, e, b)$ is altered in two ways: its meaning, the utility band [$\hat{p}/e, \hat{p}e$], may be revised, and its rectangle, the precondition or r may be refined (differentiated or split). Learning and regions are detailed in the next section.

3.2 Learning Element Mechanisms

While [Re83a] details the original system PLS1, the main notions are summarized here. The incremental three step operation is pictured in Fig. 11. First, given some training problems and an evaluation function, the *solver* extracts penerance statistics from the resulting search trees. Secondly, the *clusterer* modifies the cumulative

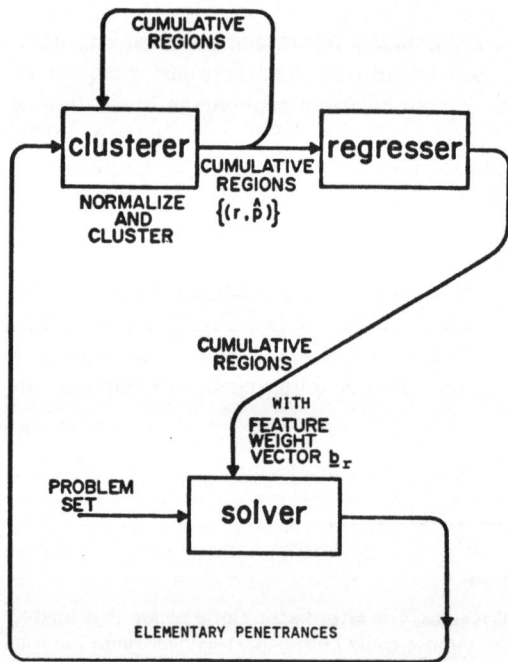

Fig. 11. Probability learning system PLS. The simplest control structure for a solver guided by an evaluation function is a vector of coefficients or weights for the function's feature vector. Based on probability statistics from searches of training problems, the learning element can revise its blackboard structures, (e.g. feature coefficients). The essence of PLS knowledge is a set of feature space regions, used to determine this heuristic and to accumulate experience. Regions associate object descriptions with their task utility or probability of class membership

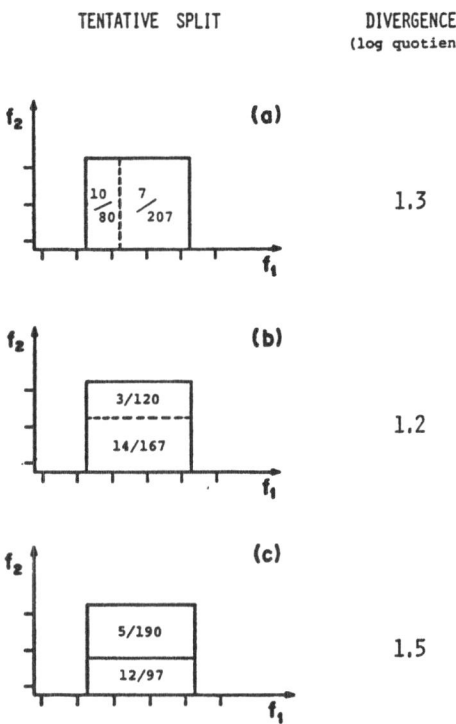

Fig. 12. Operation of the clusterer. This splitting algorithm chooses the best of all boundary insertions parallel to one of the feature space axes. Here there are a total of 287 points (nodes developed), with 17 of them in a solution. Shown are three of many possible tentative dichotomies; they are compared using a distance measure d which quantifies the dissimilarity in utility or probability. Based on d, the best of the three splits is (c), which would be made permanent. If the subregions are not different enough, no split is retained. Otherwise, subdividing continues until no longer warranted by the data. The exact definition of d also accounts for error

region set based on these measures. Finally, the new cumulative region set becomes data for the *regresser,* a curve fitting algorithm that generates an improved heuristic H for the next iteration. Derived from these repeated observations and incremental computations, this evolving evaluation H is designed to predict utility. Together the clusterer and regresser form the learning element.[16]

The clusterer is complex. New regions are formed when probability data are found to diverge within any existing region. This *region refinement* is accomplished by an efficient algorithm that repeatedly splits rectangles, until further dif-

---

[16] In addition to the learning element, one of the components of a learning system described in Sect. 2.1 was the *critic*. This element was considered in [Bu 78] to assess the current behavior of the performance element, i.e. to evaluate the active control structure. In this sense, PLS1 has no critic. On the other hand, one of the possible functions of the critic is to localize credit to substructures of the control structure. In this sence, also, PLS1 is unusual: PLS1 does localize, but it localizes utility (penetrance or probability of success). Furthermore, this localization is within the *antecedent* of the control structure (rectangles' utilities), not the feature coefficient vector **b** itself.

ferentiation is not warranted by the recent data. (See [An 73, Ha 75] for general clustering algorithms and [Re 83] for more details of this one.)

To fomalize the criterion for splitting a region, a distance measure d is used that depends on the true probability estimate $\hat{p}$ and its error factor e. Suppose two subregions of R are $R_1 = (r_1, c_1, \hat{p}_1, e_1, b_1)$ and $R_2 = (r_2, c_2, \hat{p}_2, e_2, b_2)$, representing a tentative dichotomy. Then $d = \{\log \hat{p}_1 - \log \hat{p}_2\} - t \times \log(e_1\ e_2)$, where the constant t is a parameter of the clusterer which expresses the degree of certainty demanded.

Notice that a larger d means more assuredly dissimilar regions. If $d \leq 0$ the two regions are *similar*. This distance is computed for all boundary insertions parallel to any feature space axis. If the largest d is positive, the corresponding regions are dissimilar and the split is made permanent. The whole process is repeated while the data support the differentiation (i.e. while $d > 0$). (Typically an established region splits a few times at most within an iteration). Some detail of this clustering is provided in Appendix C, and more in [Re 81, Re 83a].

PLS1 clustering is fast: the complexity of the algorithm is O(knm) (where k is the number of data, n is the number of features, and m is the ultimate number of regions — cf. [Re 81]). See also [Re 86b], and particularly [Re 86a], which discusses the similarity between PLS1 and ID3 [Qu 83]. PLS1 clustering is illustrated in Fig. 12.

In any iteration after the first, the elementary penetrances (conditional probabilities) obtained as raw data from searches are heavily biased by the heuristic

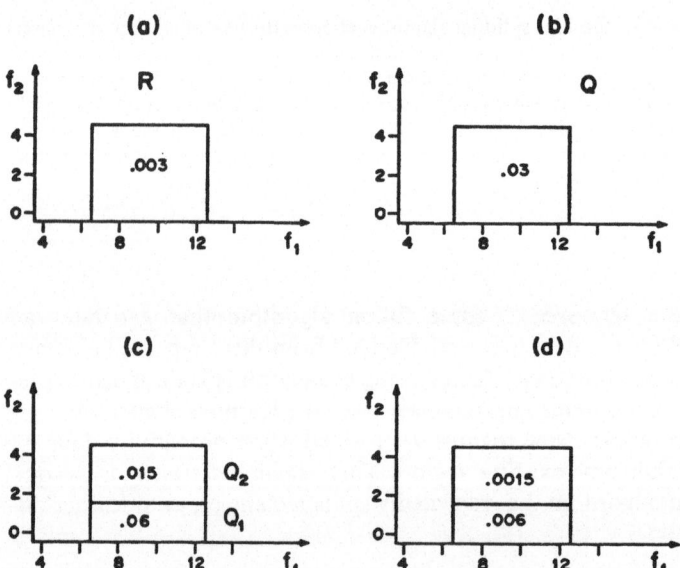

Fig. 13. Region refinement with local normalization (simplified). The region R in (a) is part of a true penetrance estimating "cumulative" set. The associated elementary region Q in (b) has a matching rectangle. The search factor s is the ratio of the two penetrances $p/\hat{p} = 0.03/0.003 = 10$. A hypothetical outcome of refining Q is diagramed in (c). To normalize the subdivided offspring set the elementary penetrances can simply be divided by 10 to give (d). (The actual procedure is somewhat more complex)

used to obtain them, so a *fine normalization* procedure unbiases values. Probabilities for newly split rectangles thereby become commensurate with the normalized estimates of the cumulative regions. The result is illustrated in Fig. 13. Region refinement is incremental; knowledge increases over several iterations, as suggested by Fig. 11.

A separate *coarse normalization* algorithm operating over the whole feature space obtains fresh probability estimates for cumulative regions. This algorithm assumes a pattern in the biased data. It smooths the probability estimates of all cumulative regions against the new elementary values within *matching* feature space rectangles to find a conversion factor to apply to all elementary probabilities, so that they also become unbiased estimates. After this normalization, each new value is averaged with the old ones to improve the estimate. In this *probability revision*, weights for the averaging depend on the accuracy of each datum. The end result is decreased error in the combination, so that cumulative probability estimates gradually become more inert (although region refinement counters this trend). The effect is shown in Fig. 14. Appendix C gives some detail of both kinds of normalization.

All this manipulation by the clusterer is designed to provide proper intermediate data (cumulative regions) to fit true probability as a function of features of the solver's heuristic. (See [DS 81] for curve fitting or regression analysis.) Each region $R = (r, c, \hat{p}, e, b)$ in the cumulative set $R = \{R\}$ has an undefined feature coefficient vector b after clustering, but the regresser (Fig. 11) determines b from R. (The contribution of each R is inversely related to its error e.) The regresser rejects any useless or less general features by zeroing their coefficients, and decides the relative importance of the discriminating features by setting their coefficients to values

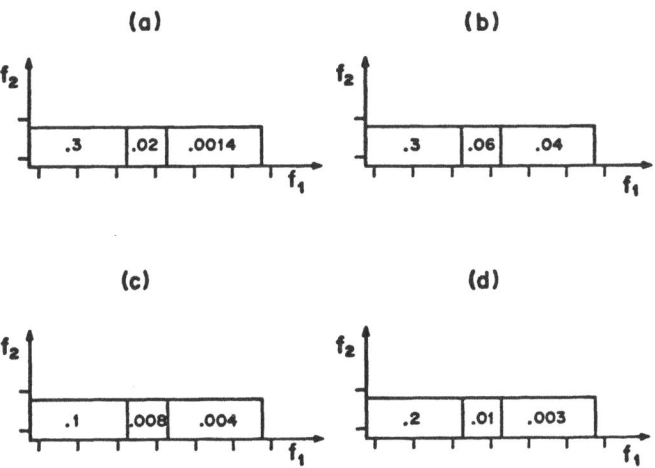

Fig. 14. Coarse normalization scheme. Penetrances are shown within rectangles. The established set of true penetrances estimating regions in (a) can be related to an elementary set (b) with matching feature space rectangles, by using the model: log true penetrance = h × log elementary penetrance. Here the constant h becomes 1.7, and the elementary regions of (b) are converted to those shown in (c). Since (a) and (c) are now commensurate, they can averaged to revise true penetrances (d)

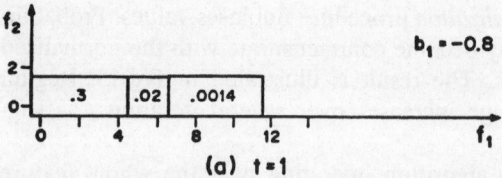

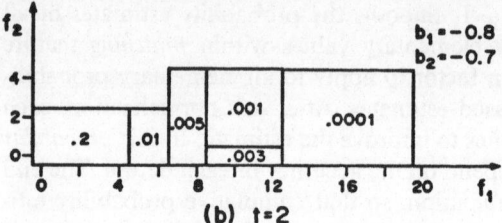

Fig. 15. Two cumulative region sets and resulting feature coefficient vectors for a simple, two dimensional case. The true probability estimates shown within the rectangles are typical of those generated in the (a) first and (b) second iterations using our two illustrative features for the fifteen puzzle (distance score and reversal score)

best suiting R. Typical results after the first two iterations for the fifteen puzzle are pictured in Fig. 15.

In the current context, the inclusion of **b** as an element of an individual region is redundant. However the next section will describe how **b** now becomes a property of individual regions R, to accomodate feature interactions.

3.3 Feature Interaction through Piecewise Linearity

Feature interaction is prevalent. For example, in experiments on evaluation functions for games, Samuel found better performance in checkers when he used signature tables to express nonlinear relationships [Sa 67]. Berliner's experience and conclusions [Be 77, Be 79] were similar.

Although there are differences in detail, signature tables are comparable to PLS1 regions: both schemes specify rectangular portions of feature space and do not restrict feature relationships. In PLS1, however, the characteristics of the cumulative region set are determined automatically: as explained in the previous section the number of regions and their size and shape are data-determined. The cumulative set could be used directly to give an evaluation function (like [Sa 67]), but in the current extension of PLS1, curve fitting is retained. This requires only a slight alteration of the regresser, and no modification of the clusterer. There is increasing departure from linearity as feature space refinement improves in later iterations (as the number of regions increases).

Instead of a single probability surface fitted over the whole of feature space, there are now as many hyperplanes as regions in the cumulative set C. In turn, each region $R_i = (r_i, c_i, \hat{p}_i, e_i, b_i)$ of C is viewed as the *principal* one for its own regression: the coefficient vector b_i is computed using an R_i-centered weighting of every other *contributing* region $R_j \in C$. As mentioned in the previous section, the regression is already weighted by error e in $\hat{p}$. In this piecewise linear design PLS1a, the former weight is multiplied by an additional factor related to the distance δ between R and Q, so that Q plays a greater role if it is near R. In the determination of δ, the feature space is essentially deformed to capture the relative importance of the various features. (Details are provided in Appendix D.)

Since each regression is still linear, the process is stable. (In contrast, permitting feature interaction by using higher order models requires many more coefficients and this "uses up" the data – there are fewer degrees of freedom.) At the same time the piecewise linear scheme PLS1a is flexible, allowing a continuously variable amount of nonlinearity in order to suit current knowledge and system power. This variability is realized by introducing a system parameter called the *localization strength* $L > 0$ as an exponent for the distance measure δ. The larger the value of δ, the stronger the localization. If $L = 0$, the nonlinear scheme degenerates to simple linearity. The localization strength L is detailed in Appendix D and its effect is illustrated in the next section.

This nonlinear capability could affect performance because of edge effects (see [Be 77]). This happens in the simplest procedure for piecewise linear evaluation, which predicts the utility of a state A according to the localized heuristic of the region into which A maps. There are discontinuities as region boundaries are crossed.

To avoid edge effects, the solver is altered slightly. PLS1a uses *all* regions in the cumulative set in *every* evaluation, empolying a distance weighting like the one used during learning. (See Appendix D for details of this weighting.) The success of both the linear method PLS1, and this nonlinear scheme PLS1a, is described in the following section.

3.4 Experimental Results

This section summarizes results of experiments with the fifteen puzzle, whose space has about ten trillion states.[17] Previously, instances of this problem had been solved consistently by computer only with two way search (working backwards from the goal as well as forward from the starting state) using the fixed problem-reduction approach of placing outer gnomons first.[18]

For the experiments, six features were selected, including the two illustrative ones described earlier, the distance score and the reversal score. Depending on the particular experiment, between 3 and 12 training puzzles were attempted in each solving step (the lower extreme was found to be sufficient). These training instances were randomly selected, but with a difficulty constraint, set to tax the current ability of the solver (see Appendix B). The final cumulative region set

---

[17] Details of the original fifteen puzzle experiments are given in [Re 81]. PLS1 was also used to improve performance for a formula manipulation problem. Experiments with games have been similarly successful.
[18] At Stanford in 1972, A. K. Chandra wrote a program (not a learning system) for the fifteen puzzle, which typically solves the puzzle after developing fewer than 1000 nodes.

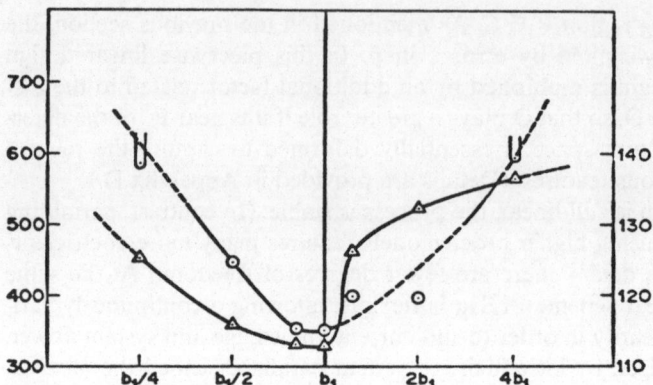

Fig. 16. Performance of a system-generated evaluation function with disturbed values of the first coefficient b_1. The graph shows the average number of nodes developed (O's and scale on left) and average solution length (×'s and scale on right) versus b_1, for a random set of 32 puzzle instances. The center line represents the coefficient computed by the system

encapsulated heuristic knowledge from all the 15–75 searches for the whole series. In a typical run, after 7 iterations the system rejected two features, and created an evaluation function whose four non-zero coefficients had converged.

In performance measurement, when the limit on generated states was 2000 (i.e. a maximum of about 1000 developed), this function solved all puzzle instances of a random sample of 50. The coefficients were found to be locally optimal (in both average nodes developed, 353, and average solution length, 113). The consequences of disturbing the coefficients are graphed in Figs. 16 and 17. (Since the original experiment a test sample of 1000 was presented and all were solved with a maximum of 1100 developed nodes.)

Three more experiments were run, using just the four discriminating features found in the first trial. Again, training instances were randomly selected with constrained difficulty (these problems were different from those in the first test run). In each case the coefficients converged to values identical with, or very close to, the same local optimum.

Comparisons were made with alternative methods of optimization. The best of these used a simpler version of PLS without clustering, for two iterations with human interpretation to adjust for probability bias (caused by informed search – see Sect. 3.1). This combined use of human and machine allowed approximate location of the optimum feature coefficient vector; the experiment was followed by response surface fitting in the coefficient space. The same local optimum was approached, but PLS1 was faster and more reliable. (Response surface fitting was briefly discussed in Sect. 2.6. More detail of the experiments is given in [Re 81]).

The greater efficiency of the PLS1 compared with response curve fitting (even after approximate location of the optimum) is perhaps explainable in terms of amount of knowledge extracted. The traditional optimization method utilized just a single performance measure per problem instance solved. In contrast, during regression, PLS1 makes use of as many data as there are regions, and, during clustering, PLS1 allows contribution from every node expanded in search. Storage

Conceptual Knowledge Acquisition in Search

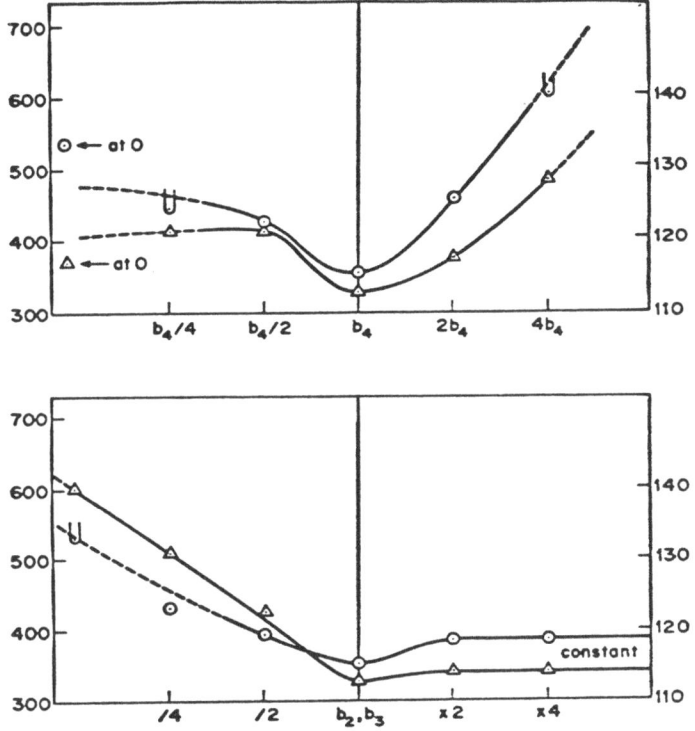

Fig. 17. As Fig. 16 (average number of developed nodes and solution lengths), but with different abscissas: (a) the coefficient b_4, and (b) coefficients b_2, and b_3 (varied together)

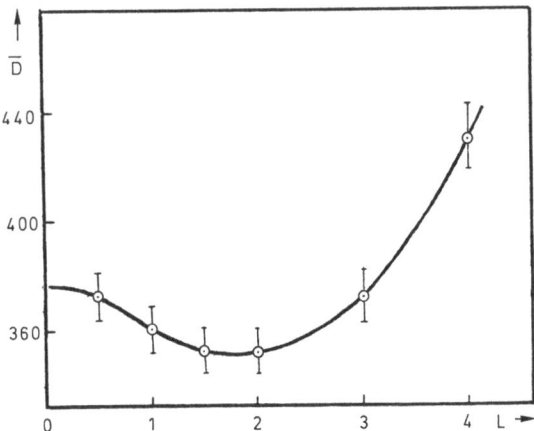

Fig. 18. Variation of performance with degree of nonlinearity. Shown is average number of nodes developed D before solution in a random sample of 1000 puzzles, vs. localization strength L. 95% confidence intervals are indicated. Feature interaction is mild here

requirements are also small: in typical experiments using a few features, only a few tens of regions are created before convergence. Splitting occurs usefully. (See the discussion of "cognitive economy" in Sect. 6.2 and the studies in [Re 86a, Re 87].)

Some program runs have also been made to study the more sophisticated, piecewise linear scheme PLS1a. In one experiment, the fifteen puzzle, the four best features, and one of the cumulative region sets described above were selected. Since these features had originally been chosen for the strictly linear system, they were deliberately selected for low interaction. Hence this is a mild test of PLS1a. Results are shown in Fig. 18, where the extent of nonlinearity is varied by choice of the localization strength L.

We might attribute the dip in this curve to two conflicting factors: As L is increased, some advantage results because the relationships are inherently nonlinear, and nearby regions now play a justifiably bigger part in the determination of each local heuristic function. However, distant regions, which formerly had a stabilizing role, now have a diminished influence, so there is some loss of stability. The inaccuracy and graininess of individual regions gradually overpower the benefit of localization. (Part 4 of this paper describes a method for increasing region accuracy.)

An important property of PLS1a is its stability. When PLS1 was used with higher order models instead of piecewise linearity, performance was significantly degraded. Moreover, PLS1a allows easy observation of the relative importance of features in any area of the space, since simple feature weighting is used. Further, relationships exemplified by Fig. 18 are useful, and the freedom to vary the localization strength L facilitates experimentation. The magnitude of the optimal localization strength is a measure of region accuracy, and indirectly, of the power of the entire learning system.

3.5 The Analogue for Games

Because of the success of PLS1, a version for games has been constructed which retains the same learning element. Also identical is the form of the information extracted from search trees — it is probabilistic information. (For other work on probabilistic evaluation in games, see [Go 77, Na 83, NU 65].)

In experiments with this variant of PLS1 for games, minimax search trees were converted to trees like those for puzzles. During the play of a game, search trees have the usual minimax form, but during learning, the trees are compressed as shown in Fig. 19.

An example of the usual game tree in which α plays opponent β is shown in Fig. 19(a). In minimax, α chooses his own move but has no control over β's, so α always assumes that β will select his best alternative. (More detail about minimax is given in Appendix A.) Beginning with the tip nodes of a lookahead tree, evaluations are backed up one level at a time, until finally the node in question is assessed. If lookahead is to the end of the game, accurate values can be assigned. Since this is not usually feasible, some static evaluation function F is applied at the tips, and these values are backed up instead. (F can be different from the evaluation function H being learned).

Conceptual Knowledge Acquisition in Search

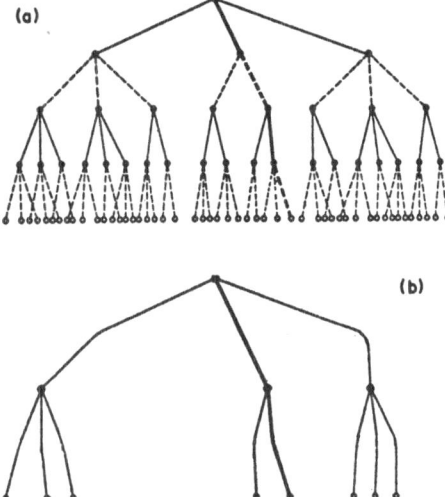

Fig. 19. Unifying learning for problems and games. A simple lookahead game tree is shown in (a) representing search to four ply. α's moves are indicated with solid lines and β's with broken lines. As described in the text, the minimax algorithm backs up values assigned to tip nodes; here α's and β's best moves are indicated with heavy lines. During the course of a game, several of these trees are normally constructed, then discarded after determining the best immediate move for α.

In (b), some information is retained from this minimax tree, forming a pruned α-tree. Here only a single β-move is saved at each choice point, while all of α's are kept. Under these conditions, β's moves need not explicitly represented. The α-tree might be constructed after a lookahead that retroactively determines β's best move at each point, or pruning might take place while search proceeds (the text describes the latter). The details of this pruning are unimportant for our purposes; what is important is that the tree for performance is not necessarily bound by the tree used for learning. (There is a distiction between learning and performance. During performance, various approaches could be used. Instead of α-trees, ordinary minimax might be used, or there might be no lookahead at all.)

Here the tree for learning is the α-tree, which is like the problem tree of Sect. 3.1. In both state space problem trees and α-trees, probabilistic values are assigned to tip nodes and backed up, taking the maximum of the offspring. In both cases, the tip value assignment can be approximate (for hard problems or games played from the beginning), or the values can be exact (for problems or end games within range of current abilities). With either backup mode, and in either domain, the learning may be identical

Now consider a slightly different approach, which, for simplicity, begins with a condensed representation of the minimax tree, the α-tree shown in Fig. 19(b). Instead of allowing β an exhaustive set of alternative moves, just a single one is selected for each β node. This choice for β might be made by a human or by an evaluation function F (which could result, for example, from previous learning as in [Sa63, Sa67]). As with PLS1 for problem solving, the search is halted when either a goal is discovered (here a win or draw) or else a preselected maximum number of moves has been made.[19]

---

[19] The condensed α-tree not only simplifies learning, it allows deeper search. To permit save more space, the α-branching factor B can be restricted by limiting development to the best B moves (e.g. according to F again; see [AIH 82]).

Once an α-tree is completed, values are assigned to the tip nodes, called *g-values;* they represent *probabilities of α's winning*. If a tip node is the end of the game, these are 0, 0.5 or 1 (lose, draw or win); otherwise the g-value is an estimate given by F. Next the g-values are backed up, assigning to each node the maximum of its offspring's g-values. If F is good enough and β has played perfectly this procedure is equivalent to minimax. If F is flawed, α will learn imperfectly (at least temporarily — see [Sa63, Sa67]). In this case, corrective learning has to rely on PLS to overcome misleading information. Overall, the assignment and back-up process is like minimax except that not all of β's moves are considered. (This simplified back-up is not critical to the method.)

In the PLS1 learning phase, information is extracted from an α-tree in much the same way as described in Sect. 3.1: by counting nodes in feature space (see Fig. 8). Recall that the elementary probability $p = g/t$, where t is the total count, and g is the good count (i.e. g is the number of nodes of the solution path). In this, each node A contributing to g can be considered as one of t samples, which either falls on the solution path or not. This event is known: its probability is 1 or 0, and this probability is the g-value. Averaging over the t samples gives individual contributions from neighboring feature space locations to improve accuracy: $p = g/t = \sum_i$ g-value$_i$/t, where i runs from 1 to t.[20]

If we extend this picture to games, the g-value should now be the probability that a given node A appears in a win. By design, this is precisely what is estimated by the evaluation function F, but a tip node offspring A_i of A. If G is the maximum of $F(A_i)$ (over all i), then (subject to the accuracy of F), G represents the predicted best outcome for α. This definition of G is equivalent to the α-tree back-up described above. G will reflect the play of β, i.e. G will estimate the probability of winning against β. (Later use of these estimates for evaluation assumes β will behave according to conditions prevailing during generation of the α-tree.) In the problem solver (Sect. 3.1) the g-value was binary, expressible as max [probability of solution appearance of offspring A_i]; in the game player, the g-value should be $G = \max [F(A_i)]$. In either case, it is success probability that is backed up, assigning the maximum of offspring values to parent nodes.

The analogy between the two domains can be completed by realizing that either the solver or the player can be operated in one of two back-up modes, *discrete* or *continuous*. If a problem or game is carried to its conclusion, discrete values are backed up (0 or 1 with a problem, and 0, 0.5, or 1 in a game). If search is not complete, the backed up values are estimates, probabilities of succeeding in a problem, or of winning in a game. When used in solving, PLS1 has usually been operated with problems roughly within range of current solver abilities, so most training instances are solved, and g-values have been binary by design. However, if a reasonable evaluation function is known, the continuous mode can be used instead. Conversely, the training of the player can begin with end games, with discrete g-values resulting. In either solving or playing, the values backed up can be

---

[20] Recall from Sect. 3.1 that the counts g and t are made within probability clusters in feature space. Regions associate probability (utility) with nearby feature values having similar utility.

accurate, the result of natural search completion (discrete mode), or the values can estimate likelihood of a solution or win (continuous mode).

α-trees encoding game experience have multiple sources of error, much like the earlier problem trees. The latter depend heavily on problems attempted and evaluation function H guiding search. Similarly, α-trees are biased by the starting point and H, but also by the play of β. The treatment in Sect. 3.1 was to abstract an ideal concept called *true penetrance*, defined in terms of unbiased search trees obtained from breadth first search of random problems. With games, the analogous ideal must additionally account for β. We could imagine a "perfect" β who would always respond with his best move. In reality, however, α's knowledge structure (the cumulative region set) embodies experience averaged in some way. Depending on the use of the system, β might be a fixed expert opponent, or a sequence of (perhaps increasingly informed) opponents, using self-play like [Sa63, Sa67].

One question is whether PLS1 can bootstrap α's play effectively if α begins with a poor opponent β. During learning, the construction of a single α-tree is tantamount to playing multiple games. Each α-offspring corresponds to a different game, so hundreds or thousands are actually represented. Consequently the statistical observation (node counting) allows comparisons to be made of the various choices. Therefore one would suspect that α can improve its play even against a β only as good as itself (cf [Sa63]). Preliminary experimental results with checkers support this assertion.

Unlike [Sa63, Sa67], PLS1 retains all information until each tree is completed or suspended, and learning occurs then with all nodes contributing to assess feature relevance. Since a suspended game can be resumed, PLS1 can learn during single game (as do [Sa63, Sa67]) with a break for continuous mode back-up and modification of the evaluation function.

The statistical PLS1 scheme for games seems to be robust. Because of increasing search depth (a consequence of improving evaluation over several iterations), the horizon effect may have a small effect on learning. This would be true if PLS1 can recover sufficiently from erroneous data, as it does with the solver.

In summary, PLS1 provides a single approach to both game playing and problem solving domains. In either case, discrete or continuous mode back-up may be used, and games or problems may be completed or else suspended then resumed. In both playing and solving, the values backed up are probabilities of success. In learning from these assignments, the same data compression and heuristic formation algorithms can be used (the original PLS learning elements).

PLS1 and [Sa63, Sa67] share important properties. Nonlinear problems are handled using feature space regions that contain results of statistical sampling. Learning is efficient, incremental, and unsuspectible to errors encountered in search.

3.6 Summary of the Basic System

PLS1 (probability learning system one) is a general knowledge acquisition scheme for uniform application to state space problems and games and to other problems of concept learning. (Here we have examined search applications; see [Re 86a, Re 87] for others). Given a set of user-defined features, PLS1 learns efficiently, often with optimal performance. Efficiency results from full use of information: every single node in a search tree contributes to the assessment of every feature. This effieciency has also been demonstrated experimentally. When used in search, PLS1 generates data in an inherently noisy environment, is driven by the data, and yet is insensitive to this error (this is contrary to some expectations [DM 83]).

The basis for learning in solving is an a goal-oriented ideal of task *utility* called the true penetrance, or unbiased, unconditional probability, the *probability of success* when attempting a random problem instance using breadth-first (unguided) search having no resource limitations. (In game playing the ideal is similar.) PLS1 approaches this ideal by accumulating normalized probabilities in localized volumes of feature space called *regions*.

A set of cumulative regions (a partition of feature space) expresses utility knowledge in a compact form intermediate between the elementary data and the evaluation function dependent on it. The cumulative region set allows both storage economy and high accuracy within current limits of experience. This knowledge structure retains appropriate information density for expressing known relationships of node utility to features.

Conceptually, probability seems a good measure of node utility since it measures extent of participation in the shortest solution or win. Experiment supports this claim: local optima have been discovered without the direct feedback about overall performance used by conventional optimization techniques. This demonstration of efficient optimization is unique in machine learning.

Although these characteristics and results are encouraging, the present state of the system is seen mainly as a basis for future work. Current limitations include the requirement of full expansion of nodes, with no explicit knowledge gained about operators. More importantly, the success experienced with the fifteen puzzle involved a favorable choice of features, and highly interactive features cause problems for the basic linear system.

Very irregular utility relationships often arise when the data are described not by high-level features, but by low-level primitives. This situation gives rise to the problem of new terms, i.e. the automatic creation of features from primitives. We examine this difficult problem in Part 5.

For moderately interactive features, the piecewise linear extension seems promising: it is flexible, stable, and easy to use and monitor. The method may benefit from a scheme designed to measure and improve the accuracy of utility estimates. The method will be examined in the next part.

4. Support from Criticized Parallelism (PLS2)[21]

This part of the paper describes PLS2 as a method for improving the performance of the original learning system PLS1. In our context, the purpose of PLS2 is to provide stability, improve accuracy, increase efficiency, and thereby increase of the power of the system. We shall discuss the use of parallelism, credit assignment, and other techniques. Detailed experimental results are analyzed in [Re 85a]; PLS2 is viewed in terms of hypothesis formation and assessment in [Re 86a, Re 87].

PLS2 is important when features are not well behaved. While the system examined in Sect. 3.3 is able to handle mild feature interaction, strong nonlinearities present a severe problem of stability unless data are accurate. Reliability and other advantages result from a genetic algorithm.

A *genetic algorithm (GA)* is an inherently parallel scheme that can efficiently locate global optima. The theory was developed by Holland [Ho 75], summarized and exemplified by Brindle [Br 81] and DeJong [DJ 80], incorporated in a learning system by Smith [Sm 80], and used in many other ways [GA 85].

Shown in Fig. 20, PLS2 is not only a GA, but also a second layer learning system that activates its performance element PLS1 multiply, with a different control structure each time. (Sect. 2.1, Part 3, and Figs. 11 through 15 describe PLS1.) Now controlled by PLS2, PLS1 executes multiply, in parallel versions, each process using its own knowledge structure (cumulative region set) selected from the competing population. Each cumulative set is recorded and modified on the PLS2 blackboard. The critic and learning component of PLS2 make comparisons to improve the population, based on a measure of merit that it derived from relative performance of the control structures (knowledge structures). The critic is able to localize credit.

4.1 The Critic

The cumulative region set C is the main knowledge structure for the entire system. This structure controls the primary task or performance element PE (the solver or player). C may be a control structure for the PE (if discrete evaluation is used), or C may determine the control structure indirectly (if the evaluation is continuous). (See Sects. 3.1 and 3.2).

In PLS2, a different region set guides each activation of the PE (Fig. 20), and a resulting performance statistic provides a basis of comparison to measure the relative worth of each of these structures. By taking advantage of performance patterns across region sets, credit can be localized to individual regions.

Suppose that K cumulative sets $C^{(k)}$ are available ($1 \leq k \leq K$). Every $C^{(k)}$ is a knowledge structure for K separate runs of PLS1, each attempting training

---

[21] As illustrated in Fig. 20, the acronym PLS2 refers to a level of learning above PLS1, or to the whole learning system comprising both levels. Apart from the link to PLS1 through the basic knowledge structure (the cumulative region set), Part 4 may be read independently of the rest of the paper.

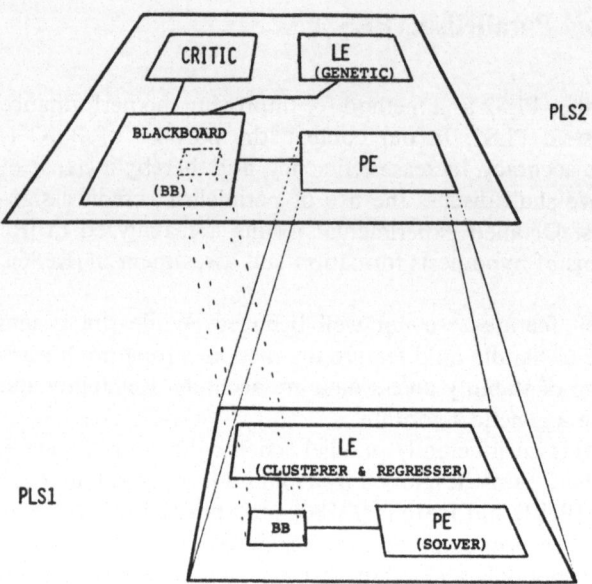

Fig. 20. The second layer of learning. The blackboard of PLS2 contains the union of PLS1 blackboards, recording PLS1 control structures (cumulative region sets) and other information. PLS2 activates PLS1 with different cumulative sets, which it continually improves. The basis for improvement is comparative. Competing cumulative regions are selected for new sets in accordance with the relative performance they exhibit. The more successful of the regions become components in new knowledge structures (region sets) after region refinement

instances of fixed difficulty d. (See Appendix B about the selection of training problems and their difficulty.)

Already calculated as a by-product by the primary task (but not used is PLS1) are two overall measures of performance: the solution or win length L and number od nodes developed D; these are stochastic functions of $C^{(k)}$ and d. Choose some functional F of L and D (e.g. simply D). Then, given some cumulative region set $R = C^{(k)}$, define its *rough merit* $\mu(R)$ to be $\bar{F}(d)/F(R, d)$, where $\bar{F}$ is the mean value of F over all K region sets. Values of μ will therefore center around one. For example, suppose K is small, say 3, and that D_1, D_2, and D_3, are 500, 380 and 710, respectively. In this simple case, the μ values are 1.0, 1.3 and 0.7 (see Fig. 21). As will be seen in the next section, μ is a typical merit, performance, or fitness measure for a genetic algorithm.

The critic is designed to extract more information than just the rough merit. To localize credit, regions are compared (pairwise). Consider first a simplification, in which each cumulative region has a counterpart in every other parallel set; i.e. feature space rectangles match precisely, and only their success probabilities or utilities differ. An example of this situation is shown in Fig. 21. For each *focus region* R, and *comparison region* Q, define the *likeness* (R, Q) to be $1 - (p_R - p_Q)/\max(p_1, p_2)$, where p_R and p_Q are the utilities of R and Q. In the general case of dissimilar rectangles, this definition becomes asymmetric, and a focus region R is compared with each cumulative *set* $Q = C^{(k)}$. Depending on the extent

Conceptual Knowledge Acquisition in Search

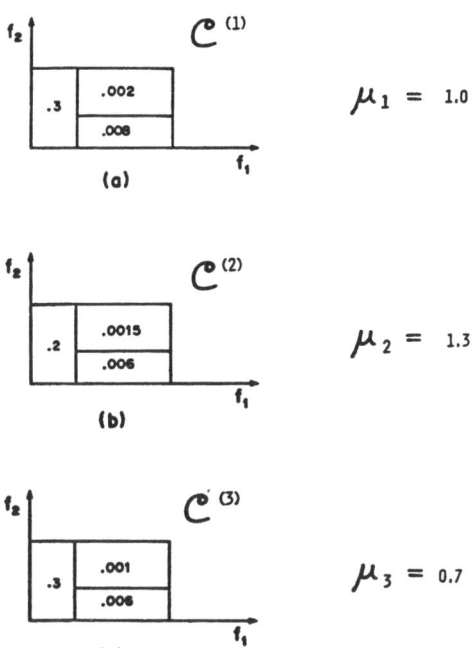

Fig. 21. Different knowledge structures (region sets) cause varying performance μ. In this simplified picture with 3 parallel sets $C^{(k)}$, the rectangles match, and only their utilities p differ (shown inside the rectangles). By comparing p values with μ values, credit can be localized to individual regions. In real cases, rectangles across cumulative sets do not match, so an elaboration is used (see text)

of its intersection with R, each $Q \in \mathcal{Q}$ contributes to a varying degree to the overall utility similarity of Q to R.

This likeness measure, together with region set performance, provide veiled information relating p_R to its accuracy. Assuming coincidence of utility with optimal merit, $R \in \mathcal{R}$ will tend to improve the performance $\mu(R)$ if R is accurate, and regions similar to R will be similarly likely to improve performance. Consider again Fig. 21. Each cumulative set $C^{(k)}$ might have a rough merits (performance measurements) as indicated. We can conclude that regions in set $C^{(2)}$ have generally better estimates than those in $C^{(1)}$ or $C^{(3)}$. For example, for the leftmost rectangle r_1 in the diagram, utility appears to be more accurately estimated by the value 0.2 than by 0.3 (since the merit is greater for p=0.2). If, for each focus region R, the rough merits are plotted as a function of likeness, a peak will likely occur at the point of greatest accuracy, and if a curve is fitted to the data, the resulting merit at likeness=1 will estimate the pure merit of $R \in \mathcal{R}$, independently of other regions in $\mathcal{R}$. In our simple example, when the focus region is $R_1^{(2)}$, the merit peak occurs at $\mu=1.3$, where the utility is 0.2.

In general the number of data K would be larger. Various outcomes are illustrated in Fig. 22, in which parabolas are fitted. The first (a) would never occur since it suggests that regions from a single location of feature space in every cumu-

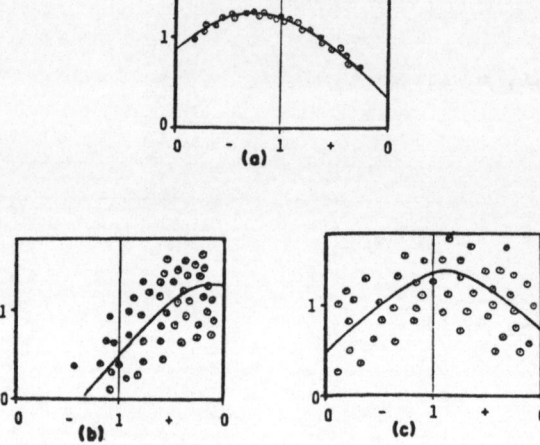

Fig. 22. Credit localization. Consideration of region similarity or "likeness" (abscissa) across multiple cumulative sets extracts performance patterns μ (ordinate). In turn, each "focus" region R is contrasted with all other "comparison" regions that intersect R. The μ value at likeness = 1 is the "refined merit" of the focus region R, independent of regions in other parts of feature space that affect μ but do not relate to R. Each individual focus region R is assessed separately

lative set are exclusively responsible for the overall performance of the heuristic. The other two diagrams are more likely: There is little merit attributable to a single focus region R (since R could be quite accurate while its neighbors degrade the heuristic). Fig. 22(b) indicates that R is inaccurate, but atypically so. Fig. 22(c) might result if regions in the set containing R are fairly accurate. Here competing sets are often poorer; in particular many rivals of R are less accurate (and therefore unlike R).

One would generally expect poor fits for individual focus regions but significant information overall, since many focus regions are assessed (all JK of them, where J is the average number in each region set and K is the number of sets). The precise mechanism for this information extraction is straightforward: perform a regression, then compute the *refined merit* $v(R)$ of focus region R which can be defined, e.g., as $\hat{\mu}^{g(K) \times r^2}$, where $\hat{\mu}$ is the predicted merit at likeness = 1, r is the correlation coefficient, and g is some nondecreasing function of population size K. $v = 1$ means mediocre or uncertain merit, while larger or smaller values of v show confidence in greater or lesser merit. If g is a constant function, the refined merits corresponding to Fig. 22(b) and (c) are 0.7 and 1.2.

4.2 The Genetic Algorithm

To utilize merit information, PLS2 incorporates a novel version of Holland's [Ho75] genetic algorithm (GA). A GA uses parallel structures called *genotypes;* each codes the *phenotype,* which is a set of attributes characterizing an individual.

Although the phenotype is the ultimate object of interest (e.g. eye color in the biological case, a coefficient vector in our case), the phenotype is determined by the genotype code, which is more suitable for computation. In the biological case, the genotype is DNA; in our case it is the cumulative region set. The *fitness* or *merit* of an individual is its performance in the *environment*. The fitness measure is used to favor selection of successful *parents* for new *offspring*, so the whole *population* evolves toward greater merit. The strength of a genetic plan its its ability to recombine successful parents for controlled exploration of the space of genotypes: constrained variation is combined with knowledge retention. Theory [Ho 75] shows that knowledge about desirable phenotypes is advantageously stored in the population itself, implicitly in surviving genotypes. A GA can locate global optima efficiently [Ho 75, GA 85].

In the design of an artificial genotype, one issue is whether to use many component *loci* (variables) with few *alleles* (values), or vice versa. To allow greater adaptability, binary alleles are generally chosen, although this can cause problems [Br 81]. This issue is irrelevant in PLS2 because of its unusual design. First, population variance is aided by the learning element of PLS1, so the alleles need not be binary to insure variability; instead the allele set is the continuous interval [0, 1], representing utility. Secondly, the loci of the PLS2 genotype correspond to feature space coordinates, but the loci are compressed to an extent depending on current knowledge refinement. The genotype is the cumulative region set. (See [Re 85a, Re 86a] for detail.)

Since regions estimate utility, and only within their own boundaries, these "loci" are independent, thus precluding another problem: inefficiency due to loci interaction [Br 81, p. 170]. The resulting phenotype, the feature coefficient vector, *can still be* nonlinear (when a high order model is used or this vector is regionalized; see Sect. 3.3).

To optimize the population, a genetic algorithm includes algorithms for parent selection and offspring generation. *Parent selection* is based on an individual's fitness measure such as the rough merit μ of the previous section. This defines a probability distribution for candidates so that successful parents are favored in weighted random selection. The fitness measure is normally a property of the individual as a whole; typical applications do not admit localization of credit since loci usually interact. In contrast, the PLS2 genotype (the cumulative region set) allows the refined merit v described earlier.

The genotypes of a population are repositories of knowledge and also sources of subtle variation for exploration. To achieve balance in this mutual role, *offspring generation* typically adopts biological *operators* such as mutation (unary) and crossover (binary or bisexual). In contrast, PLS2 is K-sexual (where K is population size): all regions are merged into a single set before selection. Moreover, alleles (utility estimates) are untouched (it is the lower level learning element PLS1 that alters these); regions are simply chosen stochastically as loci/alleles according to their refined merit. To create fit offspring region sets, the merit of every candidate region (its probability of selection) is continually adjusted to account for the current feature space cover V defined by the regions so far selected (candidates are less useful if they overlap much of V). This formation of a new set halts when a V is attained which is close to the maximum. Hence a new individual has a high likelihood of utility accuracy. Genotypes are created in this manner to replace all of the old population.

The second layer system PLS2 has been programmed; experimental results indicate better performance than the already successful PLS1. Perhaps the most obvious improvement is stability. Whereas PLS1 is sensitive to various run parameters and appropriate training sets, PLS2 overcomes any abnormalities by immediately dismissing aberrant information. PLS2 seems to be more accurate *and* more efficient. PLS2 can manage interacting features that PLS1 cannot handle alone. Investigations are continuing to discover the effects of varying system parameters such as population size and extent of credit localization. Some of these results are reported in [Re 85a].

4.3 *Summary of the Genetic Scheme*

PLS2 is promising from several viewpoints: as support for PLS1, PLS2 improves region accuracy and stability, important for feature interaction (Section 3.3). As a genetic algorithm, PLS2 is efficient because of the independence and flexibility of individual loci (regions). These characteristics avoid typical problems that can degrade efficiency, and also aid credit localization which usually improves it. Despite the absence of explicit genetic operators, the ability to discover global optima may be retained since PLS1 already provides (controlled) population variance. Finally, as a scheme for knowledge accumulation, PLS2 benefits from layering. A mediating structure, the cumulative feature space region set (storing conditional probability of success in task performance), allows both credit localization and feature interaction. The elements of this set, the regions, are independent of one another, but determine the task heuristic which can be nonlinear.

Like PLS1, PLS2 uses information well. A genetic algorithm is effective and efficient, and PLS2 improves these qualities using credit localization and amalgamation with PLS1.

The next part of the paper describes a method for the difficult problem of new terms (constructive induction). This method is similar to PLS1 and PLS2 with respect to good use of information, and with respect to the use of statistics to manage and incrementally correct error.

5. Constructive Induction and Feature Formation (PLS0)

To this point, the discussions of PLS have concentrated on the "20%" problem described in Sect. 2.3, that of creating a good heuristic from high level features (such as piece advantage, mobility, etc.). This part of the paper begins to examine the harder questions of mechanized feature formation. This is *constructive induction, the problem of new terms,* or *transformation of the original variables* [Ba 80, Di 82, Hu 75, Mc 83, So 75, To 74].

Except for relatively straightforward techniques, so little has yet been mechanized that we might even question whether the problem is solvable in practice. Can complex features be created automatically, within reasonable time constraints? What might be the essential elements in a system that could accomplish this task?

Feature formation is *induction,* abstracting particular cases to create a general rule. Unlike deduction, induction can be wrong; an *hypothesis* is an untested proposition formed by induction. The space of possible classes, concepts or hypotheses is called *hypothesis space* [Mi 82]. (See Sect. 2.3 of this paper.) Associated with an hypothesis H is its validity or *credibility* μ: $\mu(H)$ quantifies our belief in H (see [Re 86a, Wa 69a, Wa 72]). In order to permit credibilities to change incrementally, we make μ probabilistic and update it (see [Ch 85]).

Other requirements for induction are a precise language in which to express knowledge, and precise methods for hypothesis formation and testing. Some of these are considered in [Mi 82, Mc 83, Re 86a]. One characteristic of successful systems is information compression using *invariance* of some relevant quantity (e.g. the utility). Invariance has been used by Banerji [Ba 76], Ernst and Goldstein [EG 82], Christensen and Korf [CK 86], Newman and Uhr [NU 65], and Quinlan [QU 83], all in domains similar to those of PLS. Although the feature formation system *PLS0* is different from these approaches, it shares the notion of invariance with them. (See Part 6 of this paper for other aspects common to learning systems.)

Induction can be of at least two types, both related to class formation [Re 86a]. One kind is what Watanabe [Wa 72] calls *induction proper* or *recognition,* in which something is known about the classes, and the problem is to describe them. The other, more difficult kind of induction, is what he calls *abduction* or *cognition,* in which nothing is known about the classes or even how many of them there are. Abduction is also known as the clustering problem.[22] The full problem of feature formation requires abduction and constructive induction.

Despite some concrete results [EG 82, Mc 83, Re 85b], relatively little has yet been learned about abduction or constructive induction. The computational complexity is extreme (contrast the two lower levels of Fig. 4). Even in the simpler kinds of induction, when features are predefined and only determination of their coefficients is required, feasible methods are not obvious. Samuel's work on feature combination [Sa 63, Sa 67] is a quarter of a century old, yet it is still cited as one of the most impressive results [Di 82]. The PLS1/2 method is well evidenced (Parts 3 and 4 of this paper), although it is still only partially explored. The remaining "80%" problem of feature formation is still more difficult [Di 82, Art. D. 1], [Qu 79, pp. 171-2]. Because of the complexity of this problem, much of PLS0 is formative, though the scheme appears promising. It is outlined here and developed and tested in [Re 85b].

To create features, PLS0 searches for invariance of utility relationships over combinations of more basic variables than abstract features: *primitives* (illustrated

---

[22] The "inductive ambiguity" of abduction is even greater than induction proper. Inductive ambiguity [Wa 69a, Wa 69b] refers to the number of possible generalizations. As an example of the huge combinatorial problem, consider sorting only 25 objects into classes. If there are 5 classes, this induction can be done in 2×10^{15} ways. If the number of categories is unknown (abduction), there are 4×10^{18} ways. According to Fig. 4, the number of possible combinations for utility classes in checkers is immense: about 100 to the power 10^{18}! Researchers have been concerned with some means to restrict hypotheses, according to "simplicity", "elegance", etc. (see [Re 86, Wa 69, Wa 86]).

in Fig. 4). Whereas PLS1 introduced probabilistic conceptual clustering [Re 77], PLS0 uses a new technique of "higher order" clustering. From primitives, PLS0 gradually builds features using information layering to restrict complexity in a "devide and conquer" approach. This system does not just generate and test hypotheses, rather it selects simpler ones from partially constructed components. PLS0 is resilient to error, making use of mutual data support (Sect. 2.6) to strengthen hypotheses incrementally.

An hypothesized feature is valid if it can be used to improve an evaluation function. An example of a valid induction is the formation of the concept "fork" in checkers (sure capture of one of two men). To learn such a generalization requires the realization that certain spatial patterns are essential while other aspects are immaterial (e. g. extraneous pieces, and exact location of the pattern). Such a generalization also requires a description in terms of the primitives: the contents of individual squares of the board (the description becomes a feature). The emergent feature or class description should be concise and satisfied by a large number of board configurations which are invariant or similar. A function counting the number of forks would be a valid feature.

5.1 Broad Considerations and Overview of PLS0

Recalling Part 2 of this paper, let us reconsider why generalization is necessary in search domains. The most basic knowledge consists of data obtained in searches, from which observations can be made, such as the contents of each square on a checker board (see the lowest level on Fig. 4). These form a set of *primitives* or very elementary features of a state. For each and every primitive measurement vector, it would be possible to list its utility (here a probability of success) in an exhaustive table, for a complete expression of all necessary knowledge. As shown in Sect. 2.3 and Fig. 4, however, the number of table entries is immense, e. g. about 10^{13} and 10^{18}, for the fifteen puzzle and checkers, respectively. In contrast, only about 100 different utility classes would be required for a complete heuristic (evaluation function), *if* the knowledge were readily available for this utility classification. We called such high level, abstract knowledge *conceptual knowledge* (Sect. 2.4).

The space saving of this information compression is not the only reason to categorize. Operating solely with a utility table of individual measurement vectors and no conceptual knowledge, a rote learning system would never gather much useful information in practice. Playing a billion games of checkers would leave the detailed table of Fig. 4 only about one trillionth full, even if every board position arising were unique, and each somehow provided an accurate utility estimate. On the other hand, if patterns among entries can be discovered, if states can be generalized to meaningful utility categories, a twofold advantage results. First, during task performance, newly encountered states can be evaluated as being similar to other members of the class (i. e. prediction is possible). Secondly, during learning, data can support each other, resulting in greater assurance of the utility value assigned to each class. This *mutual data support* was discussed in Sect. 2.6, implemented in Part 3 as clustering and curve fitting, and will appear here as higher order clustering.

In Part 2 we discussed the advantages of using features intermediately in an evaluation function H (e.g. H = **b.f**). In theory there is nothing to prevent the formation of H in a single step, by replacing features in H with primitives. For good reason, however, typical learning methods take advantage of regularity in the relationships between dependent variable H (e.g. utility) and independent variables (here the features). As seen previously, smoothness is the utility-feature relationships permits mutual data support (Sect. 2.6): curve fitting or straightforward clustering for assured compaction during learning and for interpolation during state evaluation. This simple information compression is infeasible with basic primitives, since the utility surface in primitive space is so erratic (consider Fig. 4). Patterns of elementary primitives must be molded into manageable features, using some sophisticated kind of mutual data support to detect, reinforce, and generalize complex regularities.

Constructing a feature is logically equivalent to a classification problem: the number of utility classes is the size of the feature range (number of feature values); into each class must be placed the subset of feature arguments having the utility value of that class. In other words, each class is the set of feature arguments (primitive vectors) mapping to the utility value that is characteristic of the class (in practice, features are always surjections [Gi 76]). This is the clustering problem, or abduction. In our case, the values of primitive vectors *(measurement vectors)* are classified to form a feature. For each category (feature value), a concept is induced which is a rule for specifying that category. This concept is a set of measurement vectors.

To learn such a concept in practice, the class of measurement vectors must be built in some regular manner; otherwise the combinatorial problem is too great. This regularization should perhaps be accomplished in steps, since feature creation require several times the information compression needed beyond this stage (Sect. 2.3), and since *uniform* compression is easier [Wa 72].[23] In PLS0, feature formation is accomplished using a 3-level information hierarchy (see Fig. 23). Each level progressively generalizes the one below: each stage imposes constraints, reduces complexity, and increases regularity. Guided by this hierarchy and by the data, production of prospective feature components in PLS0 is automatically restricted to manageable numbers. Emerging and lasting components are those that exhibit worth, so a subsequent PLS0 level sees only the better prospects, leaving it efficient and effective.

Although each stage of the hierarchy uses a distinct information structure characterizing the level of knowledge at that point, the three representations have much in common. First, the basis for generalization is the same at each level; it is utility: more precisely, the *relationship* of utility to primitives. At each of the three knowledge levels, a formative feature or potential feature component is characterized by this utility relationship. For each formative feature, there is a separate hierarchy: Each formative feature is a different *pattern class*.

---

[23] The complete layered system PLS0/1/2 to create a heuristic begins with low level search data (primitive measurements) and eventually reaches the desired evaluation function expressed in terms of high level features. (A level above even the evaluation function is strategy or plan.) See Sects. 2.2 and 6.2.

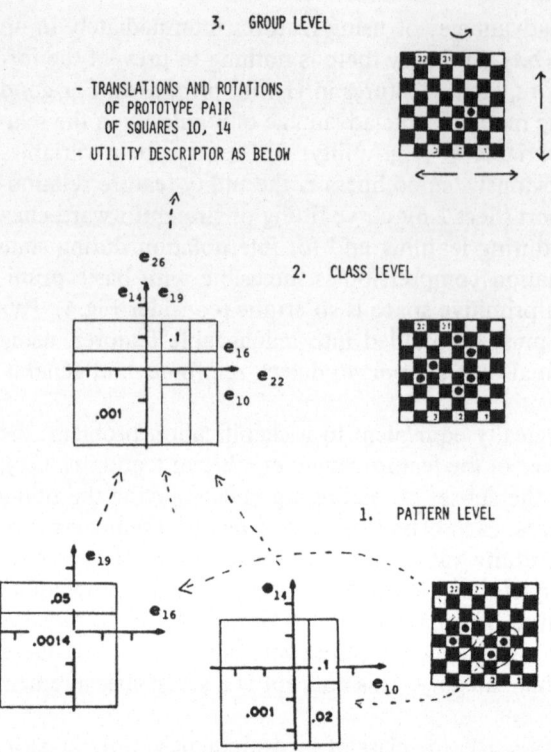

Fig. 23. The three level information hierarchy of PLS0. This example shows the construction of a hypothetical feature f which counts the number of diagonal juxtapositions of two friendly pieces in checkers. This begins with the most basic description of a board position in terms of 32 primitives e_i giving the contents of individual squares. When subspaces such as $e_i\ e_j$ are specified and corresponding utilities are CLUSTERed and recorded in region sets or utility descriptors (UD's), patterns begin to emerge (level 1). After more patterns arise, they may be superimposed in CLUSTERing trials to find supporting (similar) UD's, thus forming pattern classes (level 2). Eventually a class may be generalized as a group of transformations (level 3)

Progressive information compression unifies the three levels: feature components are built first upon primitives, then from elements formed at the level below (see Fig. 23). The difference in the three knowledge structures is greater organization at higher levels. Higher levels *include* lower ones. At the lowest level, discriminating primitives are identified and their utility relationships are summarized. To accomplish this, data are clustered to distinguish characteristic *utility descriptors* (region sets or step functions) in primitive subspaces; participating primitives are recorded as *subspace specifiers*. At the second level, these results are categorized into sets of corresponding subspace specifiers having mutually similar utility descriptors. At the highest knowledge level, individual primitive subspaces of a given class are used to induce a complete group. A general rule is discovered for transforming one member of the class into another, and missing elements are inferred, to induce a complete feature. Fig. 23 illustrates this overall design.

Any inductive method is likely to encounter noisy or anomalous data and therefore be prone to error. As with PLS1 and PLS2, statistical methods for PLS0 seem appropriate to counter inaccuracies. Stochastic treatment is used at each level of PLS0. Since this involves the information hierarchy, the system is both data- and model-driven.

5.2 Knowledge Level 1: Primitive Patterns

To illustrate PLS0 knowledge structures, their relationships, and the emergence of features, let us consider two simple examples. One (f_1) is the distance score for the fifteen puzzle; it was used in Sect. 2.1 and Fig. 2. The other feature (f_2) is the number of instances of diagonal juxtapositions of two friendly men in checkers. Slightly more complex than f_1, this feature reflects some degree of support or insurance against being jumped; it is shown in Fig. 23. We shall follow the hypothetical generation of f_1 and f_2 at each of the three knowledge levels.

To begin, let us consider the primitive form of the data, and how the primitives can be logically combined to form features (ignoring, for the moment, how any learning might occur). The fifteen primitives q_i for the fifteen puzzle might be the city block distances of each tile from home. These can be indexed in a left-to-right, top-to-bottom fashion, so that, for example, in Fig. 2, $q_1(A_0)=0$ (since "1" is properly placed), $q_2(A_0)=4$, $q_3(A_0)=1$, etc. Hence $f_1 = \sum q_i$. As for the other illustrative feature, the thirty-two primitives e_i can be similarly indexed, to give standard checkers notation. Suppose $e_i(B)=0$ means that board B has no piece currently occupying square i, while $e_i(B)=c$ indicates the presence of a man if $c=1$, or of a king if $c=2$ (with corresponding negative values if the piece is the opponent's). Then f_2 would be the number of cases in which $e_i>0$ and $e_j>0$ for certain i and j (i.e. so that the squares are diagonally adjacent – see Fig. 23).

One step in creating f_1 is to recognize that (as a first approximation) the utility of a q_i value is independent of i. Similarly, in forming f_2, it must be realized that the condition ($e_i>0$) and ($e_j>0$) is uniformly good, for certain i and j. A prerequisite for mechanizing these inferences is some language in which to express the single primitive q_i, distinct from other coordinates in q space, and in which to represent the two dimensional subspace determined by e_i and e_j, separate from the other primitives e_k.

To permit this structuring, *knowledge level 1* incorporates s-dimensional projections of the whole n-dimensional primitive space. More precisely, a *subspace specifier SS* is a string $e_{i_1}, e_{i_2} \dots e_{i_s}$ of length $s \leq n$ (with no repetitions). Both our examples (f_1 and f_2) are can be expressed with a combination of equal-length specifiers ($s=1$ for f_1 and $s=2$ for f_2). The total number of possible SS's is 2^{15} for the fifteen puzzle and 2^{32} for checkers. Despite the seemingly prohibitive combinatorial problem, there are uniform and unobtrusive methods for reducing the complexity.

The first step in recognizing meaningful subspace specifiers is to detect useful utility descriptors; for this, clustering is suitable. The algorithm CLUSTER of Sect. 3.2 is now made to operate on data in primitive space rather than in feature space. The output of this algorithm is a primitive space region set which often differentiates utility in just some of the n primitive dimensions;[24] these are called the *active* primitives for current data.

The s active primitives e_{i_1}, e_{i_2}, ..., e_{i_s} define a subspace specifier $SS = e_{i_1} e_{i_2} \ldots e_{i_s}$. The region set output by CLUSTER is the *utility descriptor (UD)* which describes the relationship of utility to SS. A subspace specifier together with its utility descriptor is a *primitive pattern*. For example, Fig. 23 (level 1) shows two different primitive patterns, each comprising an SS ($e_{10}e_{14}$ or $e_{16}e_{19}$) along with its UD. This simple CLUSTERing in primitive space is called *ground* CLUSTERing, to distinguish it from a more elaborate form to be described shortly.

Since CLUSTER preferentially selects variables (here primitives) that more strongly differentiate utility, only those specifiers emerge which, according to current data, play an important part in its discrimination. While primitive utility relationships are very complex, experiments show that data samples do tend to cluster in primitive space during this ground operation. As we shall see, the utility descriptor is instrumental in further identification of regularities: it helps to discover related SS's.

5.3 Knowledge Level 2: Pattern Classes

Knowledge level 2 facilitates search for uniform relationships in utility so that primitive patterns exhibiting similar behavior can be merged, eventually to produce a sensible feature. Regularities are recorded in *pattern classes*. A pattern class is a *set* of subspace specifiers with a *common* utility descriptor (i.e. a region set in primitive subspace like the level 1 primitive pattern — see Fig. 23, level 2). One of the subspace specifiers of a pattern class is its *prototype*, which corresponds directly to the utility descriptor for the class (coordinates of other SS's must be mapped into the prototype in order to decipher relationships between these secondary specifiers and the utility coded in the descriptor).

With our simpler (f_1) example, the subspace specifier q_7 might have been discovered as the first coordinate discriminating utility; being the first, it becomes the prototype. Subsequent (secondary) specifiers might be q_2, q_8, and q_{11}. Each would have a UD (i.e. a primitive region set, at knowledge level 1), the SS/UD pairs forming an unstructured collection of primitive patterns (possibly mixed with spurious, unrelated patterns). Providing that all for utility descriptors corresponded when coordinates q_7, q_2, and q_{11} were matched up (i.e. if superimposition of these dimensions gave coinciding utility surfaces), these four SS's would be classified together in a single pattern class, with q_7 the prototype. (Superposition or overlaying of variables in primitive-utility space will soon be described more precisely.)

This classification would result in a unification of the separate utility descriptors corresponding to q_7, q_2, q_8, and q_{11}: coordinates of the common UD would be chosen to relate directly to prototype q_7, and indirectly to q_2, q_8, and q_{11} (via a

---

[24] Sect. 3.1 and Fig. 6 described a region basically as a rectangle in feature space with its associated utility. In other words, a region is primarily a utility class. See also Sect. 2.4. Here the most obvious analogue of a feature space region's class descriptor is a primitive space rectangle. As will be seen in Sect. 6.3, however, a primitive descriptor is more flexible in that rectangles may be superimposed.

change of variable in each case). The four primitives would henceforth be treated indistinguishably in this pattern class, whose existence records their similarity.

Similar utility surfaces are discovered through the CLUSTER procedure. The ground clustering finds low level primitive-utility relationships but does little to form larger, more meaningful patterns. However an elaboration of CLUSTERing extracts more structured information, discovering complex mutual support in data.

For this more elaborate algorithm we need to reconsider CLUSTERing. Recall from Sect. 3.2 that CLUSTER dichotomizes a region R when utility data within it are found to diverge. The criterion for splitting involves a dissimilarity (distance) measure d. If p_1 and p_2 are the two utilities for a tentative dichotomy, and e_1 and e_2 their errors, then $d = |\log p_1 - \log p_2| - \log(e_1 e_2)$. The dissimilarity d is computed for all boundary insertions parallel to any feature space axis. If the largest d is positive, the corresponding split is retained. The process is repeated until additional refinement is unwarranted by the data (until $d \leq 0$).

Notice that larger d means more assuredly dissimilar regions. If the values of d are summed for successive permanent splits of R, the result is a measure of reliability (credibility) of the complete clustering operation, the *discrimination assurance* D. D increases directly with the quotient u_1/u_2, and inversely with the error e. One factor affecting the error e is sample size N (number of observed objects): as N increases, e decreases and D improves.

As an example, consider Fig. 6, and suppose that the two leftmost rectangles from $(0 \leq f_1 \leq 6) \cap (0 \leq f_2 \leq 2)$. Assume that the sample size N in each new rectangle is 100, and that the error e is $\log[1 + 1/\sqrt{N}]$. Then the total discrimination assurance D is just the dissimilarity $d = |\log[20/100] - \log[1/100]| - \log[(1.1)(1.1)] = -1.6 - 4.6 - 0.2 = 2.8$. If the sample size were 10, D would be 2.5, still a high credibility.

Now let us return to formation of pattern classes and consider another example. With the f_2 example, subspace specifiers would arise consisting of two coordinates (discrimination assurance D would be greater when e_{10} and e_{14} are separated). Other specifiers detected might be $e_{16}e_{19}$ and $e_{22}e_{26}$ (see Fig. 23). Again these would be mixed with extraneous specifiers, likely of different length. However, analysis of all data, based on similarity of utility descriptors and SS length would unite primitive patterns based on these regularities. Here the pattern class would include $e_{10}e_{14}$, $e_{16}e_{19}$, and $e_{22}e_{26}$ (and possibly spurious patterns). This pattern class would indicate similar utility behavior of each pair and also inseparability into single coordinated e_{10} and e_{14}, etc.; i.e. certain primitives are meaningful in *pairs*.

The fusion of SS's into classes is accomplished either with extant UD's and new data, or else with a single data set (i.e. over more than one system iteration or within a single iteration — see Fig. 11). Here we outline the latter which uses the discrimination assurance D and begins with straightforward ground CLUSTERing that determines D_g.

To discover meaningful relationships among components of the board (i.e. among subspaces of primitive space), certain arrangements A of variables from the active set S are considered. Suppose the size of S is s; each A is a *relation* [Gi76] over S^k, where $k < s$. For example, suppose the active set is $S = \{e_2, e_6, e_{10}, e_{14}, e_{15}\}$ (s = 5). One arrangement A might be $\{(e_2, e_6), (e_{10}, e_{14}), (e_{10}, e_{15})\}$ (here k = 2); $(e_2,$

e_{10}	e_{14}	e_{16}	g	t	e_{10} v e_{16}	e_{14}	g	t	e_{10} v e_{14}	e_{16}	g	t
0	1	1	3	5	0	1	6	13	0	1	4	11
1	0	1	1	6	1	0	2	12	1	0	6	16
1	1	0	3	8	1	1	6	13	1	1	4	11
⋮					⋮				⋮			

Fig. 24. Discrimination assurance D measures similarity in domain structures using superpositions of primitive subspaces. D depends on the extent of agreement of utility-primitive relationships when primitives are overlaid, and also on error, which decreases with larger sample size t. The value of t becomes larger with more superpositions, and providing that the corresponding structures are really similar, utility relationships may be strengthened. This simplified example shows the ground case (leftmost), and two overlays. The central case is supported by D (relative to the ground case − note the g and t values), but the rightmost case is not. Hence e_{10} and e_{16} are similar but e_{10} and e_{14} are not

e_6), determines the SS $e_2 e_6$, etc., and A defines a *superposition* of primitive subspaces, i.e. a *class* of SS's (here $\{e_2e_6, e_{10}e_{14}, e_{10}e_{15}\}$, a precursor of f_2 − see level 2 of Fig. 23).

Given such a superposition of active primitives, CLUSTER is now run with these overlaid primitives treated as one. In other words, it is patterns *within* states that are counted. Because of this superposition, the total counts t (Sect. 3.1) are effectively increased (by a factor roughly equal to the number of superpositions. This idea is illustrated in Fig. 24 which delineates three possible conditions for three hypothetical CLUSTER activations: the first five columns show data for the ground case (a), and the two other groups of four columns each (b and c) show data for two one-dimensional superpositions: (b) $A_b = \{e_{10}, e_{16}\}$ and (c) $A_c = \{e_{10}, e_{14}\}$. Notice that the g and t counts for the ground values (a) increase in overlays (b) and (c). Referring to the dissimilarity or distance formula, and assuming an error factor of $1 + 1/\sqrt{t}$ (cf. [Re83a, p.390]), we have $d = |\log p_1 - \log p_2| - \log[(1 + 1/\sqrt{t_1}) \times (1 + 1/\sqrt{t_2})]$.

Suppose the only data are those in the three rows of Fig. 24; in this case (a) and (b) would each result in exactly one split (in the e_{14} dimension), while (c) would remain undifferentiated. Applying $D = \sum d$ and the dissimilarity formula giving the value of d, we obtain discrimination assurance values: $D_a = D_g = 0.43$, $D_b = 0.59$, and $D_c = 0$. D_c is zero because no splits occur; D_b is larger than D_g because of the increased data counts (the counts are doubled here since two primitive dimensions are overlaid).

In general, since larger counts imply lower errors, the discrimination assurance is higher in cases where primitive patterns coincide (i.e. when utilities match up in the overlaid dimensions and merged UD's support each other). If, instead, utility behavior differs, the mutual support is weaker, and if misalignment is extreme, D is even lower than the ground value D_g. When various superpositions are examined, certain of them are found to stand out (having high D's); these become candidates for pattern classes. This overlaid CLUSTERing extracts utility commonalities in components of the board description, and discovers and strengthens patterns of invariances in utility relationships.

Examining superpositions is extremely complex if search is exhaustive, but general and uniform heuristics can be used. Heuristic guidance and some experimental support are described in [Re 85b]. One speed-up is apparent: knowledge level 1 simplifies level 2 investigation since only active primitives are pursued. Another heuristic involves the examination of only pairs of primitives. For example, while the final pattern class might include the subspace specifiers $e_{10}e_{14}$ and $e_{16}e_{19}$ (as in Fig. 23), this knowledge begins with favorable discrimination assurance for the one-dimensional superposition $A_b = \{e_{10}, e_{16}\}$ (as in the above paragraph and Fig. 24b).

The overall purpose of knowledge level 2 is to unify similar components within states of a problem or game, i.e. to allow subspace specifiers to be classed together if their associated utility descriptors agree when superimposed. This strengthens knowledge about primitive-utility relationships by the amalgamation of their utility descriptors (mutual data support).

5.4 Knowledge Level 3: Pattern Groups and Features

Knowledge level 3 completes features formation. A level 2 pattern class is augmented by a set of transformation operators which, when applied to subspace specifiers (SS's) in the class, produces some new ones. Those operators are selected that produce the best closure, giving a meaningful *group* [Gi 76] or related SS's. Some of the SS's are already present and others are induced, to fill in "missing elements" of the *pattern group*.[25]

The set of transformations representing a complete pattern class can be quite complex, including, for example, various deformations (e.g., consider the game of GO). For many domains, however, level 3 learning seems to be feasible. For our f_1 example (distance score for the fifteen puzzle), the process would be straightforward since any primitive pattern q_i can be obtained from another q_j simply by translation. The induction might take place with only a few subspace specifiers q_i present in the pattern class to induce all fifteen. The second illustrative feature f_2 (adjacency of two friendly men in checkers) requires not only translation but also rotation (of 90%). Several pairs like $e_{10}e_{14}$, etc. might be needed for confidence in the general transformation, which induces a group of 49 primitive patterns. In practice, even exhaustive search for suitable operators is not prohibitively complex in these search domains.

Features are produced from pattern classes (knowledge level 2) or from pattern groups (level 3). In either case, the associated utility descriptor (UD) for the category provides the necessary information about a formative feature f. An object x to be assessed by f is first mapped into primitive space, then for each SS $e_{i_1}, e_{i_2}, \ldots e_{i_s}$ of the class, the utility given by its utility descriptor is summed. As an example, for f_2, a formative pattern class might include $e_{10}e_{14}$, $e_{16}e_{19}$, and $e_{22}e_{26}$. Suppose (i) $e_{10}(x) = -1$ (enemy piece), $e_{14}(x) = 0$ (clear square), while (ii) $e_{16}(x) = e_{19}(x) = 1$, and (iii) $e_{22}(x) = e_{26}(x) = 1$ (all friendly pieces). Typical utilities given by the UD for (i)

---

[25] Our feature formation approach may be compared with *grammatical inference*, for which limited techniques are available [Fu 78, Fu 82].

might be $u = .001$, but for (ii) and (iii), $u = .1$ (as in Fig. 23). Then the formative feature $f_2(x)$ is the sum of these, or .201. To give a more natural form agreeing with our earlier conception, f_2 can be made integer. This final form might approximate a count of instances of some characteristic of x: for f_2, multiplication by ten gives the number of diagonal juxtapositions of friendly pieces. In general, given a pattern class or group, a feature is generated by summing utilities, as in this example.

A feature is tentative until enough evidence is found for its determinative pattern class. This support increases gradually as experience is gained (additional data result in more regions per utility descriptor and in more primitive pattern per class). Once defined, features are independently assessed and selected by PLS1 (Part 3).

5.5 Summary of Feature Formation
(Abduction or Constructive Induction)

PLS0 feature formation uses a tractable "divide and conquer" scheme having three hierarchical stages, each of which builds from the previous level. The induction is probabilistic and incremental. Knowledge structures are generated, assessed, and improved (refined and revised) so that the generate-and-test cycle of inductive inference is meaningfully constrained. A by-product is constructive induction: PLS0 discovers relationships.

The basis for generalization is classification of utility descriptors and geometric patterns: double invariance − of task utility and of utility relationships − is used to extract regularities (under transformation of primitive measurements on problem states). Progressive compression is *mutual data support,* implemented by the clustering of utilities and of patterns: information is simultaneously regularized and reinforced (and doubly so). This stochastic process is insensitive to error. Simplification of pattern classes is not limited artificially, but rather depends on data. In limiting the huge number of possible hypotheses, PLS0 imposes few artificial constraints. Rather, the data themselves help to simplify hypotheses while gaining confidence of these generalizations (mutual data support).

At knowledge level 1, primitive data are clustered to distinguish relevant subspace specifiers. At level 2, these results are categorized into set of comparable subspace specifiers having mutually similar utility descriptors. These pattern classes become prospective feature elements whose components exhibit common subspace geometries. At level 3, individual primitive patterns of a class induce a complete pattern group. A general rule is discovered for transforming one member of the class into another, and missing elements are inferred, so that a complete feature results.

PLS0 scores high according to criteria for induction [DM 83]. Although other problems and games would require elaboration such as nonuniform primitive specifiers, the system appears *extensible* to these and other domains. The three level knowledge *representation* appears *adequate. Rules of generalization* are fully general for domains considered and extensible for other domains. Finally, the process is *efficient.*

Induction methods are likely to encounter noisy data. Resulting inaccuracies can be countered by statistical techniques. Complex clustering allows the necessary structuring and *change of knowledge representation,* in a system which is both model- and data driven. As discussed in [Re 85b], the computational complexity of the generalization problem may be reducible from intractably exponential to practically polynomial.

6. Relationship of PLS to Biological Systems

This part of the paper discusses some parallels between PLS and research in other fields. Our brief discussion will include notions and results from pychology, phylosophy, and neuroscience. For some readings in these fields, see [Ar 72, BGA 56, Chr 64, CM 84, De 80, DW 80, El 71, Ga 65, GHS 79, Hf 79, HT 81, Ko 64, Ma 76, MS 84, Rk 83, RM 75, Rt 62, Se 66, Si 62, We 57].

If we integrate apparently different ideas we may accelerate discovery and development of general principles of intelligence. While details in various research areas are dissimilar, the differences are sometimes superficial and models can be profitably compared at an abstract level. Among the important characteristics common to PLS and abstract studies are the use of probability [BGA 56, Ch 85, Go 77], active goal-oriented perception [Ar 72, BGA 56, Ko 64, Rk 83], extraction and use of features [BGA 56, DK 82, Hu 75], abstraction and information compression [An 73, BGA 56, Ca 82, Ro 76, Wa 72], concept formation [BGA 56, CM 84, MS 84, SM 81], hierarchical structuring [Ar 72, Ko 64, LHK 79, Si 62], and cognitive economy [LHK 79, Ro 76].

6.1 Goal Orientation, Features, and Discrimination[26]

One behavioral aspect of biological organisms reflected in PLS and many other learning systems is *goal orientation*. In his analysis of the relationship of brain theory to cybernetics and AI, Arbib [Ar 72, pp. 16, 17] emphasized

> ... action-oriented perception ... which is oriented toward the future as much as the present ... the animal perceives its environment to the extent that it is *prepared to interact* with that environment ... the primary purpose of recognizing objects is not to classify them, but to be prepared to interact with them.

Similarly, his extensive study of perception and cognition, Koestler [Ko 64, pp. 468, 537, 646] summarized

> [Motivation guides] perceptual organization [by] generalization of the input ... [Mechanisms for generalization] de-particularize or strip the input for purposes

---

[26] This section relates to most of the paper, but particularly to Sects. 3.1 and 3.2, and Part 4 (probability combined with goal orientation or utility); to Sects. 2.2 and 2.4 (features); and to Sect. 3.2 and Appendix C (discrimination).

of recognition and storage according to ... criteria of relevance ... [This is not] free: there are motivations ... which give it direction.

This goal-oriented activity is modeled is PLS1 using *utility*, measured as probability of node usefulness in a solution or win (i.e. the penetrance − see Sect. 3.1). Some means must be available for differentiating utility. Again from [Ar 72]:

... features of the current environment [are explored] which may be incorporated ... to guide action more and more adaptively.

Relating this notion of *feature* to our earlier definition of feature as function, we see that a feature is not just any such function, but one capable of distinguishing a desired property or outcome.[27] In a biological context, Bruner et al [BGA 56, p. 36] defined an attribute [feature] to be

... [some aspect of an event] that is susceptible of some *discriminable* variation from event to event ... most higher organisms are highly sensitive to changes in the probability relations in their environment and will tend to use any cue [feature] that does better than chance.

PLS1 selects features that are relevant or *salient* (see Sect. 3.4 and [DW 80, p. 154]).

In biological organisms, of course, discrimination is learned (e.g. animals have often been trained to respond to features such as shape or colour). Animals become more discerning with accumulating experience, i.e. *differential sensitivity* improves.[28] Similarly, the learning algorithms of PLS1 gradually refine feature knowledge: utility clusters increase in number, permitting more precise induction of relationships (see Fig. 15). Discrimination and induction seem to be opposite sides of the same coin [Ko 64].

An organism's environment allows such a large number of features, that not all of them can be managed [Gib 69, pp. 3, 4]. Consequently, the animal must choose among them; this is *selective perception* [Bi 76, pp. 210, 211]. The *discriminability* of a feature is its capacity to differentiate utility; those with better discriminability are more likely to be selected (see [Bi 76 pp. 210, 211]).

One measure of discriminability is the utility dissimilarity d, used in PLS clustering (Sect. 3.2). Divergent values are recorded in utility clusters, which are split according to *assured dissimilarity* of probability of usefulness observed in feature space: the dichotomy is selected that has the greatest utility difference. Since differentiation by more than one attribute is sometimes required, the process continues, selecting the next feature (possibly the same one again), repeating until no more splitting is warranted by the data. Like animal discrimination, PLS1 cluster-

---

[27] As defined earlier in this paper, a *feature* is a function mapping objects of interest into some description set, e.g. shapes or numbers. In PLS, states in a problem or game are mapped into the integers, which in turn are used to differentiate utility. In contrast to our terminology here, the *value* of the function is often called a feature in psychology.

[28] There are many natural examples of discrimination and its improvement over time. Experiments with human subjects have shown that ability to discriminate musical semitones increases with age, and that skill in distinguishing two tones, closely spaced in frequency, improves with practice [We 57, pp. 101–103]. A more abstract example: another person's state of mind can be inferred from nuances in posture, voice, etc., and the ability to read these cues can be developed.

ing results in high similarity within classes, and high dissimilarity among members from different classes [An 73, Ch. 1, 2], [Ro 76, p. 384].[29]

PLS clustering uses discrimination in the production of utility classes, i.e. categorization follows discrimination. These two phenomena were viewed as two aspects of a single process in [Ko 64] and were seen as sequential in [Ga 65, Ga 71].

6.2 Categories and Concepts[30]

In its clustering (i.e. categorization or discrimination of utility), PLS1 exhibits *cognitive economy* [Ro 76]: the number of stored classes (utility categories) is small relative to the number of data encountered. The characteristics of the class descriptions (i.e. size and shape of feature is directly related to domain realities: an existing class is differentiated just when necessary for proper expression (i.e. feature space cluster is subdivided only if utility is found to diverge within it − see Part 3 and Figs. 12, 15). Similarly, according to Rosch et al [Ro 76, pp. 384, 428]

> ... one purpose of categoriation is to reduce the infinite differences among stimuli to behaviorally and cognitively usable proportions. It is to the organism's advantage not to differentiate one stimulus from others when that differentiation is irrelevant to purposes at hand ... [it should] yield the most information for the least cognitive load.

In our context, this cognitive economy is information compression (Sect. 2.3), formed into conceptual knowledge (Sect. 2.4), using statistical clustering (Sect. 3.2).[29] Feature selection (Sects. 3.4 and 6.1) is another means to maximize discriminability with limited recources.

In their discussion of cognitive economy, Rosch et al define *category* in terms of nested subsets, or hierarchical taxonomies (e.g. felines and primates are mammals; mammals, fish, and birds are animals, etc.). Within a given subset, members are considered equivalent for current purposes. A more inclusive category implies a higher *level of abstraction*. In terms of conceptual knowledge (Sects. 2.3 and 2.4), if "bird" comprises $512 = 2^9$ different genera, the information compression in "bird" is 9 bits. In PLS, compressed structures are equivalent with respect to utility; utility invariance results from the clustering criterion that maximizes utility dissimilarity (Sect. 3.2). In PLS1, only one level of nesting occurs as feature space data are compressed into clusters; in PLS0/1 the hierarchy is deeper as elementary primitives are gradually compressed into high level features.

Cognitive economy promotes time efficiency. Fewer extant classes may mean faster access, particularly important for constructive induction. In Part 5 of this paper we argued that efficiency improves if simple clusters are overlaid and com-

---

[29] Related to feature discriminability is *cue validity* which is the basis for placement of an object into a class. Cue validity can also be used as a discriminability measure [RM 75].
[30] This section has to do with Sections 2.3, 2.4, and 3.2, and Part 5 (classification as well as induction and concept formation).

plex structures are built gradually and tentatively. The idea of overlaying subspaces is reminiscent of Koestler's "bisociation" [Ko 64].

The notion of class, category or cluster relates to a term introduced in Sect. 2.3: a *concept* was said to be an intentional (logic) expression of a frequently used class. A concept should assert categorization of objects, examples, or cases that have *uniform* importance to a current goal (see [Wa 72], [BGA 56, pp. 243-245], [DW 66, p. 153], [GHS 79, p. 326ff.], and [MS 84]). In PLS1, a concept is expressed as a hyperrectangle in feature space, or equivalently, as a conjunction of feature ranges; each rectangle is associated with a single utility value (see Sect. 3.1).

There are various models of concept representation in cognition [MS 84, GHS 79, SM 81]. One is the defining attribute model having rigid categories (e.g. a bird has wings, a certain range of possible sizes, etc.). An object is either in the class or not. Another model uses feature space proximity to a *prototypical* instance of the concept as a determining criterion for class membership (e.g. a typical bird has wings, is six inches long, etc.). Since a continuous distance measure is involved in this latter view, it admits uncertainty.

Most machine learning research in AI has been based on the defining attribute model [CMM 83, Di 82, DM 83, Mi 77, Mi 82, Mc 83, Wi 84], which does not facilitate recovery from error. In contrast, PLS (and a few recent systems like it, such as LR 86) are probabilistic. The PLS1 knowledge structure is rigid in the sense that feature space rectangles are precise, but flexible in that both rectangles and their utilities are subject to change. These ideas are pursued in [Re 86, Re 87].

6.3 Hierarchical Structuring[31]

Glass and Holyoak [GH 75], [GHS 79, p. 341] suggest that both psychological models are valid: the prototype/feature model being "popular", learned early in life, and the defining attribute model being "technical", learned later. Perhaps both are used by adults, but each on a different level of abstraction: the former for pattern recognition and lower level learning, and the latter for concise communication and higher level knowledge acquisition. Fluid interaction between the two levels would allow precise assertion when appropriate (at the higher level), yet subtle distinction and error resilience during dynamic learning (mainly at the lower level).

This idea of degrees of abstraction has been investigated in numerous contexts, such as [AIH 82, Ar 72, BB 82, Ca 82, Ga 71, Hf 79, Ko 64, Rk 83, Si 62]. Koestler states [Ko 64, pp. 467, 515]

> The word "hierarchy" is used here [to mean] a special type of organization in which the overall control is centralized at the apex of a ... tree ... each suborganization [has a] certain amount of autonomy ... [In a given hierarchy,] operations strip the input of what appears to be irrelevant [for the particular hierarchy].

---

[31] This section relates to Sect. 2.3 and Part 5.

Koestler develops this model very extensively, arguing its impact on effectiveness and efficiency in human intelligence, from perception to creativity. Similarly, Arbib [Ar72, Ch.5] describes in detail how

> ... hierarchical organization [reduces] the burden of computation at higher levels [of abstraction] ... more time is available ... more space is available [and] information flow is substantially reduced in comparison to an organization having only one level of command.

These ideas are reiterated in such as [Ar72, Hf79, La51, Rk83], which assert that hierarchical organization underlies animal nervous systems. Several detailed implementations have used this approach, e.g. the pyramid structure for vision described in [BB82, AIH82]. These notions also relate to "modes of learning".

Gagne [Ga65, Ga71] described human learning in terms of a hierarchy, a sequence of cumulative knowledge involving first discrimination, followed by concept attainment, then rule formation. Some order seems to exist not only ontogenetically (developmentally in an individual human), but also phylogenetically (over the evolution of species). For example, lower animals do not communicate explicit rules but do discriminate goal-related aspects of their environment. This hierarchy might be profitable in mechanical learning systems.

PLS1 conforms to the first two stages of this model: performing discriminations and generating concepts. PLS automates discrimination and concept formation using clustering. For this, Sects. 3.2 and 6.1 assume the prior existence of features, but clustering also seems to be a key in the creation of features. This was argued in Part 5, which discussed a multilayered hierarchy for complex clustering (overlaying simpler cluster in primitive subspaces).

While PLS1 creates knowledge as feature space regions, it does not form explicit rules; the latter could be added as a new layer by observing performance of the evaluation function; i.e. an implicit strategy can be made explicit (see Sect. 2.4 and [FHN72, Ge83, Sac74].)

We could compare mechanical formation of features, clusters and evaluation functions with a human's unconscious, intuitive, primarily right hemisphere activity; and automated creation of a specific plan or strategy with conscious, explicit, primarily left hemisphere thinking [Ca82, HT81].

6.4 Summary of Biological Parallels

Researchers in various fields have stressed that certain ideas and relationships may become principles of learning. Some of these are: hierarchical organization is ubiquitous in nervous systems [Ar72, Ko64]; hierarchy and generalization reduces computational complexity [Hf80, Re85b] and improves cognitive economy [Ro76]; generalization and discrimination are twin phenomena [Ko64]; discrimination uses probability [Ar72, BGA56]; and these processes are goal-oriented [Ar72, Ko64].

One of the reasons for studying natural systems is that they are the only known means for effective and efficient inductive inference. This is an important research goal in AI which may be guided and facilitated by appropriate modeling. One such approach is the clustering used in PLS as a tool for discrimination, concept formation. Cognitive theory coincides with the PLS approach: both have similar characteristics such as efficiency. Simultaneous study of artificial and natural systems may promote of principles of intelligence.

7. Conclusions[32]

This paper has adressed effective and efficient methods for inductive learning in incremental situations involving error and uncertainty. Both conceptual analysis and experimental results support the approach. Conceptually, the probabilistic learning system PLS is compact, and coincides with psychological theory (Part 6). Empirically, PLS1 has been uniquely successful: local optima have been discovered for task performance, and the learning is more efficient than other algorithms (Part 3). Two extensions are promising: the genetic system PLS2 (Part 4) for stable, accurate, and efficient induction from typical data, and the feature formation system PLS0 (Part 5) for tractable constructive induction from primitive data.

We have suggested that *conceptual knowledge acquisition* is measurable, and that its quantification helps learning. (Part 2 of the paper introduces these ideas).

For practical and scientific reasons, we have studied conceptual knowledge in heuristic search domains. The task of search has not been restrictive, but rather illuminating, since it requires incremental and uncertain learning, and demands that these issues be addressed. One result of our study is that learning an evaluation function and learning a concept are basically the same problem (although learning a function is harder). Another result of our investigation is the view is that the traditional logic representation for concepts is best considered a final product od probabilistic learning, which is more effective and efficient.

Although current versions of PLS are quite general, this paper emphasizes induction from data rather than induction using domain specific knowledge. While Part 5 considered background knowledge to some extent, learning systems must integrate varied knowledge sources more fully (see [MKK 86]).

This paper has addressed some general issues of effective and efficient inductive learning. Some emerging principles may be summarized:

(1) *Appropriate mediating structures between data and result facilitate learning*.
Since the data are often massive, while the desired concept is usually concise, a large amount of induction is required. To alleviate this difficulty, intermediate knowledge structures can compress the information in steps.

This and other characteristics of mediating structures may promote efficacy and efficiency. Mediating structures are often probabilistic; they gradually capture and flexibly develop invariances and similarities. (The probabilistic

---

[32] This is a very brief summary of the approach, methods and results in this tutorial paper. An overview is given in the Introduction (Part 1). Comprehensive summaries appear at the end of each major part of the paper.

conceptual clusters of PLS1 and the layered structure-inducing clusters of PLS0 combine multiple benefits of mediating structures.)

(2) *Efficient and effective learning depends on good use of data.* Techniques based on statistics or information theory permit every datum to contribute to the assessment of every relevant hypothesis. Probabilistic methods control uncertain data and utilize normal data: predominating tendencies become underlying truths.

Information may be compressed while invariances are sought, described, and verified. Efficiency, information compression, and error resilience go hand-in-hand.

(3) *Data, models, uncertainty, induction, and its credibility are bound up together. Good learning methods extract and combine knowledge from all available resources.* Combined statistical and AI methods for induction, such as probabilistic conceptual clustering and second order relationship clustering, accomplish *mutual data support,* the efficient, simultaneous emergence of credibility, confidence, and concept.

Bibliography

[AIH82] Barr, A, Cohen, PR, Feigenbaum, EA (ed.) The Handbook of Artificial Intelligence (3 volumes), Kaufmann, 1982

[An73] Anderberg, MR, Cluster Analysis for Applications, Academic Press, 1973

[Ar72] Arbib, MA, The Metaphorical Brain: An Introduction to Cybernetics as Artificial Intelligence and Brain Theory, Wiley, 1972

[Ba71] Banerji, RB, Some linguistic and statistical problems in pattern recognition, Pattern Recognition 3, (1971), 409-419

[Ba76] Banerji, RB, Learning to solve games and puzzles, in Simon, JC (ed.), Computer Oriented Learning Processes, Noordhoff-Leyden, 1976, 341-363

[Ba78] Banerji, RB, Pattern recognition: Structural description languages, in Belzer, J (ed.), Encyclopedia of Computer Science and Technology 12 (1978), 1-28

[Ba80] Banerji, RB, Artificial Intelligence: A Theoretical Approach, Elsevier North Holland, 1980

[Ba82] Banerji, RB, Theory of problem solving: A branch of artificial intelligence, Proc. IEEE 70, 12 (1982), 1428-1448

[BB82] Ballard, DH, Brown, CM, Computer Vision, Prentice-Hall, 1982

[Be73] Berliner, H, Some necessary conditions for a master chess program, Proc. Third International Joint Conference on Artificial Intelligence, 1973, 77-85

[Be77] Berliner, H, Experiences in evaluation with BKG — a program that plays backgammon, Proc. Fifth International Joint Conference on Artificial Intelligence, 1977, 428-433

[Be79] Berliner, H, On the construction of evaluation functions for large domains, Proc. Sixth International Joint Conference on Artificial Intelligence, 1979, 53-55

[BF78] Buchanan, BG, Feigenbaum, EA, DENDRAL and Meta-DENDRAL: Their applications dimension, Artificial Intelligence 11 (1978) 5-24

[BGA56] Bruner, JS, Goodnow, JJ, Austin, GA, A Study of Thinking, Wiley, 1956

[Bi76] Bindra, D, A Theory of Intelligent Behavior, Wiley, 1976

[BM80] Bratko, I, Michie, D, An advice program for a complex chess programming task, The Computer Journal 23, 4 (1980), 353-359

[Br81] Brindle, A, Genetic algorithms for function optimization, C.S. Department Report TR81-2 (PhD Dissertation), University of Alberta, 1981

[Bu78] Buchanan, BG, Johnson, CR, Mitchell, TM, Smith, RG, Models of learning systems, in Belzer, J (ed.), Encyclopedia of Computer Science and Technology 11 (1978), 24-51

[Ca 82] Campbell, J, Grammatical Man: Information, Entropy, Language, and Life, Simon and Schuster, 1982
[CM 83] Campbell, MS Marsland, TA. A comparison of minimax tree search algorithms, Artificial Intelligence 20, 4 (1983), 347-367
[CMM 83] Carbonell, JG, Michalski, RS, Mitchell, TM, Machine learning: A historical and methodological analysis, AI Magazine 4, 3 (Fall 1983), 69-79
[Ch 85] Cheeseman, P, In defense of probability, Proc. Ninth International Joint Conference on Artificial Intelligence, 1985, 1003-1009
[Chr 64] Christensen, R, Foundations of Inductive Reasoning, Entropy, Ltd., 1964
[CK 86] Christensen, J, Korf, RE, A unified theory of evaluation functions and its application to learning. Proc. Fifth National Conference on Artificial Intelligence, 1986, 148-152
[CM 84] Cohen, B, Murphy, GL, Models of concepts, Cognitive Science 8 (1984), 27-58
[CR 84] Coles, D, Rendell, LA, Some issues in training learning systems and an autonomous design, Proc. Fifth Biennial Conference of the Canadien Society for Computational Studies of Intelligence, London, Ontario, May, 1984, 99-102
[Da 77] Davis, R, King, J, An overview of production systems, in Elcock, EW and Michie, D (eds.), Machine Intelligence 8, Halsted Press (Wiley), 1977, 300-332
[De 80] Dennett, DC, Brainstorms: Phylosophical Essays on Mind and Psychology, MIT Press, 1980
[Di 82] Dietterich, TG, London, B, Clarkson, K, Dromey, G, Learning and inductive inference, STAN-CS-82-913, Stanford University, also Chapter XIV of The Handbook of Artificial Intelligence, Cohen, PR, Feigenbaum, EA (eds.), Kaufmann, 1982
[DJ 80] DeJong, KA, Adaptive system design: A genetic approach, IEEE Transactions on Systems, Man, and Cybernetics SMC-10, (1980), 566-574
[DK 82] Devijver, PA, Kittler, J, Pattern Recognition: A Statistical Approach, Prentice/Hall, 1982
[DL 82] Davis, R, Lenat, DB, Knowledge-Based Systems in Artificial Intelligence, McGraw-Hill, 1982
[DM 83] Dietterich, TG, Michalski RS, A comparative review of selected methods for learning from examples, in Michalski, RS et al. (eds.), Machine Learning: An Artificial Intelligence Approach, Tioga, 1983, 41-81
[Do 66] Doran, J, Michie, D, Experiments with the graph-traverser program, Proc. Roy. Soc., A, 294 (1966) 235-259
[DS 81] Draper, NR, Smith, H, Applied Regression Analysis (2nd Ed.) Wiley, 1981
[Du 73] Duda, RO, Hart, PE, Pattern Classification and Scene Analysis, Wiley, 1973
[Du 83] Duda, RO, Shortliffe, EH, Expert systems research, Science 220, 4594, (1983) 261-268
[DW 80] Dodd, DH, White, RM, Cognition: Mental Structures and Processes, Allyn and Bacon, 1980
[EG 82] Ernst, GW, Goldstein, MM, Mechanical discovery of classes of problem-solving strategies, J. ACM 29, (1982) 1-33
[El 71] Eliot, J (ed.), Human Development and Cognitive Processes, Holt, Rinehart and Winston, 1971
[FHN 72] Fikes, RE, Hart, P, Nilsson, NJ, Learning and executing generalized robot plans, Artificial Intelligence 3 (1972) 251-288
[Fu 78] Fu, KS, Pattern recognition: Discriminant and syntactic methods, in Belzer, J (ed.), Encyclopedia of Computer Science and Technology 12 (1978) 28-49
[Fu 82] Fu, KS, Syntactic Pattern Recognition and Applications, Prentice-Hall, 1982
[FY 74] Feldman, JA, Yakimovsky, Y, Decision theory and artificial intelligence: I. A semantics-based region analizer, Artificial Intelligence 5 (1974) 349-371
[Ga 65] Gagne, RM, The Conditions of Learning, Holt, Rinehart and Winston, 1965
[Ga 71] Gagne, RM, Contributions of learning to human development, in Eliot, J (ed.), Human Development and Cognitive Processes, Holt, Rinehart and Winston, 1971, 111-128
[GA 85] Proc. International Conference of Genetic Algorithms and their Applications, Carnegie-Mellon University, July, 1985
[Gas 79] Gaschnig, JG, Performance measurement and analysis of certain search algorithms, Dept. of Computer Science CS-79-124 (PhD thesis), Carnegie-Mellon University, 1979
[Gd 77] Good, IJ, Dynamic probability, computer chess, and the measurement of knowledge, in Elcock, EW and Michie, D (eds), Machine Intelligence 8, Halsted Press (Wiley), 1977, 139-150

[Ge83] Georgeff, MP, Stragegies in heuristic search, Artificial Intelligence 20, 4 (1983), 393–425
[GH75] Glass, AL, Holyoak, KJ, Alternative conceptions of semantic memory, Cognition 3, (1975), 313–339
[GHS79] Glass, AL, Holyoak, KJ, Santa, JL, Cognition, Addison-Wesley, 1979
[Gi76] Gill, A, Applied Algebra for the Computer Sciences, Prentice-Hall, 1976
[Gib69] Gibson, EJ, Principles f Perceptual Learning and Development, Appleton-Century-Crofts, 1969
[GL75] Goldin, GA, Luger, GF, Problem structure and problem solving behavior, Proc. Fourth International Joint Conference on Artificial Intelligence, 1975, 924–931
[Ha75] Hartigan, JA, Clustering Algorithms, Wiley, 1975
[Har74] Harris, LR, The heuristic search under conditions of error, Artificial Intelligence 5 (1974) 217–234
[HDP80] Huyn, N, Dechter, R, Pearl, J, Studies in heuristics, part 6: Probabilistic analysis of the complexity of A*, Artificial Intelligence 15 (1980) 241–254
[Hf79] Hofstadter, DR, Godel, Escher, Bach: An Eternal Golden Braid, Basic Books, 1979
[HNR76] Hart, P, Nilsson, NJ, Raphael, B, A formal basis for the heuristic determination of minimum cost paths, IEEE Trans. Sys. Sci. and Cybernetics SSC-4 (1968) 100–107
[Ho75] Holland, JH, Adaption in Natural and Artificial Systems, University of Michigan Press, 1975
[HT81] Hampden-Turner, C, Maps of the Mind, Macmillan, 1981
[Hu75] Hunt, EB, Ch. VIII: Feature extraction, Artificial Intelligence, Academic Press, 1975
[Kf85] Korf, RE, Depth-first iterative deepening: An optimal admissible tree search, Artificial Intelligence (1985)
[Ko64] Koestler, A, The Act of Creation: A Study of the Conscious and Unconscious in Sciene and Art, Macmillan (hard cover) or Dell (paperback). 1964, Other editions do not contain the important Book Two.
[Ku62] Kuhn, T, The Structure of Scientific Revolutions, University of Chicago Press, 1962
[La51] Lashley, KS, The problem of serial order of behavior, in Jeffress, A (ed.), Cerebral Mechanisms in Behavior – The Hixon Symposium, Wiley, 1951
[Le82] Lenat, DB, The nature of heuristics, Artificial Intelligence 19 (1982), 189–249
[LHK79] Lenat, DB, Hayes-Roth, F, Klahr, P, Cognitive economy in artificial intelligence systems, Proc. Sixth International Joint Conference on Artificial Intelligence, 1979, 531–536
[Lng83] Langley, P, Learning search strategies through discrimination, International Journal of Man-Machine Studies 18 (1983), 513–541
[LR86] Lee, WD, Ray, SR, Rule refinement using the probabilistic rule generator, Proc. Fifth National Conference on Artificial Intelligence, 1986, 442–447
[Ma76] Marr, D, Early processing of visual information, Philosophical Transactions of the Royal Society of London B 275, (1976) 483–524
[Mc80] Michalski, RS, Pattern recognition as rule-guided inductive inference, IEEE Trans. Pat. Rec. and Mach. Intel. 2, 1980, 349–361
[Mc83] Michalski, RS, A theory and methodology of inductive learning, Artificial Intelligence 20, 2 (1983), 111–161; reprinted in Michalski, RS et al (eds.), Machine learning: An Artificial Intelligence Approach, Tioga, 1983, 83–134
[MCM83] Michalski, RS, Carbonell, JG, Mitchell, TM (eds.), Machine Learning: An Artificial Intelligence Approach, Tioga, 1983
[Mi77] Mitchell, TM, Version spaces: A candidate elimination approach to rule learning, Proc. Fifth International Joint Conference on Artificial Intelligence, 1977, 305–310
[Mi82] Mitchell, TM, Generalization as search, Artificial Intelligence 21 (1982), 203–226
[Mi83] Mitchell, TM, Learning and problem solving, Proc. Eighth International Joint Conference on Artificial Intelligence, 1983, 1139–1151
[MKK86] Mitchell, TM, Keller, RM, Kedar-Cabelli, ST, Explanation-based generalization – a unifying view, Machine Learning Journal 1, 1 (1986)
[MR70] Michie, D, Ross, R, Experiments with the adaptive graph traverser, in Meltzer, B, Michie, D (eds.), Machine Intelligence 5, American Elsevier, 1970, 301–318
[MS84] Medin, DL, Smith, EE, Concepts and concept formation, Annual Review of Psychology 35 (1984), 113–138

[Na 83] Nau, DS, Pathology on game trees revisited and an alternative to minimaxing, Artificial Intelligence 21, 2 (1983), 221-244

[Ni 71] Nilsson, NJ, Problem Solving Methods in Artificial Intelligence, McGraw-Hill, 1971

[Ni 80] Nilsson, NJ, Principles of Artificial Intelligence, Tioga, 1980

[NU 65] Newman, C, Uhr, L, BOGART: A discovery and induction program for games, ACM Proc. 20th National Conference, 1965, 176-185

[Pe 83] Pearl, J, Knowledge versus search: A quantitative analysis using A*, Artificial Intelligence 20, 1 (1983), 1-13

[Pe 83a] Pearl, J, On the nature of pathology in game searching, Artificial Intelligence 20, 4 (1983), 427-453

[Po 70] Pohl, I, First results on the effect of error in heuristic search, in Meltzer, B, Michie, D (eds.), Machine Intelligence 5, American Elsevier, 1970, 219-236

[Qu 79] Quinlan, JR, Discovering rules by induction from large collections or examples, in Michie, D (ed.), Expert Systems in the Microelectronic Age, Edinburgh University Press, 1979, 168-201

[Qu 83] Quinlan, JR, Learning efficient classification procedures and their application to chess end games, in Michalski, RS et al (ed.), Machine Learning: An Artificial Intelligence Approach, Tioga, 1983, 463-482

[Re 77] Rendell, LA, A locally optimal solution of the fifteen puzzle produced by an automatic evaluation function generator, Dept of Computer Science CS-77-36, University of Waterloo, 1977

[Re 81] Rendell, LA, An adaptive plan for state-space problems, Dept of Computer Science CS-81-13, (PhD thesis), University of Waterloo, 1981

[Re 82] Rendell, LA, State-space learning systems using regionalized penetrance, Proc. Fourth Biennial Conference of the Canadian Society for Computational Studies of Intelligence, Saskatoon, Saskatchewan, May, 1982, 150-157

[Re 83a] Rendell, LA, A new basis for state-space learning systems and a successful implementation, Artificial Intelligence 20, 4 (1983), 369-392

[Re 83b] Rendell, LA, A learning system which accomodates feature interactions, Proc. Eighth International Joint Conference on Artificial Intelligence, Karlsruhe, West Germany, August, 1983, 469-472

[Re 83c] Rendell, LA, A doubly layered, genetic penetrance learning system, Proc. Third National Conference on Artificial Intelligence, Washington, DC, August, 1983, 343-347

[Re 83d] Rendell, LA, Toward a unified approach for conceptual knowledge acquisition, AI Magazine 4, 4 (Winter 1983), 19-27

[Re 83e] Rendell, LA, Conceptual knowledge acquisition in search, University of Guelph Report CIS-83-15, Dept. of Computing and Information Science, Guelph, Ontario, Canada, November, 1983

[Re 84] Rendell, LA, Burgess, J, A uniform learning system for problems and games, CIS Dept. Report CIS84-6, University of Guelph, 1984

[Re 85a] Rendell, LA, Genetic plans and the probabilistic learning system: Synthesis and results, Proc. International Conference on Genetic Algrithms and their Applications, Carnegie-Mellon University, July, 1985, 60-73

[Re 85b] Rendell, LA, Substantial constructive induction using layered information compression: Tractable feature formation in search, Proc. Ninth International Joint Conference on Artificial Intelligence, University of California at Los Angeles, August, 1985, 650-658

[Re 86a] Rendell, LA, A general framework for induction and a study of selective induction, Machine Learning Journal 1, 2 (1986, in press)

[Re 86b] Rendell, LA, Induction, of and by probability, Proc. Workshop on Uncertainty and Probability in Artificial Intelligence, University of California at Los Angeles, August, 1985, 129-134, revised version to appear in Kanal, LN, Lemmer, J (eds.), Uncertainty in Artificial Intelligence, North Holland, 1986

[Re 87] Rendell, LA, Representations and models for concept learning, University of Illinois Dept. of Comp. Sci. Report no. UIUCDCS-R-87-1324, 1987.

[Rk 83] Rock, I, The Logic of Perception, MIT Press, 1983

[RM 75] Rosch, E, Mervis, CB, Family resemblances: Studies in the internal structures of categories, Cognitive Psychology 7, (1975), 573-605

[Ro76] Rosch, E, Mervis, CB, Gray, WD, Johnson, DM, Boyes-Braem, P, Basic objects in natural categories, Cognitive Psychology 8, (1976), 382-439
[Rt62] Rosenblatt, F, Principles of Neurodynamics: Perceptrons and the Theory of Brain Mechanisms, Spartan, 1962
[Sa63] Samuel, AL, Some studies in machine learning using the game of checkers, in Feigenbaum, EA, Feldman, J (eds.), Computers and Thought, McGraw-Hill, 1963, 71-105
[Sa67] Samuel, AL, Some studies in machine learning using the game of checkers II-recent progress, IBM J. Res. and Develop. 11 (1967) 601-617
[Sac74] Sacerdoti, ED, Planning in a hierarchy of abstraction spaces, Artificial Intelligence 5 (1974) 115-135
[SB68] Slagle, JR, Bursky, P, Experiments with a multipurpose, theorem-proving heuristic program, JACM 15 (1968) 85-99
[Sc67] Schofield, PDA, Complete solution of the 'eight puzzle', in Collins, NL, Michie, D (eds.), Machine Intelligence 1, American Elsevier, 1967, 125-133
[Se66] Selfridge, OG, Pandemonium: A paradigm for learning, in Uhr, L (ed.), Pattern Recognition, Wiley, 1966, 339-348
[SF71] Slagle, JR, Farrel, C, Experiments in automatic learning for a multipurpose heuristic program, C. ACM 14 (1971) 91-99
[Sh50] Shannon, CE, Programming a computer for playing chess, Philosophical Magazine (series 7) 41, (1950) 256-275
[Si62] Simon, HA, The architecture of complexity, Proc. Am. Phil. Soc. 106, 6 (1962), 467-482
[SL74] Simon, HA, Lea, G, Problem solving and rule induction: A unified view, in Gregg, L (ed.), Knowledge and Cognition, Erlbaum, 1974, 105-127
[SLM82] Sleeman, D, Langley, P, Mitchell, TM, Learning from solution paths: An approach to the credit assignment problem, AI Magazine, 3, 2 (Spring 1982) 48-52
[Sm80] Smith, SF, A learning system based on genetic adaptive algorithms, PhD Dissertation, University of Pittsburgh, 1980
[SM81] Smith, EE, Medin, DL, Categories and Concepts, Harvard University Press, 1981
[So75] Solomonoff, RJ, Inductive inference theory – A unified approach to problems in pattern recognition and artificial intelligence, Proc. Fourth International Joint Conference on Artificial Intelligence, 1975, 274-280
[Wa69a] Watanabe, S, Knowing and Guessing: A Formal and Quantative Study, Wiley, 1969
[Wa69b] Watanabe, S, Pattern recognition as an inductive process, in Watanabe, S (ed.), Methodologies of Pattern Recognition, Academic Press, 1969, 521-534
[Wa72] Watanabe, S, Pattern recognition as information compression, in Watanabe, S (ed.), Frontiers of Pattern Recognition, Academic Press, 1972, 561-567
[Wa85] Watanabe, S, Pattern Recognition: Human and Mechanical, Wiley, 1985
[We57] Werner, H, Comparative Psychology of Mental Development, 1957
[Wi84] Winston, PH, Artificial Intelligence (2nd Ed.), Addison Wesley, 1984

Appendix A – Basic Search Methods for Problems and Games

This appendix provides some details of common search paradigms. See also [AIH82, Ni71, Ni80].

A.1 State Space Formalisms

A *state space problem* is one that can be formulated in terms of explicitly describable, distinct configurations or *states*. In a tree representation, states become nodes. *Operators* of the problem are applied to *develop* or *expand* a node: when an operator is applied to a *(parent)* node, an *offspring* node results. A problem *instance* is specified by a given *starting state* and a *goal state* (sometimes a set). A *solution* is a sequence of operator applications, found when a goal is eventually reached from the starting state. In the *search* for a solution, operators are branches of the tree, and the solution is a path. Many significant problems are state space, e.g. deduction.

One such problem, the fifteen puzzle, is a four-by-four array containing fifteen labeled square tiles and a space into which an adjacent tile can be slid. The goal is some particular ordering (see Fig. 2). The fifteen puzzle has been the subject of experiment in [Do 66, Kf 85, MR 70, Po 70, Re 83a]. Schofield [Sc 67] gave a complete solution of the simpler eight puzzle, which Gaschnig [Gas 79] also studied in his clear and extensive analysis. Investigation of the fifteen puzzle has been frequent because it is easy to formulate but difficult to solve by machine, and also because such board puzzles easily admit heuristic abstraction, having considerable "structure", a concept examined in [GL 75] in terms of symmetry groups and equivalence classes of states.

Since unguided or *breadth-first* search is generally infeasible because of the exponential growth of nodes, some way of narrowing search is required. The *evaluation function* has often been used as a heuristic to order and select states for development in what is called *best-first* search. When a heuristic function H is formulated as a distance-to-goal estimator, it is frequently merged with the stabilizing distance-already-from-start term, either directly, to give the well known A* algorithm schema [HNR 68, Ni 71, Ni 80], or with weighting, for greater flexibility [Po 70]. Experimental and theoretical analyses [Gas 79, HDP 70, Pe 73] have quantified the dependence of search performance on the accuracy of H. Under certain conditions, search is *admissible,* i.e. it always results in a shortest solution [HNR 68, Ni 71, Ni 80].

Instead of path distance to the goal, an alternative choice for the conceptualization and construction of a heuristic evaluation function is the probability for a node's being in a solution. This approach is used in [Re 83a, Re 83b, SB 68, SF 71], and in this paper. The path distance approach can be related to utility, probability, and true penetrance (see Sect. 3.1). For example, breadth-first search is admissible, so the associated statistics are disposed toward short solutions.

Some experiments involving evaluation functions are described in [Be 73, Be 77, CK 86, Do 66, MR 70, Re 83a, Re 83b, Re 85a, Sa 63, Sa 67, SF 71]. A standard technique is to combine several more elementary functions or *features,* often linearly, to form the heuristic H = **b.f**, where **b** is the *coefficient* vector and **f** is the feature vector. Features also appear in control theory and pattern recognition (see [DK 82]), and in cognition (see Sect. 6.1). Two simple features for the fifteen puzzle are shown in Fig. 2.

A.2 Minimax

Corresponding to search for problems is a well known technique for games described first by Shannon [Sh 50], and successfully applied by Samuel [Sa 63, Sa 67]. This method, called *minimax,* is more elaborate than problem search since two players are involved. Minimax has two aspects. The first begins with the ideal approach of obtaining perfect knowledge about node A simply by looking ahead, considering all possible moves (branches in the search tree). Eventually the game must be won, lost or drawn, so to these tip nodes, the corresponding values 1, 0 and .5 can be assigned. (Our values are different from the standard values of 1, -1 and 0.)

Our minimax values estimate the probability of winning. Once an assignment is made, the values are "backed up", using the maximum of all offspring of A when α (the favored player) has a free choice, and the minimum when β (the opponent) is uncontrolled by α. Assuming both players always make the best move, this procedure assigns the proper value to parent node A. The node A can be compared with other nodes that are candidates for development, and the move is chosen that has the greatest value. See Fig. 19(a), Sect. 3.5, and [AIH82, Be77, Na83, Ni71, Ni80, Pe83a, Re84, Sa63].

The growth of nodes is exponential unless search is guided. This brings us to the second aspect of the minimax technique. The traditional cure for the combinatorial problem is to look ahead only so far, then apply guesses at the tip nodes. Instead of relying on certain knowledge, the minimax values are estimates obtained from a *static function* like that for puzzles or "one person" games. Many improvements have been made to the basic algorithm; see [AIH82, CM83].

Appendix B - Selection of Problems for Training

Learning systems are sometimes categorized as being *supervised* (in which a teacher presents positive and negative examples of a concept), or *unsupervised* (not knowing what class examples correspond to). The distinction seems to be more subtle and interesting than it first appears, however (this is one of the topics discussed toward the end of [Re86a].

Here we are interested in just one aspect of training: a human may select and present search problems to the learning system, the training (problem selection) may be fully mechanized, or there may be degrees between these two extremes [Bu78]. In the case of PLS (and for [Sa63, Sa67]), the individual states from which statistics are compiled are determined partly by the system's current evaluation function, and partly by the training instance (see the discussion of utility in Sect. 3.1). Early versions of PLS1 required training problems to be input by the user, but later versions have automated this [CR84].

When the performance element (solver or player) is operated in the mode that backs up binary utility values (Sect. 3.5), it is important to present problems or games of appropriate difficulty to the learning system. If the training instances are too hard for the current capabilities of the solver or player, no information whatever is obtained since only zeroes are backed up then. On the other hand, if instances are too easy, little information becomes available, because novel situations tend not to arise in easy search, and discriminations that might otherwise appear, remain unknown. To maintain a balance requires some familiarity with current performance capability, which can be time consuming.

To automate the burden of selecting appropriate training problems or games, a mechanical instance selector or *trainer* has been implemented which samples the ability of the current control structure (evaluation function) for the performance element. (In the case of parallel operation using PLS2 (Part 4) several of these control structures (individuals in the population) are randomly sampled.) The trainer is designed to work with any control structure and problem domain; it is necessary only to supply a set of standard training instances, each paired with a measure of its difficulty, or else to provide a means to generate instances of a specified difficulty.

Problem generation is easy with the fifteen puzzle since moves can simply be made backwards from the goal, to a given depth (difficulty) d. The procedure is a little more complicated with a game such as checkers, although still straightforward, since games can be played to the end, then paths traced back d moves.

Once the trainer has these training instances graded by difficulty, it can test the current control structure within a "window" of very easy problems or games. The trainer increases the difficulty d until the response D (performance — e.g. nodes developed to achieve the goal) is close to the desired value D* (the target). Regression (curve fitting) is used to fit a linear relationship between log D and difficulty measure d. Extrapolation plays a (restricted) role, to fix a revised approximate range of d. A new window is then placed somewhat below the estimated location of the target performance D*. Within the window, only interpolation is used. After a (short) series of window placements, the approximate value of d is found which gives the target value D'; this d is the information required by the performance element.

Since costs increase with D, and since underestimates are used, this exploration is inexpensive, accurate and stable (see [CR 84]). The trainer needs only existing PLS1 elements and a means for ranking or generating training instances by difficulty. With the trainer, PLS1/2 becomes fully automated.

Appendix C – Details of Clustering and Normalization

This appendix oulines the induction algorithms of Sect. 3.2, which are basic to PLS1.

C.1 Splitting Regions

This section details of the clustering algorithm outlined in Sect. 3.2 and illustrated in Fig. 12. The distance d between two regions was defined as an inverse measure of their similarity. Regions are allowed to split only if they are sufficiently dissimilar and adjacent in the feature space.

The algorithm CLUSTER (R, H, P) generates a refined *offspring region set* from the *parent* region R. CLUSTER is based on probability statistics from searches governed by the heuristic (i.e. the control structure) H when solving problems P. This is the algorithm:

Let the rectangle of R be r.
Exhaustively insert hyperplanes, oriented with the axes at integer points, to find the best of all possible splits, as follows:
While any such hyperplane boundaries remain untried do
   Choose a hyperplane not previously selected, to become a tentative boundary for two subrectangles of r, r_1 and r_2.
   Find the elementary utilities (conditional probabilities) p_1 and p_2 of r_1 and r_2, and their error factors. The quantities p_1 and p_2 are defined as the quotient of the two counts $g(r_i, H, P)$ and $t(r_i, H, P)$.
   If this tentative dichotomy produces a distance d larger than any previous, note the hyperplane.
When all dichotomies have been tested, check if the best d was positive (this means that the two regions are "assuredly dissimilar" — see Sects. 3.2 and 5.3 for details and examples). If $d > 0$, then
   Create two permanent offspring regions R_1 and R_2 with the noted best boundaries and probabilities.
   Call CLUSTER (R_1, H, P) and CLUSTER (R_2, H, P) recursively.
else
   Place R in the offspring set and quit.

When regions are being refined (i.e. probability classes differentiated), each in turn becomes a parent for CLUSTER. Since regions are rectangular and aligned with feature space axes, the algorithm is quite economical: it is cheaper than the problem solving step even with many features, the cost increasing with the product of the number of data, features, and eventual regions. With very large feature sets, the algorithm can be speeded by spacing out trial hyperplanes. Often CLUSTER splits a region once or twice, and frequently not at all. Fig. 15(a) shows a typical result. See also [Re 86a] and [Re 86b].

C.2 Probability Normalization

As discussed in Sect. 3.1 and illustrated in Fig. 9, elementary penetrances (conditional probabilities) are heavily biased by the associated evaluation function (control structure). This section gives a short description of the methods used for normalization. Details such as detrimental effects of ignoring biases are explained in [Re 81, Re 83a].

Coarse normalization corrects over the whole feature space. The elementary penetrances p, just available from recent search, are compared with established true estimates $\hat{p}$ obtained from breadth-first search or from earlier normalization treatment. Once a relationship is established, the new data are converted: within each established rectangle r, corresponding probability pairs ($\hat{p}_r$, p_r) are constrained to fit a standard model $\hat{p} = p^h$, where $\hat{p}_r$ and p_r are true and elementary values, and h is a constant whose value is discovered through a regression. Fig. 14 illustrates a typical case. The constant h is called the *search power* whose value reflects the quality of the evaluation function H associated with $\{p_r\}$. Given an estimating region set R and elementary set E with matching rectangles, the algorithm

COARSE NORMALIZE finds h and then unbiases all regions of E by raising their probabilities to the power h, as shown in Fig. 14(c).

A different procedure, *local* normalization, is required when rectangles are refined. Regions are subdivided according to fresh elementary penetrances (Sect. 3.2), but this splitting results in a mixture of true with elementary penetrances. The values must be made commensurable for meaningful treatment. Fig. 13 illustrates the basic situation. If an unconditional probability (true penetrance) estimating region R defines the rectangle r for a matching elementary region Q and CLUSTER has split Q into offspring $\{Q_1, Q_2, \ldots\}$, this elementary set is modified to reflect unconditional probability as follows: Let $R = (r, \hat{p})$, $Q = (r, p)$, and the offspring $Q_i = (r_i, p_i)$. The *search factor* (for evaluation function H) within rectangle r is defined to be $s = p/\hat{p}$. As a first approximation, the true probability of each offspring region Q_i can be estimated as p_i/s. The algorithm FINE NORMALIZE is constructed to implement the conversion. This normalization is actually more complex than suggested here; in [Re 83a] the search factor is corrected for bias within r.

Appendix D – Localization and Piecewise Linearity

While Sect. 3.3 gives a general picture of the piecewise linear method, this appendix details the localization. Suppose the feature-probability relationships are to be established for a region $R = (r, c, \hat{p}, e, b_r)$, from the cumulative set C. R is the *principal* region. Recall that the true probability estimate $\hat{p}$ and the feature space centroid c are used along with others from C in a regression to determine b_r for the true probability predictor $H_r = \exp[b_r \cdot f]$.

Next H_r is regionalized. The weight for each region $Q \in C$ contributing to the R-centered regression depends on the distance of Q from R. Before constructing this distance measure, we need to consider that features are not uniformly important; in fact a feature can be completely irrelevant. Hence the distance, itself, is weighted by b_r. This, of course, is circular since it is b_r that is to be determined.

To circumvent this circularity, the procedure is iterative. First the global coefficient vector b is calculated, weighting each region equally. Then b_r is estimated (initialized): $b_r^{(1)} = b$. This value of the regionalized coefficient vector is next used to perform the regression again, and so on, repeating until the value converges. Even this doubly multiple regression costs little compared with the time required by the performance element.

The exact weighting is as follows: The *distance factor* is $1/\text{dist}(R, Q)$. If $R = Q$, the function $\text{dist}(R, Q) = d_r$. If $R \neq Q$, $\text{dist}(R, Q) = |b_r^{(i)} \cdot (c_r - c_p)|^L$, where $b_r^{(i)}$ is the ith estimate of b_r in the iterative procedure, and where c_r and c_q are the centroids of R and Q, and d_r is the average value of $|(C_r - x)|^L$ over all points x within r. The exponent $L > 0$, the *localization strength*, decides the degree of non-linearity.

The solver or player uses one of two evaluation methods. The first, *discrete piecewise linear* procedure simply predicts the true probability of a state A to be $H(A) = \exp[b_r \cdot f(A)]$, where f is the feature vector and $f(A) \in r$. The more complex evaluation mode, *smooth piecewise linear,* uses all regions Q in the cumulative set C, each one weighted according to its distance from f(A). If $d_j = \text{dist}(f(A), Q_j)$ for each of the J regions Q_j of C ($1 < j < J$), with the localization power L here fixed at 2, and if the coefficient vector Q_j is $\mathbf{b_j}$, then the predicted true probability of A is $H(A) = \exp\left(\sum_j [\mathbf{b_j}.f(A)/d_j] / \sum_j [1/d_j]\right)$ (where $1 \leq j \leq J$). This avoids edge effects at region boundaries, resulting in the good performance described in Sect. 3.4.

Acknowledgements

I would like to thank Jim Burgess and Dave Coles for their helpful criticism of early drafts of this paper. I would also like to thank the National Science and Engineering Research Board of Canada, who funded this work.

Cognitive Development as Optimisation[1]

J. G. Wolff[2]

Abstract

This article reports the latest phase of a research programme whose long-term goal is the creation of a comprehensive theory of linguistic/cognitive development. A partial theory, and computer models embodying aspects of it, were developed in previous phases of the programme (Wolff, 1982) and tested in restricted domains using artificial languages in the main. The aim here is to show how the previously established framework of ideas may be extended to explain the learning of more realistic cognitive structures.

Working assumptions which constrain the form of the theory include: 1) Knowledge structures must be bootstrapped from a small base of primitives; 2) The learning system must be able to operate without reinforcement, error correction by a "teacher" or other kinds of training regime; 3) Structures built by the learning process must be usable in both language comprehension and language production; 4) One formalism to be used for both syntax and meanings and for their integration.

The central idea in the theory is that learning is a process of building and refining a knowledge structure towards a form which is optimally efficient for the several functions it must serve. The foundation of the optimisation process is the proper application of a small range of data compression principles - just six seem to be enough for the efficient representation of a wide variety of cognitive structures. The six principles are: 1) The formation of AND groups (chunking), 2) The formation of OR groups, 3) The application of frequency and size heuristics to find the best groupings, 4) Recursion/iteration, 5) Discarding information (related to generalization) and 6) Schema-plus-correction. The theory incorporating principles 1 to 5 can explain a wide range of phenomena in cognitive/linguistic development (Wolff, 1982).

This article extends the earlier discussion to consider how all six principles may be applied to the representation and learning of syntactic agreements, class-inclusion hierarchies, part-whole hierarchies, "relational" concepts, English auxiliary verbs and the integration of syntactic structures with meaning structures.

Other issues considered include the use of partial matching and probabilities in language analysis and a comparison of the optimisation idea with hypothesis-testing views of learning. The article concludes with a summary of empirical evidence bearing on the theory.

1. Introduction

Learning, by natural or artificial systems, may usefully be seen as the development and refinement of knowledge structures towards a form which is optimally efficient for the several functions to be served. This heuristic has already provided answers to several problems in language learning and other aspects of cognitive development. The theory which has been built around this idea and a computer

---

[1] The research reported in this article was supported in part by Personal Research Grant HRP8240/1 (A) to J. G. Wolff from the British Social Science Research Council.
[2] Department of Psychology, The University, Dundee DD1 4HN, Scotland, U.K. Now at Praxis Systems plc, 20 Manners St., Bath, BA1 1PX, U.K.

model in which the theory is embodied is described most fully in Wolff (1982). (To be referred to here as W82. There is also a shorter account of the theory in Wolff, 1980a). The present article is mainly a report of the most recent phase of research, a project to extend and refine the ideas in W82. The emphasis will be on psychological modelling but most of the ideas are relevant to the construction of computational learning systems for other applications.

To help bootstrap a theory in a complex domain, artificially simplified data and knowledge structures have been the main test-bed for the theory in work prior to this project. The latest phase of the research has explored how ideas about learning which were developed using simplified structures may be applied to more realistic kinds of syntactic and semantic knowledge. The outline of a new learning system is now fairly clear but a working model embodying these latest ideas has not yet been completed.

Let us begin with an outline of the presuppositions and working assumptions of the research programme.

1.1 Theoretical Presuppositions, Working Hypotheses and Research Strategy

1.1.1 In terms of the distinction promoted by Noam Chomsky and others, the theory is empiricist rather than nativist in flavour. A working assumption is that children are born with only a little innate knowledge about the structure of language and about the world: perceptual primitives plus procedures for learning new things. The main reason for favouring this kind of theory over one in which a child is supposedly equipped at birth with relatively large amounts of knowledge about language structure and other things is the need to postulate processes which are flexible enough to learn any natural language as children evidently can.

This research may be seen as a continuation of a research programme conducted in the 1940s, '50s and early '60s by structural linguists (e.g., Fries, 1952; Harris, 1961) and by behaviourist psychologists (e.g., Osgood, 1963) which was interrupted by Chomsky's influential criticisms and is only now recovering its stride. Readers acquainted with the history of psychology will recognise ideas (the significance of frequency and contiguity in learning, for example) with a fairly venerable provenance.

1.1.2 Some computer models of language development (e.g., Anderson, 1981; Langley, 1982) treat the problem as one of mapping surface structures to independently established semantic or deep structures. The models are supplied with semantic structures together with corresponding sentences and they have to work out the relationship between the two.

This is a reasonable posture to adopt as means of simplifying a difficult problem providing the dangers are recognised. There is a risk of creating spurious solutions to learning problems (the learning of phrase-structure groupings, for example) by putting structure into the model implicitly which the model should be constructing for itself.

The contrasted strategy adopted in this programme is to look for learning principles which are general enough to embrace the learning of semantic structures and syntactic structures and their integration. The aim is to develop a system which can bootstrap a realistic knowledge structure starting with only a minimum of given knowledge – perceptual primitives and procedures for building knowledge structures which are not domain-specific in any way. Most work up to the beginning of the project concentrated on syntax learning but the generalization of those ideas to handle semantic knowledge and the integration of syntax with semantics has now been much more fully explored.

1.1.3 A related point may be made about the social context of learning. While it is recognised that language learning is closely bound up with social interactions between children and adults and with pragmatic aspects of communication, no attempt has been made to make these things part of the foundation of the theory. Rather than suppose that social or pragmatic or conceptual or syntactic knowledge is the key to language learning, it seems preferable to search for structure-abstracting principles which may eventually provide a theory of learning broad enough in scope to embrace all these domains.

1.1.4 It seems that children can probably learn a first language without reinforcement in any ordinary sense of that word, or correction by a "teacher" or samples of language containing "negative instances" (items marked somehow as "wrong") or graded sequencing of language samples or any other kind of training regime. It seems prudent as a matter of research strategy to develop a theory which does not depend on any of these aids but which may take advantage of them if they are available. This requirement has raised some ticklish problems concerned with the generalization of grammatical rules and the correction of overgeneralizations but outline solutions to these problems seem now to be reasonably clear.

1.1.5 Unless one is adopting a Skinnerian "white box" approach to learning which ignores processes and structures between stimulus input and response output, any theory of learning must presuppose a theory of knowledge representation. And any theory of knowledge representation needs to be framed to fit in with what is known about how people use their knowledge in such tasks as language comprehension and language production. In this research programme efforts have been made to develop a learning theory and associated theory of knowledge representation which is compatible with the broad facts of language comprehension and production (much in the spirit of the "generative semantics" school). The implications of this posture for one's choice of representation system will be considered in more detail later in the article.

1.1.6 Two general points about knowledge representation may be made immediately. Both of them derive from Occam's razor. This principle leads us to look for a system of knowledge representation which allows knowledge used in language comprehension to serve also in language production whenever that is appropriate. Obviously there are likely to be some kinds of knowledge or skill which are specific to each domain. Feedback processes, for example, are probably more important in language production than in comprehension. But there are clearly large amounts of knowledge which are relevant to both activities equally and it would be unreasonable to suppose that this knowledge could not be shared between them.

1.1.7 The second working assumption which has been made for reasons of theoretical parsimony is that there are uniform principles of knowledge representation governing the storage of syntactic knowledge and semantic/pragmatic/world knowledge, auditory, visual and tactile knowledge. There may well be domain-specific principles operating also but we should only postulate such special principles when we have exhausted the explanatory scope of the domain-independent principles.

There are two other reasons for seeking uniformity in the representation of different kinds of knowledge:

a) Most everyday concepts seem to be a blend of auditory, visual and other kinds of knowledge. It is difficult to see how the necessary blending of knowledge from disparate sources can occur if it is expressed, so to speak, in a variety of mental languages. The close integration and interdependency of syntactic and semantic knowledge which has been evident for some years (McCawley, 1968), apparently demands some uniformity in representational systems.

b) A single formalism for all kinds of knowledge paves the way for a theory of learning which can embrace the learning of all kinds of knowledge and their integration. As before, we need not rule out the possibility of differences existing in the way different kinds of knowledge are learned but we should postulate such differences only when it is necessary so to do.

The quest for a single formalism may strike the reader as trivial: the advent of digital recording techniques has made familiar the notion that all kinds of knowledge may be translated into binary code. "Learning" in this case would be the digitising and storage of raw data; "interpretation" would be achieved with simple template-matching techniques and "production" would be simple play-back.

What leads us to reject such a theory of knowledge, of course, is that, apart from the many ways in which it does not correspond with the facts of human knowledge acquisition and use, it is exceedingly inefficient. Redundancies of all kinds would be stored exactly as they appeared in the raw data; huge stocks of sentences would be needed to serve anything but the most rudimentary production or comprehension of language; the slightest perturbation in a sensory pattern would prevent its being recognised; and so on. What is needed is a single formalism which allows comprehension, production and other cognitive functions to be performed *efficiently*. With this point in mind we may proceed to the next section where the theoretical framework is described.

1.2 Outline of the Theoretical Framework

The choice of a suitable formalism does not in itself guarentee *efficiency*. Given a representational system which allows knowledge to be encoded efficiently, the encoding itself still has to be done. Learning may be seen as a process of exploiting the facilities offered by the formalism to develop a knowledge structure which is optimally efficient for one's needs.

The kinds of factors which one may consider under the rubric of efficiency include storage costs of information, usefulness of the stored information, speed of retrieval of information, reliability of cognitive operations and others. Only the first two have yet been considered in any detail. The storage cost of a knowledge structure (which has been termed **Sg**) may be measured in bits of information. If we are going to make comparisons between **Sgs** for different knowledge structures we need some slight sophistication in the way **Sgs** are calculated but we need not discuss this here. The "usefulness" of a body of knowledge depends, of course, on the things a person wants to do. But, independent of any specific goals, there does seem to be a general need to encode new information economically. Existing knowledge seems to be the key to the economical encoding of new knowledge: if a new pattern can be seen as an instance of an already stored pattern then it may be encoded as the address of the existing pattern. If the new pattern is similar to but not identical with the existing pattern then "corrections" may be stored alongside the address.

One general measure of usefulness, then, is the effectiveness of a knowledge structure for compressing incoming data. It has been termed "compression capacity" or **CC** and defined as **(V-v)/V** where **V** is the size of a body of data (in bits) before it has been compressed and **v** is its volume after compression. **CC** is not the only criterion of usefulness of course – the emotional significance of information (carrots and sticks) must play a part at times. But for hum-drum knowledge something like **CC** seems to be the best guide to what information is worth storing for future use.

Measures like **Sg** and **CC** may be used for precise quantitative comparisons of grammars and quantitative evaluations of discovery procedures for grammars. Some work along these lines has been done but the treatment here will be informal.

There is usually a trade-off between **Sg** and **CC** in that small grammars tend to have a poor **CC** and *vice versa* (see Horning, 1969; Feldman, 1972; Cook and Rosenfeld, 1976; Coulon and Kayser, 1978; Michalski, 1982). This point may be seen most clearly if we consider two primitive grammars at opposite ends of the trade-off spectrum. The first one consists of one re-write rule of the form **£→A,£ ¦ B,£ ¦ C,£ ¦ ... ¦ Z,£ ¦ 0** and the other has one re-write rule of the form **£→a corpus of raw data**. The first grammar is very compact but it can only encode (alphabetic) data in its original form and it cannot therefore compress the data at all. The second grammar is not at all compact but it can encode the given corpus using just one bit of information. A realistic grammar is some kind of compromise between the two extremes.

A priori we do not know what balance is optimal for a given individual. However, it seems clear that, for any given **Sg**, the **CC** should be maximised. Learning may be seen as a process of taking in information, organising it and discarding much of it so that only the most useful material is left. In this way a body of generally useful knowledge is gradually built up.

The decision to concentrate on the storage cost of information and its usefulness has been made mainly as a means of exploring optimisation ideas in a simplified domain before attempting to generalize them. But the other factors mentioned above may in fact be relatively unimportant in optimisation.

If one assumes that information is retrieved by some kind of serial process then there is likely to be a strong link between the speed with which information can be retrieved and the size of a body of knowledge. Likewise, retrieval times can be strongly influenced by the way in which information is stored. However, if one assumes that retrieval of information from the brain is done by multiple processes working in parallel (and it is hard to avoid the conclusion that this is at least partly true) then the link between retrieval times and the size of a knowledge structure may disappear. The link between retrieval times and the way in which information is stored may, likewise, be much reduced, perhaps to vanishing point.

The standard engineering technique for increasing the reliability of some operation is to multiply the structures which can fail. It is conceivable that all of one's mental knowledge is replicated many times throughout the brain in the same kind of way that there are billions of copies of the genetic code distributed throughout our bodies. There is no conflict between this idea of multiple copy memory and the idea that each copy should be compact. Indeed, if a knowledge structure is going to be multiplied then there is likely to be more of a premium on finding a compact representation of the material which is to be copied. A working assumption in this research programme is that the need to find the best CC for a given Sg is largely independent of any mechanism for introducing error-reducing redundancy into memory and that the latter factor may be ignored.

1.3 Six Principles of Data Compression

The processes of organising a long-term knowledge structure to achieve the best CC for any given Sg seem to be governed by a limited range of data compression principles: just six seem to be sufficient to handle the learning of a wide range of features of linguistic and other knowledge. All of these principles have been used from time to time in psychology, linguistics, computer science and AI. Identifying them explicitly and abstracting them from the several guises in which they appear may help us to develop a general theory of learning and knowledge representation.

All six principles will be briefly described in this section although only the first five had been explored up to the beginning of the project. As it turns out the project has been largely an investigation of how the sixth principle may be applied to the learning of realistic syntactic and semantic structures.

[1] The Formation of Conjunctive (AND) Groupings
A body of information like:

$$ABCDPQRABCDABCDPQRABCDPQRPQRABCD$$

may be reduced to **xyxxyxyyx** and the two rules **x** → **ABCD** and **y** → **PQR**. This is chunking.

[2] The Formation of Disjunctive (Exclusive OR) Groupings
A grammar like

$$1 \rightarrow \text{ABCDPQRSEFGH} \qquad (1)$$
$$2 \rightarrow \text{ABCDLMNOEFGH}$$

may be changed to

$$1 \rightarrow \text{ABCD3EFGH} \qquad (2)$$
$$3 \rightarrow 4 | 5$$
$$4 \rightarrow \text{PQRS}$$
$$5 \rightarrow \text{LMNO}$$

(where "|" stands for exclusive OR).
Although new structures have been created and new symbols introduced, there is an overall saving of space because ABCD and EFGH are each stored only once.

[3] Searching for the best Groupings
In general there are many alternative AND groupings one might choose. The ones giving the most compression are those having the largest product of *frequency* and *size*. Similar principles apply to the choice of OR groupings.

For reasons discussed in W82, frequency should take precedence over size in a search for optimal groupings.

[4] Recursion and Iteration
A pattern which repeats itself in a regular way (e.g., **ABCABCABC**...) may be reduced to an iterative rule or a recursive rule (e.g., $x \rightarrow$ **ABC, x**) or a group of rules with that effect.

[5] Generalization
A body of data may be compressed by discarding information (or not recording it in the first place). There is a close connection between this compression mode and the phenomena of syntactic and semantic generalization (see W82). The discarding of information and selective recording of information also figure in the choice of AND and OR groupings.

[6] Schema plus Correction
Where two or more patterns are similar but not identical they may be collapsed into a single pattern or schema as we saw under 2. If we want to specify one of the patterns subsumed under the schema whilst taking advantage of the compressed representation we may simply identify the schema together with one or more "corrections". For example, the grammar in (2) may be used to specify ABCDPQR-SEFGH in a compact form as 1 (4). This schema-plus-correction idea has a long history in psychology; it has been widely used in the world of computing where a general purpose program, sub-routine or procedure is rendered more specific by the application of switches, parameters or arguments.

1.4 Computer Models

These six compression principles are the foundation of the learning theory as it stands now. It is important to understand how they can be incorporated in working models which can meet pre-established criteria of success. Two main models, MK10 and SNPR, were developed in work prior to this project and they will be described briefly as a necessary introduction to the developments which will be proposed later in the article.

1.4.1 Program MK10

This program is an embodiment of compression principles 1, 3 and 5. It was developed to explore how children might come to know the word structure and the phrase structure of language despite the apparent paucity and unreliability of cues from pause, stress or semantics. The extent to which children do in fact use any of these cues is an open question but it is useful to know whether and how they may learn the segmental structure of language without them. The model performs well at identifying word structure in unsegmented text (Wolff, 1975, 1977) and also at identifying phrase-structure groupings in semantics-free unsegmented text (Wolff, 1980b). And it exhibits other properties which correspond quite well with features of children's language development. (These are described in detail in an "overview" article in preparation).

In outline, the program works like this:-

1. Parse a sample of text using the dictionary of segments as it has been built so far. Initially this dictionary contains only the character set used in the text. (The data structure built by this program is made of modules or *elements* comprising the original character set together with the AND groupings built by the program. The term *element* will also be used to cover OR groupings built by SNPR).

The parsing routine is designed to find the AND element which will match the longest portion of text starting at any given point. This is a strategy which leads to occasional "garden-path" errors; it is an approximate solution to the problem of finding the most economical encoding of the text for a given dictionary (see Olivier, 1968). It is itself a compromise between the need to minimise the computational cost of parsing and the need to avoid errors in parsing.

2. During the parsing, keep a record of the number of each distinct pair of contiguous elements. For example, a text **ABCAB** would have these counts: **AB (2), BC (1), CA (1)**.

3. At the end of the sample, take the most frequent pair and add it to the dictionary as a new AND element. Discard all other information about frequencies.

4. Repeat 1 to 3 as often as is necessary. The point at which this process should be stopped depends on criteria of optimisation which need not be discussed at this point.

Cognitive Development as Optimisation

The effect of the program is to seek out a set of elements in which the total product of size and frequency for all elements ($\sum_{i=1}^{i=s} f_i \, l_i$; where **f** is the frequency of element **i**, **l** is its length (in symbols) and **s** is the size of the set of elements) is at or near a maximum. For any given value of **s** (and also, depending on how the elements are stored, for any given value of **Sg**) the compression capacity (**CC**) of the set is also maximised.

One feature of this program (and SNPR) which deserves special attention is the way the combinatorial explosion is handled. For most values of **s** there is a huge number of possible dictionaries. The number of alternative groupings that have to be considered at any one time is constrained by the fact that only pairs of neighbouring elements are recorded. This restriction does not prevent the program from building arbitrarily large elements by successive pairings. The number of possible pairs which have to be recorded at any one time is never more than **n-1** (where **n** is the number of characters in the sample) and is often much less than this. There is never any risk of being swamped by the number of possible groupings. The technique can be characterised as a hill-climbing search of the space of possible dictionaries.

1.4.2 Program SNPR

Program SNPR is like MK10 in the way it searches for AND groupings. But it combines this search with a search for OR groupings in such a way that arbitrarily complex structures may be built up containing both kinds of element. Although complex patterns of AND and OR relations may be represented in these structures, *the constituents of any given element are related in only one of these two ways.* Keeping the two kinds of relation in separate modules seems to facilitate processes of building, modifying and using the knowledge structures.

The AND and OR elements formed by the program function as context-free phrase-structure rules. The program can form recursive rules as a by-product of these search processes. It generalizes its rules and corrects overgeneralizations without any external error correction or provision of negative instances. Here is an outline of the program:

1. Parse an unsegmented sample of text using the current grammar. As in MK10, the initial grammar is only the character set used in the text. The parsing routine is a little more complex than that in MK10 because it has to deal with OR elements as well as AND elements. But it retains the principle of seeking the element which matches the largest amount of text starting at any point and it will, as a consequence, make occasional garden-path errors in parsing. These are not normally enough to disturb the process of grammar abstraction.

2. During the parsing, keep a record of the frequencies of pairs of contiguous elements and the frequencies of individual elements.

3. Also during the parsing, keep a record of how the constituents of OR elements are used. The aim is to identify those constituents of OR elements which are *not* used *in particular contexts* (see 4 (a) below).

4. At the end of the data-gathering phase there is a process of editing and refining the grammar like this:

(a) "Rebuilding". AND elements which contain OR elements as constituents may be "rebuilt". The records kept during parsing may show, for example, that element **R** was never used in the context of the structure **AxB** (where $x \rightarrow P \mid Q \mid R$). In that case it is remade as **AyB** (where $y \rightarrow P \mid Q$). Element x may be retained in the grammar if all its constituents are used in at least one other context. This process of removing elements from contexts where they are not used is the way that overgeneralizations are corrected.

An important feature of this mechanism, *apparently unique amongst formal models of learning,* is that it removes some generalizations and leaves others intact without any kind of external error correction or provision of negative samples. (An example will be given shortly). It is a possible explanation of how "correct" generalizations may be distinguished from "incorrect" generalizations given positive samples only, despite the fact that both kinds of generalization, by definition, have zero frequency in the corpus from which the grammar is abstracted. There is support for this idea both in terms of how it can contribute to optimisation and from the performance of SNPR (see W82).

Despite superficial similarities, the rebuilding mechanism in SNPR is *not* equivalent to the "discrimination" mechanism employed by Langley (1982) (personal communication). The latter mechanism, if given free reign, will eliminate generalizations of all kinds in a way that the rebuilding mechanism will not.

(b) Any elements in the grammar that have not been identified at all during parsing are removed from the grammar.

In (a), elements are removed from a context if their frequency in that context is zero and in (b) they are removed from the grammar if their absolute frequency is zero. This mode of removing elements is obviously too sensitive to the quirks of particular samples. It is an approximation to a more realistic mode of operation in which the absolute and contextual "accessibility" of elements would be governed by absolute and contextual frequencies monitored over a long period. The least accessible elements may be removed whenever storage space may be used more profitably for other things.

(c) A search is made within the grammar for opportunities to reduce the size of the grammar by the formation of OR elements (compression principle 2). Where alternative groupings are possible then the ones giving the most compression are chosen.

(d) Whenever a new OR element is formed in (c) it is substituted for all instances of each of its constituents occurring as constituents of AND elements throughout the grammar. For example, an OR element like **the | one** would replace instances of **the** and **one** in structures like **the man, one day** etc. The program generalizes by saying, in effect, "If **the** is valid in this context then **one** is also valid in the same context; and *vice versa.*"

In many cases these generalizations are wrong and they are then corrected by rebuilding on the next cycle. When the generalizations are correct, as they often are, then there is a gain in terms of optimisation: the **CC** of the grammar will be increased without any cost in increased **Sg**.

Recursive rules can be formed by this generalization process. For example, an OR element **x → y∣z∣0**, (where **y → very** and **z → very, very**) may be derived from structures like **D, A, N, D, very, A, N** and **D, very, very, A, N** with the consequent formation of a composite AND element **D, x, A, N**. **x** replaces **very** in the structure **D, very, A, N** and *also* in **z**, giving **z → x, x**. The recursive properties of the word **very** are now correctly described by the rules **x → y∣z∣0, z → x, x** and **y → very**.

(e) As in MK10, the most frequently occurring pair of neighbouring elements is formed into a new element which is added to the grammar. The frequency data for all other pairs are discarded.

5. Repeat stages 1, 2, 3 and 4 as often as necessary to achieve a knowledge structure which is optimally efficient or nearly so.

Because of the existence of OR groupings in the grammar, the concatenation of elements in 4 (e) can lead to generalizations additional to those formed in 4 (d). For example, **Ay** (where **y → P∣Q**) and **Bz** (where **z → R∣S**) may be joined to form **AyBz** even though the text contains only instances of the strings **APBR, AQBR** and **APBS**; the string **AQBS** would then in effect be predicted as being an acceptable "utterance" in the language.

This is an example of one of those generalizations which the rebuilding mechanism would not remove from the grammar. Because Q has appeared in AQBR and has thus been called from the context of AyBz, it would not be removed by rebuilding and AQBS would remain as a permanent part of the grammar's generative range whether or not it occurs in future language samples.

Program SNPR performs quite well at abstracting plausibly "correct" context-free phrase-structure grammars (PSGs) from unsegmented samples of language-like text created from simple PSGs.

$$\begin{aligned}
&1 \to 2 \mid 3 \\
&2 \to 4, 5, 6 \\
&3 \to 7, 8, 9 \\
&4 \to \text{DAVID} \mid \text{JOHN} \\
&5 \to \text{LOVES} \mid \text{HATED} \\
&6 \to \text{MARY} \mid \text{SUSAN} \\
&7 \to \text{WE} \mid \text{YOU} \\
&8 \to \text{WALK} \mid \text{RUN} \\
&9 \to \text{FAST} \mid \text{SLOWLY}
\end{aligned} \tag{3}$$

Sample: DAVIDLOVESMARYJOHNHATEDMARYYOURUNSLOWLY...

(3) is an example of a grammar which has been successfully retrieved from unsegmented text like the sample shown. The grammar is simple but the processing required to find the "correct" conjunctive and disjunctive groupings is quite complex.

The sample text supplied to SNPR as data was constructed from the grammar but all instances of two sentences (JOHNLOVESMARY and WEWALKFAST) were omitted. In this situation, when the program's data contains less than the complete range of sentences which the original grammar can generate, the program does a good job of predicting the missing sentences and correcting all overgeneralizations. There is some validation here of the mechanism for correcting overgeneralizations and, in particular, for the way it can distinguish putatively correct generalizations from others despite all of them having zero frequency in the sample corpus. Whether a grammar which is "correct" in terms of optimisation is also correct in terms of human psychology presents a number of difficult methodological problems if it is to be answered rigorously; only informal evidence on this question has been obtained so far.

SNPR handles the potential risk of a combinatorial explosion in the same way as MK10. At any one time it only considers pairs of *contiguous* structures - there is an echo here of the principle of contiguity in associationist psychology. This restriction prevents any undue expansion in the number of possible structures needing to be evaluated at any time but it still allows arbitrarily large and complex structures to be assembled. Discontinuous dependencies, like those between "put" and "on" in "Put the kettle on" or between "if" and "then" in their familiar uses, can be discovered through this stepwise discovery process.

2. Extending the Theory to the Learning of more Realistic Knowledge Structures

The overall aim in developing the SNPR model was to explore the kinds of process which would enable a child to learn a natural language. Simple language-like texts generated by PSGs were used as a test-bed for the model because they exhibit a number of features of natural language without its full complexity. They may also be seen as analogues of the non-linguistic world and the model may be viewed as a learning process for structures in that domain. Looking at the performance of SNPR from both perspectives it does apparently have some useful things to say about quite a wide range of phenomena in learning and in people's use of mature knowledge. Many of these have been considered in W82 (and in the "overview" article mentioned earlier). They will be summarised later in the article together with some other phenomena which the theory can now address.

The chief shortcoming of SNPR and its associated theory is that it is geared to unaugmented PSGs; it is well known that these are not sufficient to handle realistic structures in an efficient way. What is needed is a representational system which can express realistic structures efficiently and which marries with the learning principles as they have developed so far. For reasons given earlier, it would be nice if one representational system would serve for both syntax and semantics and if it would marry with theories of language comprehension and production, allowing knowledge used in comprehension to serve also in language production.

There is a large number of formalisms which may be considered, each developed for particular purposes and each having particular strengths and weaknesses: transformational grammar, case grammar, stratificational grammar, augmented transition networks, generalized phrase structure grammars, systemic grammars, functional, dependency and categorial grammars, KRL, FRL, production systems, conceptual dependency theory, semantic networks, predicate calculus and others. No attempt will be made here to review these systems exhaustively. Comments will be made on some of them before discussing the system which is apparently most favourable to the goals which have been set in this research programme.

Strong claims have been made for transformational grammar and its relevance to language acquisition. It is associated, of course, with Chomsky's view that children are born with relatively elaborate knowledge structures which are differentiated or "triggered" by environmental influences. The implications of this view have been explored most notably by Wexler & Culicover (1980).

From the present perspective, the main drawback of TG is that it is hard to see how it could be incorporated in an empiricist theory of learning in which minimal innate knowledge is postulated. Also, it does not apparently lend itself well to incorporation in a theory of language comprehension and it seems to require distinct formalisms for syntax and semantics.

The concept of a Generalized Phrase Structure Grammar (GPSG; Gazdar, 1980) has been developed chiefly to handle representational problems and no claims have been made for its relevance to language acquisition. However, given the ideas already developed about how PSGs may be learned and given the way that PSGs lend themselves to interpretation and production processes, it is natural to ask whether a GPSG would be a suitable formalism for incorporation in an extended version of the current theory.

The main problem with GPSGs from the point of view of learning seems to be the postulation of "meta-rules". These are distinct from, but similar in many ways to transformational rules and they seem to complicate learning in a similar way. Another drawback of GPSGs is that they postulate distinct formalisms for syntax and semantics – although these two formalisms do have quite a lot in common.

Production systems have been and continue to be popular in models of learning. Typically these are collections of rules of the form: "IF condition1, condition2, ... THEN action1, action2, ...". A rule for recognising the written word **table** might, for example, be the formalised equivalent of "If you see T followed by A followed by B followed by L followed by E then register an occurrence of the word **table**". A rule for creating the word might be: "If you want to create an instance of **table** then write T followed by A followed by B followed by L followed by E." The chief merit of production system, which PSGs share, is that the process of building and modifying knowledge structures is facilitated by having knowledge parcelled into discrete modules.

If-then rules are, in effect, AND groupings in which some constituents are classified as conditions and others as actions. This distinction seems to be the main drawback of such rules. If it is strictly observed it can lead to redundancies in the system. Information required in one place may have to be duplicated in another as was the case with the pattern T, A, B, L, E in our two example rules given above. It seems preferable to record this grouping once, giving it some kind of label or code as one might do in a PSG, and allow it to be used in interpretation or production or other processes as required. Another advantage of registering AND groupings independently of whether the constituents are going to function as conditions or as actions will be seen later when "partial matching" is discussed.

In practice, production systems can be used very much like PSGs. It is perhaps no accident that the several formalisms mentioned above are often not as distinct, one from another, as their distinct names might suggest. If problems of knowledge representation are chiefly problems of efficiency and data compression as the present thesis suggests then it should not be surprising to find one set of devices appearing in a variety of guises in the several representational systems.

We have seen how an unaugmented PSG allows the expression of compression principles 1, 2, 3, 4 and 5. The theme of the next section is that augmentation of a PSG with the sixth compression principle described earlier is apparently sufficient to allow the efficient representation of most kinds of syntactic and semantic knowledge in a psychologically plausible way. We shall consider one formalism which embraces the six compression principles and how it may be used to represent various kinds of knowledge. Then we shall examine how the previously developed learning principles may operate to build up the kinds of knowledge structures which have been presented.

2.1 Definite Clause Grammars

Definite Clause Grammars (DCGs) are grammars based on the programming language Prolog, which is itself based on predicate calculus. For most of the questions we shall be considering, the three formalisms may be treated as one and termed DCG or Prolog.

The DCG/Prolog formalism or something like it seems to meet our needs quite well. Pereira & Warren (1980) have shown with examples how the one formalism may be used for the efficient representation of syntactic knowledge and semantic knowledge and how the two kinds of knowledge may be integrated. A knowledge structure of this kind can be used to parse a sentence (create a labelled bracketing of its surface structure) and at the same time it can create a representation of sentence meaning. Given a meaning representation, the same knowledge structure may be used to create one or more corresponding sentences (and a labelled bracketing of its surface structure). Chart parsing methods and other refinements may well prove to be useful adjuncts to the basic formalism.

In terms of the principles which were outlined earlier, a DCG may be regarded as a PSG which has been augmented with *arguments*. The PSG is a more-or-less complex *schema* embodying some or all of compression principles 1, 2, 3, 4 and 5. Arguments are the mechanism for realising the sixth principle. They are the means by which the general patterns in the schema may be "corrected" or rendered more specific. As indicated earlier, they can promote data compression by allowing two or more similar patterns to be collapsed into one without the identity of the specific patterns being lost.

The processes of language comprehension and production may themselves be seen as processes of constraining a schema: finding a specific pattern amongst the

Cognitive Development as Optimisation

many alternatives covered by the schema. Arguments may be used to feed constraining information into the schema (the surface form in the case of comprehension or some kind of semantic structure in the case of language production). Arguments are also used as the vehicle by which the results of constraint are output or "returned". All arguments can be used in either way. Readers familiar with the system may skip the next few pages which give an informal outline of how DCGs are organised.

Consider a very simple grammar written in the Prolog formalism which can be used to produce a labelled bracketing of surface structure.

    1 sentence(Number, s(NP, VP)):-   (4)
       noun-phrase(Number, NP), verb-phrase(Number, VP).
    2 noun-phrase(singular, np(it)).
    3 noun-phrase(plural, np(they)).
    4 verb-phrase(singular, vp(runs)).
    5 verb-phrase(plural, vp(run)).

This example illustrates several points about the formalism.

The grammar is composed of five rules *(clauses)* which are themselves composed of basic building blocks or *terms*. These are of three types:

1. Constants (e.g., **noun-phrase** and **it**) distinguished in this notation with lower-case initial letters.

2. Variables (e.g., **NP** and **VP**) shown with an upper-case initial letter (an initial underline character may be used instead of an initial capital letter or, if the variable requires no name, an underline character by itself will do). These variables are, in effect, boxes or slots into which constants or structures may be put. Within any one clause, and only within one clause, repeated instances of any variable name refer to one single box or slot. This means that if the variable is given a value in any part of the clause then that value applies throughout the clause, as we shall see.

3. Structures (e.g.,**s(NP, VP)** and **noun-phrase(singular, np(it))**). These have the format: **functor(component,...)** where the *functor* is always a constant and each *component* may be any term: constant, variable or structure. Predicates are named by the functors and arguments are represented by the components.

The first rule in (4) is composed of a *head* (to the left of the ":-" symbol) and a *body* (everything to the right of :-). The other rules are clauses, each composed of a head without a body. These latter rules may be read as "facts", e.g., **noun-phrase (singular, np(it))** means "One form for a singular noun-phrase is the structure np(it)". One or more clauses which share the same principal functor (e.g., **noun-phrase** or **verb-phrase**) and which have the same number of components is called a *procedure*.

The first rule in (4) can be read as a declarative statement: "A sentence is composed of a noun-phrase followed by a verb-phrase". It may also be read procedurally: "If you want to construct a sentence, make a noun-phrase using the instructions in the relevant part of the grammar and then make a verb-phrase using appropriate instructions". In the DCG/Prolog formalism there is usually no distinction between declarative and procedural knowledge. Data and program may be expressed in the same format.

At the heart of the method for using a DCG in interpretation or production are the Prolog mechanisms of *pattern matching* and *unification*. Two structures match if their functors match and if all their components, taken in order, also match. A symbol for a constant matches only with another identical symbol. A variable matches with any term: constant, variable or structure; if it is matched with a constant or a structure it takes that term as its value and is said to be *instantiated* to that term. If a variable is matched to a variable it remains a variable. When two structures have been successfully matched (and any consequent instantiations have been made) then they are said to be *unified*.

The first step in using our simple grammar to produce a labelled bracketing is to choose a constant (**singular** or **plural**) as the value of the first argument in the first clause and (by matching) to assign this value to the variable. When the **Number** argument has been instantiated in this way it will behave as a (**singular** or **plural**) constant. If, for example **Number** has been instantiated as **singular** then the noun-phrase structure has the form: **noun-phrase(singular, NP)**. This matches with the first noun-phrase clause (**noun-phrase(singular, np(it))**), and the variable **NP** becomes instantiated to **np(it)**. Since all instances of the **NP** symbol in the first clause of the grammar refer to a single entity, the structure **s(NP, VP)** now has the form **s(np (it), VP)**.

The next and last step is to find a match for the verb-phrase structure in a similar way. The **Number** variable already has the value **singular** so a match has to be found to the structure **verb-phrase(singular, VP)**. The result of matching in this case is that **verb-phrase(singular, VP)** becomes unified with **verb-phrase(singular, vp(runs))**, **VP** is instantiated to the structure **vp(runs)** and **s(np(it), VP)** becomes **s(np(it), vp(runs))**; this is a labelled bracketing as was required.

Like any grammar, this one represents a set of alternative structures. Prolog is designed to facilitate a search amongst these alternatives and to construct them in a systematic order if required. If the "number" arguments in (4) were omitted from the grammar then there are four alternative structures which may be found: two grammatical ones – **s(np(it), vp(runs))** and **s(np(they), vp(run))** – and two ungrammatical ones – **s(np(it), vp(run))** and **s(np(they), vp(runs))**. With the "number" arguments in place, the set of alternative structures which may be found is reduced to two (a singular sentence structure and a plural one). This is how arguments serve to "correct" or "constrain" a general pattern or schema. The second argument in the first rule of (4) (**s(NP, VP)**) is the vehicle for returning the structure or structures produced by the grammar. In general, arguments may be used to feed in constraint or to output one of the structures implicit in the grammar. Any argument may be used in either way, as we shall see.

We may now proceed to consider some refinements. Our small grammar is modified in (5) so that it can analyse a surface string of symbols or output such a string (in addition to the labelled bracketing).

   1 sentence(Number, s(NP, VP), SO, S) :-   (5)
      noun-phrase(Number, NP, SO, S1), verb-phrase(Number, VP, S1, S).
   2 noun-phrase(singular, np(it), [it | S], S).

3 noun-phrase(plural, np(they), [they | S], S).
4 verb-phrase(singular, vp(runs), [runs | S], S).
5 verb-phrase(plural, vp(run), [run | S], S).

Two extra arguments have been added to several structures in the grammar. Each of these extra arguments is either a *list* or a variable which may be instantiated as a list. A DCG/Prolog list (shown by the use of square brackets) is the same concept as a list in Lisp. Although it appears to depart from the regular Prolog formalism it is actually a short-hand notation for structures made out of functors and components like other structures in Prolog.

The details of how these two extra arguments are used to handle surface strings of morphemes need not concern us. The reader may refer to Pereira & Warren's paper or Clocksin & Mellish (1981, Ch.9). The two arguments are often disguised by another notational shorthand as seen in (6).

1 sentence(Number, s(NP, VP)) → (6)
   noun-phrase(Number, NP),verb-phrase(Number, VP).
2 noun-phrase(singular, np(it)) → [it].
3 noun-phrase(plural, np(they)) → [they].
4 verb-phrase(singular, vp(runs)) → [runs].
5 verb-phrase(plural, vp(run)) → [run].

The Prolog system translates a grammar in the form shown in (6) into a grammar with the format shown in (5). The user need not bother about the two extra arguments except when a surface string of symbols is to be fed in for analysis or returned as a result of computation. If the right-hand side of any rule contains structures which should not have the two extra arguments then these must be enclosed in curly brackets ({and}).

With this brief introduction to DCGs and Prolog we are in a position to see some of the power of the system for expressing syntactic and other kinds of knowledge. This expressive power derives from our six compression principles. AND groupings or elements are represented in the bodies of clauses; the first clause in (4), for example, expresses the AND relation between an initial noun-phrase and a following verb-phrase. OR groupings are represented as procedures containing two or more clauses with the same principal functor and the same number of arguments. Our third compression principle (the use of size and frequency heuristics) may be applied to find optimal groupings as previously discussed. Recursion and generalization can be expressed in the same way as in a PSG. Arguments are the means by which specific patterns can be retrieved from generalized schemata.

1 sentence → noun-phrase, verb-phrase. (7)
2 noun-phrase → determiner, noun.
3 verb-phrase → verb, adjective.
4 verb-phrase → verb, preposition, noun-phrase.
5 preposition → [sur]. ("on")
6 preposition → [sous]. ("under")
7 verb → [est]. ("is")
8 verb → [sont]. ("are")

```
 9 determiner → [la]. ("the")
10 determiner → [le]. ("the")
11 determiner → [les]. ("the")
12 noun → noun-sing, suffix1.
13 noun-sing → [plume]. ("pen")
14 noun-sing → [papier]. ("paper")
15 suffix1 → [].
16 suffix1 → [s].
17 adjective → adj-sing, suffix2.
18 adj-sing → [noir]. ("black")
19 adj-sing → [vert]. ("green")
20 suffix2 → [e].
21 suffix2 → [].
```

Let us see now how arguments can promote the economical representation of information (see also Clocksin & Mellish, 1981, Ch. 9). The grammar shown in (7) is written in Prolog but without any arguments other than the covert arguments needed to handle the surface string of morphemes. In this form it is essentially an unaugmented PSG. This grammar generates a variety of grammatical sentences but it also generates many ungrammatical sentences such as *La papiers est verte* and *Le plume sont sur la papiers* ("The papers is green" and "The pen are on the papers" – with gender errors too).

What is missing, of course, is any sensitivity to syntactic "agreements": number agreement between subject and verb, gender agreements amongst determiners, nouns and qualifying adjectives. It is possible to construct a PSG without arguments which will honour the agreements but at a cost: many redundancies have to be introduced and the grammar has to be a good deal larger than the one shown in (7). Rules for singular patterns have to be repeated with small changes for plural patterns and likewise for masculine and feminine patterns. A much more compact solution is to add arguments for number and gender agreement as in (8). (The symbols **sentence**, **noun-phrase** etc. have been abbreviated to **s**, **np** etc. and arguments to return labelled bracketings have been added). When the number and gender arguments (**Num** and **Gen**) are instantiated at the top level to **singular** or **plural**, **masculine** or **feminine**, then all agreements within structures generated by the grammar are correctly specified.

```
 1 s(Num, Gen, s(NP, VP)) → np(Num, Gen, NP), vp(Num, Gen, VP).        (8)
 2 np(Num, Gen, np(D, N)) → d(Num, Gen, D), n(Num, Gen, N).
 3 vp(Num, Gen, vp(V, A)) → v(Num, V), a(Num, Gen, A).
 4 vp(Num, Gen, vp(V, P, NP)) → v(Num, V), p(P), np(X, Y, NP).
 5 p(p(sur)) → [sur].
 6 p(p(sous)) → [sous].
 7 v(singular, v(est)) → [est].
 8 v(plural, v(sont)) → [sont].
 9 d(singular, feminine, d(la)) → [la].
10 d(singular, masculine, d(le)) → [le].
11 d(plural, _ , d(les)) → [les].
12 n(Num, Gen, n(Ns, Suf1)) → ns(Gen, Ns), suf1(Num, Suf1).
```

13 ns(feminine, ns(plume)) → [plume].
14 ns(masculine, ns(papier)) → [papier].
15 suf1(singular, suf1(0)) → [].
16 suf1(plural, suf1(s)) → [s].
17 a(Num, Gen, a(As, Suf2, Suf1)) →
    as(As), suf2(Gen, Suf2), suf1(Num, Suf1).
18 as(as(noir)) → [noir].
19 as(as(vert)) → [vert].
20 suf2(feminine, suf2(e)) → [e].
21 suf2(masculine, suf2(0)) → [].

The use of arguments does not, of course, guarantee an economical grammar and there are occasions (the grammar in (4), for example) where one could write an equivalent grammar more simply without them. For the majority of reasonably complex knowledge systems there is no doubt that the use of arguments allows a much more compact representation than is possible otherwise.

2.1.1 Other Examples

In this section some other examples will be given to show how DCGs may be used to represent syntactic knowledge and semantic knowledge and how the two kinds of knowledge may be integrated in a structure which can be used for language comprehension and language production. These examples are intended merely to illustrate techniques; they are not exhaustive or even particularly accurate representations of any area of knowledge.

2.1.1.1 Class-Inclusion Hierarchies and Part-Whole Hierarchies

$$\begin{aligned}&\text{1 animal(Sub1, Sub2)} \rightarrow\\&\quad\text{head(Sub1, Sub2), body(Sub1, Sub2), legs(Sub1, Sub2).}\end{aligned} \quad (9)$$

2 head(Sub1, Sub2) →
   eyes(Sub1, Sub2), nose(Sub1, Sub2),
   mouth(Sub1, Sub2), voice(Sub1, Sub2).
3 body(Sub1, Sub2) →
   surface(Sub1, Sub2), shape(Sub1, Sub2).
4 legs(Sub1, Sub2) →
   joints(Sub1, Sub2), claws(Sub1, Sub2).
5 cat(Sub) → animal(cat, Sub).
6 siamese-cat → cat(siamese).
7 eyes(_,_) → [green].
8 eyes(_,_) → [black].
9 eyes(_, siamese) → [blue].
10 nose(cat,_) → [whiskered].
11 nose(_,_) → [not-whiskered].
12 mouth(_,_) → [bovine].
13 mouth(_,_) → [feline].
14 voice(_,_) → [barking].

15 voice(cat,_) → [mewing].
16 surface(_,_) → [scaly].
17 surface(_,_) → [furry].
18 shape(_,_) → [oblong].
19 shape(_,_) → [squat].
20 joints(_,_) → [3].
21 joints(_,_) → [4].
22 claws(cat,_) → [retractile].
23 claws(_,_) → [non-retractile].

The schema-plus-correction idea may be applied to the representation of semantic/non-linguistic knowledge in much the same way it was used in (8) to represent syntax. The grammar in (9) shows a general schema for the parts and sub-parts of an animal mimicking the parts and sub-parts of a sentence. This schema is a crude intensional description of the class of animals (amoebae, round-worms and sundry low creatures excluded). The arguments at the top level (**Sub1** and **Sub2**) may be used to constrain the schema to become an intensional description of a sub-class. If **Sub1** is instantiated as **cat**, for example (see clause 5) then the animal schema is constrained to describe a creature with whiskered nose (we need not worry about great accuracy here), mewing voice and retractile claws. If **Sub** of **cat** is instantiated as **siamese** then the schema is constrained yet more by the specification of blue eyes. With the addition of more arguments this class-inclusion hierarchy may have multiple levels and may, in principle, extend down to the lowest level where individual cats ("Tibs", "Fluffy" etc.) are specified. Notice how economical our description of a cat or a siamese cat can be if we use a corrected schema - even allowing for the **cat** arguments distributed through the grammar.

Another way of representing the same part-whole hierarchy with the same classes and sub-classes is shown in (10). In this case the arguments are specified in terms of parts and sub-parts rather than classes and sub-classes but the overall effect is much the same.

1 animal(Eyes, Nose, Mouth, Voice, (10)
  Surface, Shape, Joints, Claws) →
  head(Eyes, Nose, Mouth, Voice),
  body(Surface, Shape),
  legs(Joints, Claws).
2 head(Eyes, Nose, Mouth, Voice) →
  eyes(Eyes), nose(Nose), mouth(Mouth), voice(Voice).
3 body(Surface, Shape) →
  surface(Surface), shape(Shape).
4 legs(Joints, Claws) →
  joints(Joints), claws(Claws).
5 cat(Eyes, Mouth, Surface, Shape, Joints) →
  animal(Eyes, whiskered, Mouth, mewing,
  Surface, Shape, Joints, retractile).
6 siamese-cat(Mouth, Surface, Shape, Joints) →
  cat(blue, Mouth, Surface, Shape, Joints).

7 eyes(green) → [green].
8 eyes(black) → [black].
9 eyes(blue) → [blue].
10 nose(whiskered) → [whiskered].
11 nose(not-whiskered) → [not-whiskered].
12 mouth(bovine) → [bovine].
13 mouth(feline) → [feline].
14 voice(barking) → [barking].
15 voice(mewing) → [mewing].
16 surface(scaly) → [scaly].
17 surface(furry) → [furry].
18 shape(oblong) → [oblong].
19 shape(squat) → [squat].
20 joints(3) → [3].
21 joints(4) → [4].
23 claws(non-retractile) → [non-retractile].
22 claws(retractile) → [retractile].

A word here about the psychological relevance of such knowledge structures. There is no guarantee of course that everyone or even anyone organises their knowledge of animals in these kinds of way. But, given the strong intuitive feel which most people have for part-whole hierarchies and class-inclusion hierarchies, it seems likely that structures something like these are fairly widespread. There is relevant laboratory evidence which we will touch on later.

One infelicity in (10) is the rather cumbersome listing of arguments at every level for all choice points at lower levels. Arguments can also proliferate in a system like (9) when, for example, the number of levels in the class-inclusion hierarchy is increased. Some streamlining may be achieved with a system in which arguments can be omitted whenever a default value will do or when the value of the argument can be left unspecified. One possible way of improving (9), for example, is to replace arguments like **Eyes**, **Nose**, **Mouth** etc. with a single argument at each level which may be instantiated as a *list* of arguments like

[nose(whiskered), voice(mewing), claws(retractile)].

This list is passed from clause to clause in the part-whole hierarchy and, at each level, all components of the list are matched with a structure within the given clause which is distinctive for that clause (e.g., **nose(whiskered)**). When a match succeeds this has the effect of selecting the given clause from amongst the alternatives in the same procedure. Thus arguments need be specified only when they are needed. A system like (10) may be improved in a similar way. Prolog does not lend itself very well to this mode of operation and there may be a case for some redesign of the language. It really needs a mechanism (like "objects" and "classes" in the Simula and Smalltalk computer languages) which is designed to handle class-inclusion hierarchies and inheritance of attributes in a streamlined way.

2.1.1.2 Relational Concepts
The distinction between relational and non-relational concepts is reasonably natu-

ral if not very clear cut. Predicate calculus is very suitable for representing the kinds of concepts normally regarded as being relational and has been popular for some time for that purpose. (11) is an example (adapted from Clocksin & Mellish, 1981) showing how the concept of a "sister" may be represented in Prolog.

 1 sister(X, Y) :- female(X), parents(X, M, F), parents(Y, M, F).   (11)
 2 female(X) :- voice-pitch(X, Y), high(Y), has-womb(X).
 3 parents(X, M, F) :- born-of(X, M), fathered-by(X, F).

The relationship "ancestor" may be represented in a grammar containing a recursive rule:

 1 ancestor(X, Y) :- parent(X, Y).   (12)
 2 ancestor(X, Z) :- parent(X, Y), ancestor(X, Y).
 3 parent(X, Y) :- born-of(X, Y), female(Y).
 4 parent(X, Y) :- fathered-by(X, Y), male(Y).

The relational concept "on" might be represented something like this:

 1 on(X, Y) :- above(X, Y), touches(X, Y).   (13)
 2 above(X, Y) :- height(X, H1), height(Y, H2), greater-than(H1, H2).
 3 touches(X, Y) :- boundary(X, B1), boundary(Y, B2), meet(B1, B2).

These examples are more-or-less crude definitions of the sample concepts and may be considerably refined. The formalism gives unlimited scope for specifying relational (and other) concepts in as subtle and detailed form as desired.

2.1.1.3 English Auxiliary Verbs

The next example (14) is a grammar for the major features of English auxiliary verbs. What has to be captured in any grammar for this part of English syntax is the interesting pattern of interlocking constraints. All the auxiliary verbs and the main verb are optional but constraints operating between them are not. If a modal verb (**will, would** etc.) is used then whatever verb follows it must have a "bare infinitive" form (**to go, to have** etc. with **to** omitted); if the "have" auxiliary is chosen (**have, has, had** etc.) then the next verb, whatever it is, must have the "en" form (**been, seen** etc. plus irregular forms like **hit, had, said** and so on). Likewise, the first "be" option (forms of the verb **be**) requires an "ing" verb to follow and the second "be" option requires "en" verbs to follow.

These constraints are discontinuous in the sense that they must be able to operate across intervening adverbs or **not**; or across an intervening noun phrase in the case of question forms (e.g., "Will it have been washed"). Constraint may also be seen in most of the cases where a "have" or "be" verb selects a following "en" verb: if the latter is constructed in a regular way from a stem and an **-en** or **-ed** suffix (e.g., **washed**) then constraint may be seen as operating across the stem (e.g., between **been** and **-ed** in ...**been washed**). Likewise for "be" and **-ing**.

Chomsky's "affix hopping" solution (1957), which at the time was a persuasive example of the need for transformational rules, specified these constraints with groupings like **(have + en)**, **(be + ing)** and **(be + en)**. A transformational rule was used to change the order of morphemes so that a correct surface structure sequence could be achieved.

More recently, Gazdar, Pullum & Sag (1980) have discussed how the patterns of constraint amongst English auxiliary verbs may be described without using transformations. The grammar in (14) follows their analysis in the use of a recursive rule (vx). However, it differs from their proposals because it makes no use of "meta rules" and some other devices that they propose. It seems that meta rules are unnecessary in the sense that equally perspicuous and parsimonious grammars can be written using only the devices in Prolog. As already noted, such rules seem not to fit easily into a learning theory.

1 s(Num, s(Np, V)) → np(Num, Np), vx(Num, m, fin, V).   (14)
2 s(Num, s(V1, Np, V)) →
   vl(Num, m, fin, X1, Y1, V1), np(Num, Np), vx(Num, X1, Y1, V).
3 np(singular, np(it)) → [it].
4 np(plural, np(they)) → [they].
8 vx(Num, X, Y, vx(V1, V)) →
   {not(Y=stop)}, v1(Num, X, Y, X1, Y1, V1), vx(Num, X1, Y1, V).
9 vx(_, _, _, _, [], []).
10 v1(Num, m, Y, X1, Y1, v1(0)) → {X1=h, Y1=Y},[].
11 v1(Num, m, Y, X1, Y1, v1(M)) → m(Num,_, M),{X1=h, Y1=inf}.
12 v1(Num, h, Y, X1, Y1, v1(0)) → {X1=b1, Y1=Y},[].
13 v1(Num, h, Y, X1, Y1, v1(H)) → h(Num, Y, H),{X1=b1, Y1=en}.
14 v1(Num, b1, Y, X1, Y1, v1(0)) → {X1=b2, Y1=Y},[].
15 v1(Num, b1, Y, X1, Y1, v1(B1)) → b(Num, Y, B1),{X1=b2, Y1=ing}.
16 v1(Num, b2, Y, X1, Y1, v1(0)) → {X1=vy, Y1=Y},[].
17 v1(Num, b2, Y, X1, Y1, v1(B2)) → b(Num, Y, B2),{X1=vy, Y1=en}.
18 v1(Num, vy, Y, _, Y1, v1(0)) → {Y1=stop}, [].
19 v1(Num, vy, Y, _, Y1, v1(V)) → v(Num, Y, V), {Y1=stop}.
20 m(_, _, m(will)) → [will].
21 m(_, _, m(would)) → [would].
22 m(_, _, m(could)) → [could].
23 h(_, inf, h(have)) → [have].
24 h(plural, fin, h(have)) → [have].
25 h(singular, fin, h(has)) → [has].
26 h(_, en, h(had)) → [had].
27 h(_, fin, h(had)) → [had].
28 h(_, ing, h(ing(ingl(hav), ing))) → ing(ingl(hav), ing).
29 b(singular, fin, b(is)) → [is].
30 b(_, inf, b(be)) → [be].
31 b(singular, fin, b(was)) → [was].
32 b(_, en, b(B)) → {B=en(enl(be), en)}, en(B).
33 b(_, ing, b(B)) → {B=ing(ingl(be), ing)}, ing(B).
34 b(plural, fin, b(are)) → [are].
35 b(plural, fin, b(were)) → [were].
36 v(_, fin, v(wrote)) → [wrote].
37 v(_, ing, v(Ing)) → ing(Ing).
38 v(_, en, v(En, en)) → en(En).
39 v(_, en, v(H)) → h(_, en, H).

40 v(_, en, v(made)) → [made].
41 v(_, en, v(Ed)) → ed(Ed).
42 v(_, inf, v(B)) → b(_, inf, B).
43 v(_, inf, v(H)) → h(_, inf, H).
44 v(_, inf, v(write)) → [write].
45 v(_, inf, v(chew)) → [chew].
46 v(_, inf, v(walk)) → [walk].
47 v(_, inf, v(Edl)) → edl(Edl).
48 en(en(Enl, en)) → enl(Enl),[en].
49 enl(enl(brok)) → [brok].
50 enl(enl(tak)) → [tak].
51 enl(enl(be)) → [be].
52 ing(ing(Ingl, ing)) → ingl(Ingl),[ing].
53 ingl(ingl(chew)) → [chew].
54 ingl(ingl(walk)) → [walk].
55 ingl(ingl(hav)) → [hav].
56 ingl(ingl(be)) → [be].
57 ed(ed(Edl, ed)) → edl(edl),[ed].
58 edl(edl(lash)) → [lash].
59 edl(edl(clasp)) → [clasp].
60 edl(edl(wash)) → [wash].

To see how this grammar for auxiliary verbs works, consider how it may be used to create the labelled bracketing in (15) for our example sentence "Will it have been washed?" To create this question form we need to choose the second of the two sentence patterns at the top of the grammar (clause 2). The first constituent (**v1**) is realised as **m (will)** using clauses 11 and 20. Within the body of clause 11 there are two other operations besides the **m** procedure: **X1** is matched to **h** (with **X1 = h**) and **Y1** is matched to **inf** (using **Y1 = inf**). Matching in this case is simply a way of assigning **h** as the value of **X1** and **inf** as the value of **Y1**. These values are the means by which the choice of the modal "will" constrains later choices as we shall see.

```
1  s(vl(m(will))),                                            (15)
2    np(it),
3    vx(vl(h(have))),
4      vx(vl(0),
5        vx(vl(b(en(enl(be),
6                    en))),
7          vx(vl(v(ed(edl(wash),
8                      ed))),
9                      _)))))
```

After **v1** has been completed, control returns to **np** in clause 2. This is realised as **np(it)** and then control returns to **vx** in clause 2. Argument **Num** will by now have acquired the value **singular** from the singular noun phrase but it has no use in this example because it only applies to finite verbs (marked with **fin** in the grammar) and these have been by-passed.

X and Y in clause 8 inherit the values **h** and **inf** from X1 and Y1 in clause 2. **h** ensures that only the two **v1** clauses marked with **h** are used (clauses 12 and 13). **inf** ensures that only an infinitive version of the "h" verbs is chosen ("have").

As with "will", the choice of "have" constrains what comes next. In clause 12, X1 is given the value **b1** and Y1 is given the value **en**. When **vx** is entered again, **b1** constrains **v1** choices. Only the two **v1** clauses with **b1** markers can be used (14 and 15). The **en** value ensures that whatever comes next will have the "en" form.

It happens on this second cycle that the null option (clause 14) is chosen from the two **v1** clauses marked with **b1** (clauses 14 and 15). In this clause X1 is given the value **b2**: this ensures that the **b2** versions of **v1** are chosen on the next cycle through **vx**. Y1 is matched to Y and thus acquires the value contained in Y: in this case it is the constant **en** inherited from the previous cycle through **vx**. In this way the "en" constraint is made to "jump across" the null choice from **have** to whatever comes next in the auxiliary verb structure.

To complete this structure, two more cycles through **vx** are needed, one for the labelled bracketing for **been** and one to make a structure for **washed**. **vx** fails on the next cycle because Y has the value **stop**; no doubt there are more elegant ways of escaping from the recursive loop.

One final comment on this grammar concerns the way **been** has been encoded (see clause 32. Similar remarks apply to the way **being** is represented in clause 33). In clause 32 the internal structure of **been** as it may be constructed has been, so to speak, "frozen in" to the grammar as a labelled bracketing. There is no doubt that, in this case, it would be simpler to include **been** directly in the clause without attempting to construct it from its constituents in any way. But the technique is general and potentially very powerful: it is an example of the use of a corrected schema *within the grammar*. A corrected schema is a means of *representing* a structure without *constructing* it. As we saw with "cat" and "siamese cat", considerable savings in space are often possible.

It is perhaps worth noting that the same idea is exploited within the "works" of Prolog (the DEC-10 version) at a level not ordinarily accessible to the user. Structures are represented using two pointers, one pointing to a general framework (a "skeleton") and the other to a vector of values (a "frame") which specifies the corrections to the framework. This system not only allows structures to be represented economically but greatly facilitates the process of creating and modifying those representations (Warren, 1977).

2.1.1.4 Integration of Syntax and Semantics

The last example in this section (16) is an extension of the grammar in (8). It is intended to show how syntactic and semantic knowledge can be integrated in a Prolog grammar which can serve language comprehension and language production too. The example follows the style of Pereira & Warren's examples (1980) but with some features which would normally be avoided in Prolog; these features have been introduced for reasons connected with learning processes and will be discussed in the next section under that head.

1 s(Num, Gen, Rel, s(NP, VP)) →   (16)
   np(Num, Gen, X, NP), vp(Num, Gen, Rel, X, Y, VP).
2 np(Num, Gen, X, np(D, N)) → d(Num, Gen, X, Nx, D), n(Num, Gen, Nx, N).
3 vp(Num, Gen, Rel, X, Y, vp(V, A)) → v(Num, V), a(Num, Gen, Rel, X, A).
4 vp(Num, Gen, Rel, X, Y, vp(V, P, NP)) →
   v(Num, V), p(X, Y, Rel, P), np(Num1, Gen1, Y, NP).
5 p(X, Y, Rel, p(sur)) → {Rel = on(X, Y)}, [sur]. ("on")
6 p(X, Y, Rel, p(sous)) → {Rel = on(Y, X)}, [sous]. ("under")
7 v(singular, v(est)) → [est]. ("is")
8 v(plural, v(sont)) → [sont]. ("are")
9 d(Num, Gen, X, Nx, d(D)) →
   [D],{num(Num, Nrel, Nx), dkn(D, Num, Gen, X, Nrel)}.
10 num(singular, singular(Nx), Nx).
11 num(plural, plural(Nx), Nx).
12 dkn(D, Num, Gen, known(Nrel), Nrel) :- dkn1(D, Num, Gen).
13 dkn(D, Num, Gen, unknown(Nrel), Nrel) :- dkn2(D, Num, Gen).
14 dkn1(la, singular, feminine). ("the")
15 dkn1(le, singular, masculine). ("the")
16 dkn1(les, plural , _). ("the")
17 dkn2(une, singular, feminine). ("a/an")
18 dkn2(un, singular, masculine). ("a/an")
19 dkn2(des, plural , _). ("some")
20 n(Num, Gen, Nx, n(Ns, Suf1)) → ns(Gen, Nx, Ns), suf1(Num, Suf1).
21 ns(feminine, Nx, ns(plume)) → {Nx = pen}, [plume]. ("pen")
22 ns(masculine, Nx, ns(papier)) → {Nx = paper}, [papier]. ("paper")
23 suf1(singular, suf1(0)) → [].
24 suf1(plural, suf1(s)) → [s].
25 a(Num, Gen, Rel, X, a(As, Suf2, Suf1)) →
   as(Rel, X, As), suf2(Gen, Suf2), suf1(Num, Suf1).
26 as(Rel, X, as(noir)) → {Rel = black(X)}, [noir]. ("black")
27 as(Rel, X, as(vert)) → {Rel = green(X)}, [vert]. ("green")
28 suf2(feminine, suf2(e)) → [e].
29 suf2(masculine, suf2(0)) → [].

If this grammar is to be used in a production mode, the third argument in the first procedure (**Rel** in clause 1) must be instantiated to a semantic structure such as

on(unknown(plural(pen)), known(singular(paper))).

The fourth argument (**s(NP, VP)**) will then return a labelled bracketing of surface structure and the fifth argument (concealed behind the notational shorthand) will return a surface string of morphemes such as

[des, plume, s, sont, sur, le, papier]
("Some pens are on the paper").

If required, the system will, by backtracking, find an alternative surface string:

[le, papier, est, sous, des, plume, s]
("The paper is under some pens").

The grammar may also be used in reverse: if the fifth argument is specified as a list of morphemes acceptable to the grammar, like the string just given, then the third argument will return a corresponding semantic structure.

It would be tedious to spell out fully how this grammar works in interpretation or production modes. Careful tracing through the grammar keeping track of unifications and instantiations, preferably on a computer, should make its workings clear. The point to notice is that structures may be built piecemeal. For example, in the interpretation of a sentence like

[la, plume, est, sur, le, papier]
("The pen is on the paper"),

variable **Rel** in clause 1 may, after the word *sur*, acquire the value **on(X, Y)** (from clause 5) with **X** instantiated as **singular(pen)** but **Y** still unknown. The value of **Y** is filled in later (as **singular(paper)**) when the second noun phrase (**le papier**) has been analysed.

It is perhaps worth saying again that no strong claims are being made here for any of the grammars presented in this section, either in terms of optimisation or in terms of psychological reality or in terms of linguistic correctness. The aim is to show how reasonably plausible knowledge structures can be handled in this system in a reasonably perspicuous and parsimonious way. These examples will be considered in the discussion of learning processes which follows.

The principles we have been discussing seem to be very general, extending well beyond the examples which have been considered. The notions of "frame" and "script" which have been employed to handle relatively high-level knowledge about patterns of entities and events are essentially the same as what has here been called a schema. The object-attribute-value triples which are widely used in knowledge-based systems, including relational database systems, also exemplify the data compression principles we have been considering.

2.2 Semantic Issues

The DCG/Prolog version of predicate calculus seems to meet the basic requirement of any semantic theory: that it should be able to accommodate phenomena such as synonymy, ambiguity, entailment, inconsistency, analyticity, contradiction, presupposition and semantic anomaly. The supposed problem of how to handle the distinction between sense and reference seems also to have an answer. Only a sketch of the possibilities can be given here.

Taking the last question first, we may begin by distinguishing between a *referent* and a *concrete referent* (Ritchie, 1980). The latter term corresponds to some entity in the "real" world while the former applies to a symbolic entity (in a natural or artificial cognitive system) which may or may not have a corresponding concrete referent. If we confine our discussion to "referents" and ignore "concrete referents" we can sidestep such questions as whether an expression like "The present king of France" refers to anything or not.

A (natural language or DCG) expression which refers to something can be seen as a procedure which returns a constant (in the sense defined earlier), this being the referent of the expression. The sense of the expression may be defined as the expression itself (if it is already in DCG form) or the DCG expression underlying a surface string of words, or, perhaps, the computational steps invoked when the expression is used to find the referent. Hence, "the evening star" and "the morning star" will return the same symbol (e.g., "planet-venus") if the cognitive system knows, so-to-speak, that Venus can be seen at both those periods of the day. In this case the two expressions, with their two senses, will have the same referent. If the cognitive system is ignorant of the connection then they will have different referents.

Synonymy and ambiguity are easily represented in the formalism. It is only necessary in the first case to assign the same meaning to more than one surface pattern (cf. "Des plumes sont sur le papier" and "Le papier est sous des plumes"). Ambiguity is the reverse.

Whether or not any particular example really does exhibit synonymy or ambiguity may be controversial but there is no doubt that the formalism does allow one-to-many and many-to-one mappings between surface forms and meanings.

"I am an orphan" entails "I have no father" (this example and some others here from Leech, 1974). In Prolog this entailment would be captured within the definition of an orphan (if having a father means having a father who is alive):-

orphan(X):-parents(X, M, F), dead(M), dead(F).

In a similar way the inconsistency between "I am an orphan" and "I have a father" would be derivable from the definition of an orphan. Much the same may be said for the analytic nature of the statement "This orphan has no father", the inconsistency of "This orphan has a father" and the anomaly of "The orphan's father …".

"Is your father at home?" presupposes "You have a father". We may account for this connection if we suppose that the interpretation of the first sentence gives rise to a meaning representation which includes a meaning representation from which the second sentence can be derived. The phrase "your father" might, for example, translate into a predicate like **father(f1, [p1,…])** where **f1** is the referent of "your father" and **[p1,…]** is a list of **f1**'s children, **p1** being the referent of "you". It is not hard to imagine how this predicate, together with suitable pragmatic information (an indication that an assertion is required) and a suitable grammar, would give rise to the sentence "You have a father".

3. Learning

The major problem in this phase of the research programme has been to find a representational system for more-or-less realistic knowledge structures which can handle interpretation/comprehension processes and language production processes with reasonable efficiency and which fits in with the principles of learning established in earlier phases of research. The representational system discussed in the previous section is an approximate answer. There are, no doubt, many refinements and adjustments to be made in the light of psychological data and other considerations but the outline solution to this three-way puzzle seems now to be reasonably clear. The fairly full discussion of representation given in the previous section should allow a relatively straightforward account of how learning processes may apply. Let us state the argument briefly first and then examine it in more detail.

The proposed learning system may operate something like this:

1. Build up syntactic/semantic schemata (simple PSGs or AND/OR trees) from raw data very much in the way that SNPR operates. This means concurrent searches for efficient AND groupings and efficient OR groupings with the results of each kind of search feeding into the other. Here is an example of a grammar which might be built in this way:

$$\begin{aligned}
&1 \text{ noun-phrase} \rightarrow \text{determiner, noun, suffix.} \\
&2 \text{ determiner} \rightarrow [a]. \\
&3 \text{ determiner} \rightarrow [this]. \\
&4 \text{ determiner} \rightarrow [one]. \\
&5 \text{ determiner} \rightarrow [these]. \\
&6 \text{ determiner} \rightarrow [those]. \\
&7 \text{ determiner} \rightarrow [several]. \\
&8 \text{ noun} \rightarrow [pen]. \\
&9 \text{ noun} \rightarrow [paper]. \\
&10 \text{ noun} \rightarrow [table]. \\
&11 \text{ noun} \rightarrow [chair]. \\
&12 \text{ suffix} \rightarrow []. \\
&13 \text{ suffix} \rightarrow [s].
\end{aligned} \qquad (17)$$

The origin of null constituents like the null suffix in clause 12 is easy enough to explain. If the database contains patterns like *table, tables, chair, chairs* etc. then the search for OR groups leads straightforwardly to the grouping of the s suffix with a null alternative.

2. At some stage after the schema is built or perhaps while it is being built, introduce arguments. For every OR grouping create arguments at that level and higher levels to control choice amongst the constituents of that OR grouping. Here is our example with arguments added:

1 noun-phrase(X, Y, Z) → determiner (X), noun (Y), suffix (Z).   (18)
2 determiner(d1) → [a].
3 determiner(d2) → [this].
4 determiner(d3) → [one].
5 determiner(d4) → [these].
6 determiner(d5) → [those].
7 determiner(d6) → [several].
8 noun(n1) → [pen].
9 noun(n2) → [paper].
10 noun(n3) → [table].
11 noun(n4) → [chair].
12 suffix(s2) → [].
13 suffix(s1) → [s].

This grammar can be used to specify particular noun phrases: **these chairs** would be **noun-phrase(d4, n4, s1), this paper** would be **noun-phrase (d2, n2, s2)** and so on.

3. The third operation required is to apply a process like SNPR to search *amongst the arguments* for frequently occurring AND groupings and for OR groupings amongst those AND groupings. Clusters like **(d4, n4, s1)** and **(d2, n2, s2)** will occur while such groupings as **(d2, n1, s1)** ("this pens") or **(d4, n3, s2)** ("these table") will not. The end result of a combined search for AND and OR clusters in our example should be two structures like this: **(dsing, n, s1)** and **(dplural, n, s2)**, where **dsing** and **dplural** represent the disjunctive sets **(d1 | d2 | d3)** and **(d3 | d4 | d5)** respectively and where **n** is the disjunctive set **(n1 | n2 | n3 | n4)**.

In the light of these newly disovered patterns of constraint the grammar may be modified to look like this:

1 noun-phrase → np(dplural, n, s1).   (19)
2 noun-phrase → np(dsing, n, s2).
3 np(X, Y, Z) → determiner(X), noun(Y), suffix(Z).
4 determiner(dsing) → [a].
5 determiner(dsing) → [this].
6 determiner(dsing) → [one].
7 determiner(dplural) → [these].
8 determiner(dplural) → [those].
9 determiner(dplural) → [several].
10 noun(n) → [pen].
11 noun(n) → [paper].
12 noun(n) → [chair].
13 noun(n) → [table].
14 suffix(s2) → [].
15 suffix(s1) → [s].

Clauses 1 and 2 embody the two main patterns of constraint: **dplural, n, s1** and **dsing, n, s2**.

4. This grammar is now properly constrained to respect number agreements within the noun phrase but it can be significantly simplified to an equivalent form like this:

   1 noun-phrase(X) → determiner(X), noun, suffix(X). (20)
   2 determiner(singular) → [a].
   3 determiner(singular) → [this].
   4 determiner(singular) → [one].
   5 determiner(plural) → [these].
   6 determiner(plural) → [those].
   7 determiner(plural) → [several].
   8 noun → [pen].
   9 noun → [paper].
  10 noun → [table].
  11 noun → [chair].
  12 suffix(singular) → [].
  13 suffix(plural) → [s].

This grammar controls number agreement in the same way as in (6) and (8).

Notice that an argument like **singular** or **plural** may be applied to the determiner category and *also* to the suffix category. In larger grammars like (8) such a marker may be applied to verbs as well. These categories are not subsets or supersets, one of another. they may not have any constituents in common and they do not have to be contiguous. (Notice, once again, that discontinuous dependencies can be identified even though the learning process exploits contiguity as a means of simplifying its task). What the categories do have in common which the shared use of **singular** and **plural** markers is designed to show, is the thread of constraint running between them. What allows us to use one marker in diverse categories without risk of confusion is the overall framework of the grammar. As we have seen, this technique allows us to simplify the grammar without any loss of expressive power. The advantage is even more marked if other constraints, like gender agreements, have to be incorporated in the grammar as well.

Before we proceed further. something should be said about the sequencing of the operations described above. It is probably easiest to think of the four operations being done in the sequence in which they have been presented but there are other possibilities. From the point of view of psychological theory it is not very plausible to suppose that children spend a first part of their childhood building general schemata and find constraints only in a subsequent phase. It is more likely that the four operations described are all applied from the earliest stages of development. They might, for example, be applied repeatedly in rotation like the several operations in SNPR so that the building of schemata and finding constraints within them would, in effect, be inter-woven.

A point to bear in mind is that the general schemata and the patterns of constraint within them are both derived from specific patterns. It may not be necessary to obtain general schemata before searching for patterns of constraint; that sequence may be reversed or it may be possible to conduct both kinds of search concurrently in some sense of that word.

A last question to consider briefly before looking at some examples is the nature of the primitives from which knowledge structures are to be built. A working assumption is that the primitives include innate systems for identifying colours, luminancies, boundaries between constrasted regions and other aspects of visual perception, systems for discriminating amongst pitches, timbres and loudnesses of sounds, perhaps including innate analysers for formant ratios and transitions, and similar systems in other sensory domains. What these innate analysers actually are for any natural system is an empirical question which is beyond the scope of this article. The range of analysers available to the system will clearly have a strong influence on the kinds of knowledge structure which can be built – a person born blind can have only a derivative concept of colour. However, it does seem that principles can be established for deriving learned concepts from innate ones without specifying what the innate concepts might be.

3.1 Examples

Now that we have a general notion about how schemata may be built and how patterns of constraint may be found and incorporated in a developing knowledge structure, we may look at the example grammars described earlier to see how they could have been learned.

The small grammar for French syntax (8) is similar to the example we have just considered and does not require much comment. The main point of difference is that there are two independent patterns of constraint, for number agreements and for gender agreements, and corresponding arguments have to be incorporated in the grammar.

The part-whole/class-inclusion hierarchy in (9) is very similar in its general organisation to the grammar for French syntax and can, we may suppose, be learned in a similar way. The main difference in the organisation of the two grammars is that **Num** and **Gen** in (8) represent independent classes whereas **Sub1** and **Sub2** in (9) represent a class and its sub-class. This difference should not present any problems for the learning process.

Our second "animal" grammar (10) is equivalent to the first one (9) but it does perhaps give a clearer idea of the way classes and sub-classes can be defined using AND groupings of arguments. A cat (clause 5 of (10)) is an animal with the co-occurring features **whiskered** (**Nose**), **mewing** (**Voice**) and **retractile** (**Claws**). A siamese cat (clause 6) has those co-occurring features together with blue eyes.

An attractive feature of the formalism we are using is that it is just as much at home with relational structures as with other ways of organising knowledge. The learning principles that have been proposed seem to apply as readily to the learning of structures like (11), (12) and (13) as to the other examples we have been considering. The driving principle in all cases is the search for AND groupings and OR groupings in a suitable combination to create structures with "good" overall efficiency.

AND and OR are themselves relational concepts postulated as innate givens in the learning system. It is possible that these two relational concepts, together with a small range of non-relational primitives are a sufficient basis for all the varied "natural" relational concepts that people apparently use: "sister", "ancestor", "on", "meet", "greater-than" and so on. Although it would be interesting to establish whether or not AND and OR really are the only two relational concepts required in the foundations of such knowledge structures, we should not be too dismayed if the conclusion of that enquiry were negative. It is reasonable to suppose that infants might be equipped at birth with some other relational notions, perhaps including concepts like "greater-than", "above/below" and "meet". We may not know at present which relational concepts belong in the set of "givens" but we can be reasonably confident that the number of such concepts required to build a wide range of derived concepts is quite small.

The partial grammar for English auxiliary verbs (14) has been included amongst our examples because this part of English syntax represents a challenge for our formalism and also for the proposed learning processes. The formalism succeeds very well in representing syntactic constraints amongst auxiliary verbs in such a way that they can be used efficiently in language production and interpretation. Whether or not such a grammar really can be abstracted from raw data in the kind of way we have been considering is not yet established. We have some reason to think that it can because the grammar exploits principles which have proved their value in the learning of other systems.

The feature of interest in this grammar which distinguishes it from our other examples is the way in which the pattern of interlocking constraints is represented in clauses 11, 13, 15 and 17. Clause 11, for example, shows transparently how the choice of a modal verb is linked to the later choices of a "have" verb (or its null alternative) and a bare infinitive verb (which may or may not be "have"). The sequence **modal** – **"have"** – **"be"** – **"be"** – **V** (with each constituent optional) is captured in this kind of way in clauses 10 to 19. The associations of modal with infinitive verbs, "have" with "en" verbs, "be" with "ing" verbs and "be" with "en" verbs are also represented in this part of the grammar. These patterns of association have a clear basis in frequency of co-occurrence. The kinds of frequency-led search processes which have shown their worth in identifying word and phrase groupings (Wolff, 1977, 1980b) should also be able to identify the associative groupings amongst English auxiliary verbs.

The main point of interest in our final example is the way in which semantic information has been integrated with syntax. No new principles are needed to achieve this. The integration relies on the association of words with the semantic structures which they stand for using AND groupings to show these connections. Examples of these groupings are **on(X, Y)** linked to **sur** (clause 5) and **on(Y, X)** linked to **sous** (clause 6). Notice how the order of the arguments in the "on" relation is used to distinguish *sur* from *sous*. Other examples are the association of **black(X)** with **noir** and **green(X)** with **vert** (clause 26 and 27).

Normally, a Prolog grammar like this could be streamlined a little by adjustments to clauses like those containing the structures **on(X, Y)**, **black(X)** and **green(X)** (clauses 5, 6, 26 and 27). It is not necessary to specify a variable **Rel** in the head of each of these clauses and then assign a structure to it in the body. In these cases the structure could be placed directly in its proper position amongst the arguments in the head of each clause.

The reason this has not been done is to draw attention to the associative link between each semantic structure and the word which represents it. These associations are no different from all the other AND groupings which have been described. And they may be learned in exactly the same way: by a clustering process using frequency of co-occurrence as a guide.

This largely completes our survey of example grammars and how they may be learned. The theme has been that knowledge structures which are complex enough to cope with realistic tasks and which are also reasonably efficient can be abstracted from raw data given only a smallish set of primitive analysers and learning procedures embodying the six compression principles. The representational and learning problems have been considered in some detail but an exhaustive and thorough understanding of these ideas will probably not be attained until a working system has been constructed which will successfully learn grammars like these.

4. Associated Issues

The remainder of this article will briefly consider some questions which are peripheral to the main focus of this article but which are relevant to a proper understanding of the theory which is being developed. One question is how notions of uncertainty may be accommodated in a system which is based on the all-or-nothing notions of truth and falsity. A second question concerns the apparent contrast between the optimisation view of learning presented here and one of the popular alternatives - learning as a process of creating, testing and selecting "hypotheses". A summary of empirical evidence which bears on the theory will be given and a few other issues associated with the theory will be briefly considered.

4.1 Partial Matching and Probabilities

A striking feature of the way people deal with language and other perceptual inputs is that they are not unduly disturbed by errors of omission, comission or substitution provided these are not too great. The pattern PSYCHBOLOGY is easily recognised as *psychology*. The error in a string of words like *Spring as on the way* is easily detected and corrected - or the error may not be seen at all.

By contrast, the Prolog grammars presented above are all extremely sensitive to errors of any kind. A surface string of morphemes will not receive any interpretation unless it can be matched precisely with structures in the grammar.

At first sight this defect seems to stem from the way Prolog is founded on the idea of pattern matching which either succeeds or fails. The language seems to have too much rigidity built into it to cope with the messy, fuzzy way that people operate. This impression is probably wrong. It would take us too far afield to discuss this question in depth but something will be said to try to show how humanlike flexibility probably depends to a large extent on the computational resources that can be applied to interpretive processes rather than abandoning the success/failure dichotomy in Prolog.

What is the "correct" interpretation of a pattern like PSYCHBOLOGY? The answer, of course, is that there is no single correct interpretation, only a range of possible interpretations varying in probability and dependent on the pre-stored patterns which the perceiver can apply. Most people would naturally read this as *psychology* with an interpolated B; the B would probably be classified as a "typo". Much less probable but still conceivable is that two words, *psychiatry* and *biology* have been collapsed together with the omission of *iatry* in *psychiatry* and the *i* in *biology*. The string would be read as PSYCH*iatry*B*i*OLOGY. PSYCH*o*B*i*OLOGY is also a possibility. There are many other improbable but conceivable interpretations of this kind. A residual interpretation, if all else fails, is that the pattern is simply a string of independent symbols: P,S,Y,C,H,B,O,L,O,G,Y. Assuming that these basic analysers are "wired in" to the perceiver, this residual interpretation is always available if required. There is always some interpretation which can be given to any perceptual input.

How can we deal with this kind of ambiguity? In broad terms, the answer is to find all possible matchings between stored patterns and the components of the pattern requiring interpretation, and to assign probabilities to them. Here is a little more detail.

The probability of a match like PSYCH*iatry*B*i*OLOGY is the probability of the word *psychiatry* multiplied by the probability of the word *biology*. These two probabilities may be contextually conditioned or, if there is no relevant context, they can be derived quite simply from absolute frequencies. In general, the probability of any match is the product of the (contextual or absolute) probabilities of the stored patterns used in the match (see Olivier, 1968). Of course, multiplication of probabilities less than 1 leads to smaller values, especially if more than two probabilities are multiplied together. The probability of a match will be maximised if: 1) the stored pattern or patterns which are used in the match are probable in themselves and 2) if there are only a few of them, preferably only one. Stored patterns which "cover" a large amount of the input string will give a better result than smaller patterns.

Partial matching as in the examples just considered is easy enough to implement in Prolog if the constituent symbols in patterns like *psychiatry* and *biology* are matched individually against the symbols in the input string. The success/failure feature of Prolog is confined to matches at the lowest level. Finding all possible (partial and complete) matches between the input symbols and stored patterns is quite simple in principle but in all but the most trivial cases it requires a great deal of computation. There are at least two ways to alleviate the problem.

The first is to take advantage of the fact that only a minority of these possible matchings will be of interest. Search heuristics may be applied to favour stored patterns with high probability, each covering as large a part of the input string as possible. Simple versions of these heuristics operate in the parsing systems in programs MK10 and SNPR. As previously noted, these search heuristics do lead to garden-path errors on occasion. More sophisticated heuristics which allow a greater range of possibilities to be considered and which are less prone to make these errors are likely to be more expensive in the computations they require.

The other answer which does not exclude the use of heuristics and is probably needed even if search heuristics are used, is to apply a lot of computational power.

In the long run, the most satisfactory way of doing this, especially where run-time considerations are important, is to use a computational system which allows multiple searches to be done in parallel. It is no accident that human perceptual systems are organised in this way.

It should be clear from the foregoing that partial matching has an important role to play in interpretive processes. In order to deal with the messiness of perceptual data we need a perceptual system which can use parts of a pattern to activate the whole pattern. This kind of inductive interpolation of information may be seen to occur also wherever meanings have to be inferred from surface forms or where an appropriate surface form has to be chosen to express a given meaning. The association between a word and its meaning - **on(X, Y)** linked to *sur*, for example - may be viewed as a binary pattern which can be activated by just one of its components, *sur* may activate **on(X, Y)** or *vice versa*.

If-then rules, which we touched on earlier, may be seen as a means of achieving this kind of effect. The "conditions" of the rule are parts of a pattern which, when successfully matched to input data, will activate the remainder of the pattern. The trouble with this kind of rule is that the roles of the constituents are ossified - a given element is either a condition or an action. The kind of partial matching we discussed above needs a flexible system in which any sub-set of an AND grouping can activate the complementary sub-set. This kind of effect can be achieved most cleanly if, as previously suggested, the encoding of AND groupings is independent of the uses to which those groupings will be put.

4.2 Optimisation and Hypothesis Testing

The relation of this work to other work in the field is considered fairly fully in the overview article being prepared. Just one salient issue will be briefly considered here.

The optimisation view of learning contrasts most strongly perhaps with the popular view of learning as a process of creating hypotheses, testing them and retaining those that are unfalsified (e.g., Wexler & Culicover, 1980; Shapiro, 1981; Erreich, Valian & Winzemer, 1980).

Consider a learning system like the very general system which is the basis of Gold's (1967) theorems. This system receives a succession of language samples and, before each one, it guesses a grammar to generate the new sample and all previous samples. Whenever the guess is successful, that grammar is retained for the next trial. Whenever the guess fails, new grammars are tried until one succeeds. When one grammar remains valid for a specified number of samples, the system is said to have learned the language "in the limit".

Gold proved that this system could not be guaranteed to learn certain classes of language (probably including natural language) "in the limit" given positive samples only and no constraint on the order in which samples are presented. The reason that successful learning cannot be guaranteed is that the system may, at an early stage, guess a very general, over-inclusive grammar which can generate all utterances in the language and many others too. In these circumstances there would never be any reason to change the grammar. If the learning system is provided with "negative" samples (samples which are marked somehow as wrong) or has access to a "teacher" who can indicate when guesses are wrong, or if there is constraint on the order of samples which allows indirect information about negative samples, then learning can be guaranteed to succeed.

Gold's proofs are apparently at odds with the assumption made in this article, which is widely acknowledged by researchers in this field, that children can learn a first language without negative samples, correction by a teacher or constraint on the order in which samples are presented. If we retain this assumption, and there is plenty of evidence that we should, then the view of learning on which Gold's theorems are based must be replaced or modified.

One way we can try to circumvent the problems which Gold raised and retain an hypothesis-testing view of learning is to establish a minimum for the complexity of the grammar to be learned and a corresponding ceiling on its generality; we may adopt the Chomskian view that the child is equipped at the outset with a relatively complex universal knowledge structure which is a framework for language-specific knowledge acquired by hypothesis-testing processes. Versions of this view have been put forward by Baker (1979), Wexler & Culicover (1980) and Erreich *et al.* (1980), amongst others. The methodological decision adopted by Anderson (1981), Langley (1982) and others to equip their learning systems at the outset with semantic structures and knowledge of word meanings has much the same effect.

The main difficulty with this kind of approach, for which no answer has been found, is to define a knowledge structure which is general enough to be a basis for any natural language and which is at the same time specific enough to prevent over-general grammars being adopted.

Even if a solution to this problem had been found, there would be another problem which hypothesis-testing by itself cannot solve. There is nothing to prevent Gold's learning system or any other hypothesis-testing system from incorporating a mass of replicated or irrelevant rules. A grammar may be guessed which can generate all the utterances in the target language, which successfully avoids generating utterances outside the language but which is nonetheless "wrong" – because it is unnecessarily complex. If we are going to adopt an hypothesis-testing view of learning then it seems that we must also adopt notions of economy in cognitive processes.

But these notions of economy can enable us to avoid over-general grammars and unnecessarily complex grammars and at the same time they allow us, indeed require us, to dispense with the hypothesis-testing idea altogether. Rather than attempt to constrain the learning process by supplying it with a relatively rich knowledge base at the outset, we may supply it with a minimum of prior knowledge – a maximally general knowledge structure – and use the optimisation principles discussed earlier to find a compromise between the initial general grammar and overly complex grammars. By starting with a maximally general knowledge structure and retaining it as a subset of the knowledge structure we are going to build, we can guarantee that the learning system will be universal.

If we adopt this approach, the notion of hypothesis-testing as it is normally construed does not make good sense. The learning system is equipped at the outset with a set of atomic analysers which are the building blocks for more complex knowledge structures but, at all stages of learning, they are retained as a part of the system's knowledge. Because the very general grammar is a subset of the grammar being built by the system, the situation can never arise where the grammar fails. Any input can be given some kind of interpretation even if it is the back-stop option of encoding it at the lowest level as a sequence of basic symbols (cf. our PSYCHBOLOGY example, above).

To be sure, particular rules may fail in particular situations but one failure of a rule (or several failures) does not in itself provide a reason for removing the offending rule from the knowledge base. A child may observe THE and anticipate CHAIR on the basis of his rule system. If SEAT is what in fact occurs then the hypothesis is falsified. But the learner can never know whether what occurred was obligatory in that context or merely a stylistic variant of what was expected. The notion of hypothesis testing as normally understood, where one single failure is enough to eliminate an hypothesis, does not apply in this situation. The only workable strategy is to apply some kind of ordering to the rules according to their "usefulness" and to eliminate rules whose usefulness falls too low to justify the space they take up.

Similar principles seem to apply to the use of falsification in science (Lakatos, 1978). When an hypothesis is falsified we are not obliged to reject it. We may contrive a more-or-less radical restructuring of our ideas to allow the hypothesis to be salvaged. Only if we set limits to the restructuring which we will countenance, as scientists usually do, can falsification be sufficient reason to eliminate an hypothesis.

Let us summarise the arguments in this section by casting them in a different form. Learning is a search through a space of possible knowledge structures which may be defined by one or more dimensions. Figure 1 shows one possible definition using the Sg and CC dimensions described earlier. A third dimension, which may be roughly characterised as efficiency, is represented by the hypothetical family of curves (1 to 4) in the diagram. These three dimensions define a space, (perhaps more meaningfully characterised as a surface in this case) within which our search takes place.

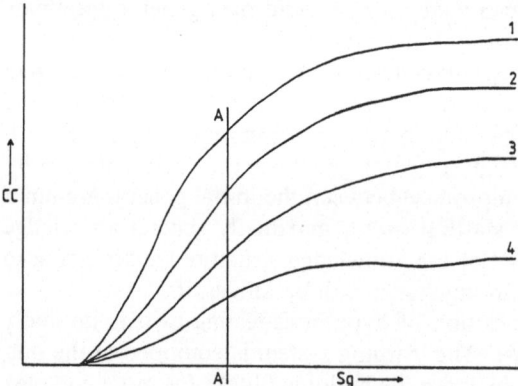

Fig. 1. Hypothetical search space of knowledge structures

Cognitive Development as Optimisation

The overall trend of the surface from left to right shows a trade-off between **Sg** and **CC**. To the left of the diagram are small grammars with small **CC**s. These are grammars with large generative ranges, too large to permit economical encoding of data. To the right of the diagram are larger grammars, some of which (curves 1 and 2) have large **CC**s while others (curves 3 and 4) have relatively poor **CC**s. For any given size of grammar. **CC** and generative range are two sides of the same coin.

No single grammar can be said to be "correct" but some are better than others. If we are interested in optimising the balance between **CC** and **Sg** then we should search along curve 1 where **CC**s for any given **Sg** are at a maximum for any given **Sg**. Which of these grammars we choose depends on the relative importance to us of small size in the grammar or good compression capacity. An "overgeneral" grammar may be defined as one with a smaller **CC** than we would like.

If we decide to equip our learning system with something more than a minimum of *a priori* knowledge or if we decide that part of a knowledge structure is immovable "fact", we are, in effect, restricting our search to the surface to the right of a line like AA in the diagram. With this restriction operating, it is reasonable to talk in terms of hypotheses being falsified. Any new component of the knowledge structure which causes **CC** to drop to zero may be regarded as a falsified hypothesis. However. although hypotheses can be falsified, that in itself does not ensure that our search is conducted on or near curve 1. We may be operating at lower levels (curves 2, 3 and 4) in the domain of over-blown grammars which contain redundant or otherwise functionless components.

We can move line AA as far to the right as we like and we can never by that means ensure that hypothesis-testing will produce a "good" grammar. When line AA is moved to the right in this way, there is progressively less likelihood that our learning system will be universal in its applications.

4.3 Empirical Validation

The optimisation view of linguistic/cognitive development which has been explored in this and earlier articles provides or suggests explanations for a wide range of phenomena observed in the way children learn a first language. There is plenty of detailed work yet to do in relating the theory to empirical data but the support which exists already is impressive. Only a summary of supporting evidence will be given here pending fuller treatment in the "overview". There will be no attempt in this article to argue the points in detail or to meet possible objections to them.

4.3.1 Learning a Grammar

Probably the most severe test for any theory of language learning which no current theory can meet is that it should be demonstrably sufficient to learn a plausible generative grammar for a natural language, including semantics, under the same conditions that apply to children's learning. The knowledge structures created by the learning processes should be able to support plausible processes of comprehension and language production. The models developed so far have shown some success in this direction. The discussion earlier in this article argued that this avenue of exploration will take us to our goal.

In the course of this work a detailed understanding has been obtained of two sub-problems within the overall problem. A process for discovering the segmental structure of language and comparable structure in other domains has been worked out in detail and validated on the discovery of words (Olivier, 1968; Wolff, 1975, 1977) and phrases (Wolff, 1980b). The theory elaborates and extends the ideas originating in taxonomic linguistics about how part-of-speech and other disjunctive categories can be established. The criticisms directed at this type of distributional analysis by, for example, Pinker (1979), have been shown to fail when the system is properly organised and integrated with a search for AND groupings.

The way in which recursive rules may be learned is reasonably clear.

Part of the grammar-learning problem is to find principled ways of generalizing grammatical rules and correcting over-generalizations. The theory explains how these effects can be achieved and offers a functional rationale. The correction mechanism appears to be the only proposal made to date which offers a principled means of distinguishing "correct" generalizations from "incorrect" ones.

4.3.2 The Rate of Acquisition of Words and Other Structures

The theory appears to provide an explanation of the pattern of vocabulary growth and the rates of acquisition of other structures through childhood and beyond.

The so-called "naming explosion" – an acceleration in the rate of acquisition of words between 18 months and 3 years – may be explained in terms of the structure-building processes in the theory. In the earliest stages, the main activity is the construction of word fragments from the smallest constituents. When a sufficient number of fragments has been created we may expect a surge in the rate of acquisition of words because relatively small amounts of processing are required to create words from the part-words that have been built.

The deceleration in the learning of new structures – fairly early in the case of phrase and sentence forms and more prolonged for words – finds an explanation also in the theory. There is reason to think that the slowing in the rate of learning of new structures is due more to a decrease in the cognitive "usefulness" of new structures as learning proceeds rather than to the increasing rarity of as-yet-unlearned structures or any sense in which the learner might be "scraping the barrel" of linguistic forms.

4.3.3 The Order of Acquisition of Words

There is a clear correlation between the order in which words are acquired and their frequency of use (Gilhooly & Gilhooly, 1979). There is a corresponding link between the order of acquisition of words and their length (Wolff, 1977). This is probably due to the well-known relationship between word length and frequency (Zipf, 1935).

The theory explains these observations but cannot yet provide a satisfactory explanation of an anomaly: that function words in English at least are acquired relatively late although they are amongst the most frequent words in the language. There are various possible ways of resolving this problem which will need exploration in the future.

4.3.4 Brown's (1973) Law of Cumulative Complexity

If a linguistic structure contains all the components of another structure plus something more, then it will probably be learned later than that other structure. This observation (Brown, 1973) accords with a commonsense view of language learning as a process of building complex forms from simpler constituents. But this incremental notion is probably not the best explanation of Brown's law. Complex structures are generally rarer than simpler ones (Brown & Hanlon, 1970) and so frequency-led search processes tend to find them later.

4.3.5 The S-P/Episodic-Semantic Shift

If a young child is asked to respond to a stimulus words with the first word he can think of, he will typically produce a word that might follow the stimulus word in a sentence or might have been heard in a similar situation or both. Older children and adults typically respond with a word which is a syntactic alternative or a semantic alternative or both (see, for example, Petrey, 1977).

The combined search for AND groupings and OR groupings proposed in the theory implies an asymmetry: OR groupings can only be found after a range of AND groupings has been established and should therefore appear later. This seems to be the explanation of a progressive shift from responses which are related to the stimulus word by an AND relation and responses which are alternatives to the stimulus.

4.3.6 Overgeneralizations

The asymmetry just noted seems to be the explanation of another observation in language development. Children typically learn irregular plurals like *geese* and *mice* and irregular past tense forms like *fought* and *hit* in their correct forms initially. Subsequently, they change them to regularized versions like *gooses* and *fighted* before eventually attaining adult usage. In terms of the theory, the original correct forms are learned by AND grouping; when enough of these have been established to abstract general rules like **V(past)** → **V, ed** then irregular forms are displaced by the new rule. Ultimately, the irregular plurals and verbs are grafted back on top of the general rules.

4.3.7 The Learning of Non-Linguistic Cognitive Structures

We have seen earlier in the article how principles of learning and knowledge representation which apply to syntax may be transferred almost without change to the domain of "concepts": *part-whole hierarchies, class-inclusion hierarchies* and so-called *relational concepts*. The theory can also apparently handle the interface between syntactic and semantic knowledge. Apart from the three mentioned, there are several other features of "natural" conceptual systems which can be accomodated in this framework of ideas.

4.3.7.1 Salience of Concepts

It has been recognised for some time (Rosch, 1977; Wolff, 1976) that natural concepts differ from the arbitrary or artificial concepts used in "concept acquisition" tasks because they are somehow salient in the experiencial data from which they are derived. On the basis of experimental evidence Rosch (1977) distinguishes "basic level" concepts from others within a hierarchy as those which stand out most prominently and naturally. "Chairs" seems to be a basic salient category compared with "furniture" and "armchair". In general, concepts like "male" and "female" are more salient than categories like "person with fair hair and handspan greater than eight inches".

In terms of the theory, salience of a concept seems likely to be a reflection of the "value" of the concept in the cognitive system: the increase in **CC** which it creates for unit increase in **Sg**.

4.3.7.2 Overlap Amongst Concepts (Cross Classification)

By contrast with category systems created by most standard clustering algorithms, natural systems may contain categories which overlap without being hierarchically related: a person may be a "woman" and a "doctor"; an item of food may be a "cake" and a "desert". The theory accomodates part-whole hierarchies and class-inclusion hierarchies and it allows categories to overlap quite readily when patterns of redundancy dictate that that is the most economical configuration. The system can accomodate heterarchies (networks) as readily as strict hierarchies.

4.3.7.3 Fuzziness of Conceptual Boundaries

Related but mutually exclusive categories may have fuzzy boundaries between them: it may be difficult to assign a given entity with confidence to one such category rather than another. For example, a particular building may not be easily classified as either a "cottage" or a "house"; at the same time one may be unwilling to classify it as both cottage and house, or neither.

The notion that concepts can have fuzzy boundaries, which corresponds roughly with Rosch's notion that exemplars of concepts may vary in their "typicality", is easily accommodated in the theory if we allow the kind of probabilistic processing discussed earlier. Whenever an entity is assigned to two or more mutually exclusive classes with roughly equal probabilities we have an instance of fuzzy boundaries.

4.3.7.4 Polythesis

Perhaps the most interesting feature of human conceptual systems is that they contain "polythetic" or "family-resemblance" concepts. What this means is that the members of a category may not have any single attribute in common. Two senses of polythesis can be recognised, one (a "weak" sense) applying to the process of recognising entities (assigning them to categories) and another (a "strong" sense) concerned with the nature of the stored specifications of the categories.

A pattern recognition system which can cope with incomplete patterns in the way discussed above would almost certainly exhibit polythesis in the weak sense. If a pattern can be recognised when any one or more of its constituent attributes is missing then the condition of polythesis as defined above is fulfilled: no single attribute is required for one pattern to be assigned to a class so no single attribute need be shared by the entities which are assigned to the class.

Polythesis in the strong sense is not as mysterious as it may at first appear. A very simple example is a class with the intensional description: $1 \rightarrow 2, 3$ with $2 \rightarrow A | B$ and $3 \rightarrow C | D$. There are only four patterns in the extension of this class: AB, BC, AD and BD. The members of the class have no single attribute in common. The key to family resemblance concepts like this is the use of disjunctive relations in the intension of the concepts; disjunctive relations do of course have a central role in the theory. They are fundamental in most concepts from the simplest to the most complex and polythesis is, correspondingly. an option at all levels.

4.3.7.5 Differential Weighting of Attributes in Recognition

Another feature of natural categories to be mentioned is the way their recognition depends more on some attributes than others. A roof and walls is more distinctive for the category "house" than the colour of the paint or the type of brick or stone used in construction. This kind of variation fits naturally into a system in which constraint (AND groupings) and choice (OR groupings) form a modulated blend in the composition of each category. Probabilistic processes of recognition will naturally accord more weight where constraint applies than where the number of alternatives is greater.

4.3.8 Nativist Arguments

The last point to be made in this section is that the theory appears to meet the objections to empiricist theories frequently voiced by proponents of nativist theories of language learning. The results that have been achieved already with very small language samples and computing resources which are miniscule compared with what a child's brain can provide is strong evidence against the nativist view that languages are too complex to be learned in the time available without assistance from a generous measure of pre-established knowledge.

An interesting feature of the kind of learning system under discussion is that it is remarkably insensitive to "errors" in its database. A process which sifts out recurrent patterns and discards exceptions is naturally stable in the face of erroneous omission, additions and substitutions in the "pure" text, all of which individually are, by their nature, rare. The nativist argument that the child's database is too corrupted to allow learning by empiricist processes does not apply in this case.

5. Conclusion

To see learning as a process of optimising a cognitive system seems to be fruitful both in the creation of artificial learning systems and in understanding how humans learn. In the first case it is difficult to see how the practical need for efficiency in cognitive systems can be met without paying attention to questions of informational redundancy and the application of data compression techniques in the management of redundancy.

The notion that people also apply these principles in learning a first language and other kinds of knowledge cannot be proved. But there is now a sizable body of empirical evidence and associated theory which fits naturally into an optimisation framework.

Throughout this research programme care has been taken to convert schematic theoretical ideas into working models as a means of sharpening, disambiguating and testing those ideas. In the phase of research reported in this article this methodology has been used to explore principles of knowledge representation in relation to learning and use of knowledge. The next step will be to create a new computer model which can not only represent the kinds of structures which we have been considering but can abstract them from "raw" data according to the principles which have here been discussed.

Acknowledgements

A number of people have contributed to this work indirectly through discussions and through comments on earlier drafts of this article or associated working papers. My thanks are due especially to Pat Langley. Philip Quinlan and Alan Wilkes for stimulus and criticism.

References

Anderson JR (1981) A theory of language acquisition based on general learning mechanisms. Proceedings of the Seventh International Joint Conference on Artificial Intelligence. pp 97–103
Baker CL (1979) Syntactic theory and the projection problem. Linguistic Inquiry 10: 533–581
Brown R (1973) A first language: the early stages. Harmondsworth: Penguin
Brown R, Hanlon C (1970) Derivational complexity and order of acquisition in child speech. In: Hayes JR (ed) Cognition and the development of language. Wiley, New York
Chomsky N (1957) Syntactic structures. The Hague: Mouton
Clocksin WF, Mellish CS (1981) Programming in Prolog. Springer, Berlin
Cook CM, Rosenfeld A (1976) Some experiments in grammatical inference. In: Simon JC (ed) Computer Oriented Learning Processes, pp 157–174, Noordhoff, Leyden
Coulon D, Kayser D (1978) Learning criterion and inductive behaviour. Pattern Recognition 10: 19–25
Erreich A, Valian V, Winzemer J (1980) Aspects of a theory of language acquisition. Journal of Child Language 7: 157–179

Feldman J (1972) Some decidability results on grammatical inference and complexity. Information & Control 20: 244–262

Fries CC (1952) The structure of English. Longmans, London

Gazdar G (in press) Phrase structure grammar. To appear in Pullum GK, Jacobson P (eds) The nature of syntactic representation. Reidel, Boston

Gazdar GJM, Pullum GK, Sag I (1980) A phrase structure grammar of the English auxiliary system. In: Sag I (ed) Stanford Working Papers in Grammatical Theory. Volume I, Stanford Cognitive Science Group, 1–124

Gilhooly KJ, Gilhooly ML (1979) The age of acquisition of words as a factor in verbal tasks. Final report to the SSRC on research grant HR/5318

Gold M (1967) Language identification in the limit. Information and Control 10: 447–474

Harris ZS (1961) Structural linguistics. University of Chicago Press, Chicago

Horning JJ (1969) A study of grammatical inference. Technical Report No CS 139. Computer Science Dept, Stanford University

Lakatos I (1978) Falsification and the methodology of scientific research programmes. In: Worral J, Curry G (eds) The Methodology of Scientific Research Programmes. Philosophical Papers Vol I. Cambridge University Press, Cambridge

Langley P (1982) Language acquisition through error recovery. Cognition and Brain Theory 5: 211–255

Leech G (1974) Semantics. Penguin Books, Harmondsworth

McCawley JD (1968) The role of semantics in a grammar. In: Bach E, Harms RT (eds) Universals in Linguistic Theory. Holt, Rinehart and Winston, New York

Michalski RS, Stepp RE (1982) Learning from observation: conceptual clustering. In: Michalski RS, Carbonell JG, Mitchell TM (eds) Machine Learning: an Artificial Intelligence Approach. Tioga, Palo Alto, pp 331–363

Olivier DC (1968) Stochastic grammars and language acquisition mechanisms. Doctoral dissertation, Harvard University

Osgood CE (1963) On understanding and creating sentences. American Psychologist 18: 735–751

Pereira FCN, Warren DHD (1980) Definite clause grammars for language analysis – a survey of the formalism and a comparison with augmented transition networks. Artificial Intelligence 13: 231–278

Petrey S (1977) Word association and the development of lexical memory. Cognition 5: 57–71

Pinker S (1979) Formal models of language learning. Cognition 7: 217–283

Ritchie GD (1980) Computational Grammar: an Artificial Intelligence Approach to Linguistic Description. Harvester, Hassocks

Rosch E (1977) Human categorization. In: Warren N (ed) Advances in Cross-cultural Psychology (Vol I). Academic Press, London

Shapiro EY (1981) Inductive inference of theories from facts. Research Report 192, Yale University. Department of Computer Science

Warren DHD (1977) Implementing Prolog – compiling predicate logic programs. Dept of AI Research Reports 39 and 40, University of Edinburgh (May)

Wexler K, Culicover PW (1980) Formal principles of language acquisition. MIT Press, Cambridge, Mass

Wolff JG (1975) An algorithm for the segmentation of an artificial language analogue. British Journal of Psychology 66: 79–90

Wolff JG (1976) Frequency, conceptual structure and pattern recognition. British Journal of Psychology 67: 377–390

Wolff JG (1977) The discovery of segments in natural language. British Journal of Psychology 68: 97–106

Wolff JG (1980a) Data compression, generalization and overgeneralization in an evolving theory of language development. Proceedings of the AISB-80 Conference on artificial Intelligence, Amsterdam. Society for the Study of Artificial Intelligence and the Simulation of Behaviour

Wolff JG (1980b) Language acquisition and the discovery of phrase structure. Language and Speech 23: 255–269

Wolff JG (1982) Language acquisition, data compression and generalization. Language and Communication 2: 57–89

Zipf GK (1935) The psycho-biology of language. Houghton Mifflin, Boston

Index

Archimedes law 42
auxiliary verbs, (English) 182–184

Black's law 35, 36, 42

Cannizarro('s law) 47, 48
censors 66
class-inclusion hierarchies 179–181
clusterer 114–116, 118
clustering 116, 120, 157
cognitive economy 93, 145
common divisors 45–49
compression (of data) 165–168
concept(s) 103, 105, 106, 134, 145
conceptual clustering 1, 13, 134, 135
conceptual knowledge 97, 102, 105, 109
constructive induction 132, 133
Coulomb's law 32, 34
credibility 133
credit localization/merit 127–132

Dalton's law/atomic theory 45, 46, 52
data compression 165–168
data-reduction heuristic 32
deductive learning 4, 7, 16
Definite Clause Grammar 174–177
discovering laws
    Archimedes' 42
    Black's 35, 36, 42
    Cannizarro's 47, 48
    Coulomb's 32, 34
    Dalton's 45, 46, 52
    empirical 50, 51
    Galileo's 24, 52
    Gay-Lussac's 45, 52
    ideal gas 32, 33, 38
    Kepler's third 24, 27, 31, 38
    Ohm's 24, 27, 34, 38, 40
    Proust's 42, 46
    qualitative 51
    Snell's 35, 36, 42
discrimination 139, 140, 143–145, 147, 148
dissimilar(ity) 115, 116, 139, 140

efficiency 97, 107, 109, 164, 165
empirical laws 50, 51
evaluation function 95, 101, 105

expectation-driven heuristics 31
expert systems 1, 2, 9, 12, 16
explanation based learning 4, 7

feature formation 133–137, 141, 142
feature interaction 118, 119
features 95, 104, 105, 143, 144
feature space 138, 139

Gay-Lussac('s law) 45, 52
Galileo's law(s) 24, 52
generalization(s), (over-) 170, 171, 201
Generalized Phrase Structure Grammar 173
genetic algorithm 127, 128, 130–132
goal-hierarchy 56
goal-state 56

heuristic(s) 56, 104
    common divisor 45–49
    data-reduction 32
    expectation-driven/based 31, 52
    for finding
        linear relations 23, 43
        multi-term relations 32
        polynomial relations 25–28
        (relations between) nominal terms
            38–44, 47
        similar relations 31
        symmetrical laws/symmetry 34, 36, 41
        two-term laws 23, 25–27
    hill-climbing 28, 29
    intrinsic property 38–48
hierarchies, class-inclusion/part-whole
    179–181
hill-climbing 28, 29
hypothesis 133
hypothesis testing 196, 197

ideal gas law 32, 33, 38
improvement 57, 58
incremental (learning) 114, 115, 117
inductive learning 1, 2, 7–9, 16
initial state 56
intrinsic properties 38–48
invariance(s) 133, 140
invariance(s), similar(ity), dissimilar(ity) 115, 116, 133, 139, 140

Kepler's third law 24, 27, 31, 38
knowledge acquisition 1, 2, 6, 9
knowledge structure(s) 91, 97-100

layering, overlaying 134, 138, 140
learning
  by analogy 4, 6, 16
  by experimentation 5
  from examples 1, 2, 5, 9, 10-12, 16
  from instruction 3, 4, 6, 12, 16
  from observation 1, 2, 5, 9, 11, 13, 16
  incremental(ly) 96, 113-115, 117
  principles 94, 96, 148
  probabilistic 110, 143-146
  strategies 1, 3, 6
  system(s) 95, 98, 148
linear relations 23, 43

machine learning 1, 2, 7, 9
mediating structure(s) 93, 97, 102, 109, 111, 148, 149
merit/credit localization 127-132
MK10 168
multi-term relations 32
mutual data support 108, 109, 142, 149

noise 25, 28-30, 32
nominal terms 38-44, 47

Ohm's law 24, 27, 34, 38, 40
operators 56

part-whole hierarchies 179-181
performance 106, 118-122
polynomial relations 25-28
polythesis 203
probabilistic learning 110, 143-146
probability of match 194, 195
problem space 56
production system 56
Prolog 174-177
proposer 65, 66
Proust('s law) 42, 46

(relations between) nominal terms 38-44, 47
rote learning 3

search 153-155
similar relations 31
similarity 116
Snell's law 35, 36, 42
SNPR 168-172
subgoals 56
symmetrical laws/symmetry 34, 36, 41

training 155, 156
transfer 58, 59
two-term laws 23, 25-27

utility (goal orientation) 102-105, 110-114, 140-142

verbs, (English) auxiliary 182-184